THE

GUINNESS BOOK OF

GOON PUMPS
LOON LUMPS
LORN LAMPS
BORN VAMPS
WORN GAMPS

WORD GAMES

WOLD NAMES
COLD DAMES
BOLD DATES
BALD PATES
BARD PATHS

BY DAVID PARLETT

GUINNESS PUBLISHING

To
John McLaughlin
friend and
(literarily)
a
gent

Published in Great Britain by
Guinness Publishing Ltd
33 London Road, Enfield, Middlesex EN2 6DJ

"GUINNESS" is a registered trademark of
Guinness Publishing Ltd.

First published 1995

Copyright © David Parlett 1995

Reprint 10 9 8 7 6 5 4 3 2 1 0

A catalogue record for this book is available from the British Library

ISBN 0–85112–679–0

Designed by Cathy Shilling
Typeset by Ace Filmsetting Ltd, Frome, Somerset

Printed and bound in Great Britain by
The Bath Press, Bath
Front cover design by DH Publicity

Acknowledgements
I thank Kevin Crossley-Holland for permission to reproduce his translation of the 'Key' riddle
from *The Exeter Book Riddles* (Penguin Classics, 1979), and, for their kind assistance in
connection with boxed word games, Messrs J W Spear & Sons plc, Hasbro UK Ltd,
Waddingtons Games Ltd, and Creative Games Ltd. The names Scrabble™, Boggle™,
Lexicon™, Upwords™, Countdown™ and Word for Word™ are registered trademarks. As it is
impossible to compile a book of this nature without drawing on existing literature, I quote all
other sources where known and appropriate and take this opportunity of expressing my debt
to them all.

CONTENTS

INTRODUCTION: WHEN IS A WORD NOT A WORD?

When it's a bone of contention ...

Many of the following games involve making words from a given set of letters. In all games of this sort the question will usually arise as to whether or not a claimed word is 'acceptable'. It may arise because the other players have never heard of it and don't know what it means. Or it may be challenged on the grounds that it is a name, an abbreviation, or slang, or foreign, or obsolete, or in some other way defective under what are considered to be generally understood rules of 'acceptability'.

In formal games like Scrabble, or games played in formal situations such as tournaments, the problem is fairly easily resolved. You look the word up in a dictionary accepted as authoritative. If it's not there it isn't acceptable. If it is, you then check to see whether it is allowed under the specific rules of the game, which may impose a ban on any of the grounds listed above. If it is listed only as a name, an abbreviation, or whatever else is held to be improper, then, again, it is unacceptable. *Voilà*!

This method of settling disputes is essentially authoritarian. It produces cut-and-dried decisions and saves time and argument. As such, it's ideal for formal games. It's also ideal for publishers, companies and tournament organizers who enjoy a vested commercial interest in encouraging the cult of 'official rules', which are of course obtainable only from themselves.

It's not ideal, however, for informal play, of the sort pursued at home by people who are generally well-known and friendly to one another, operate on much the same intellectual wavelength, and, while playing to win (which is the proper aim of any game), nevertheless prefer to moderate their cut-throat competitive tendencies in favour of having a good time and enjoying the mental exercise. Such players will not best enjoy themselves by being required to adhere strictly to rules imposed from outside by people they've never heard of. I certainly don't, and if you share this aversion, then just read on.

In my word-gaming circle we follow an alternative procedure to the Rule of Authority. It might be called the Rule of Appeal. It goes like this:

Suppose someone has offered the word *lox,* by implication claiming it as acceptable, and another has queried it. Then:

1. The claimant must, if requested, first define the word. It means both 'liquid oxygen' and (from another root), 'smoked salmon'. A precise, word-for-word definition is not required, so long as the claimant has sufficient knowledge of the word to be able to use it in context. 'A fuel used in rocket propulsion' would do for one. The point here is that in word games played for the love of words and not for the love of sheer competitiveness it is not enough merely to know that a particular combination of letters happens to be listed in a codebook called the Dictionary. If you can't define it, you don't know it. If you don't know it, you can't have it.

2. If at least one opponent recognizes the word and considers it acceptable, then it is acceptable. You may then want to check it in the dictionary to find out more about it, but this need not affect the claimant's right to count it. If not, then:

3. Check it in an authoritative reference book. This will be the nearest dictionary to hand, or any of several that may be available. If the word is there, it may be acceptable.

If it is categorized as something out of the ordinary, such as obsolete or dialectal, then, again, it is acceptable if one opponent accepts it, and not otherwise. (Defined by the claimant as 'smoked salmon', *lox* might be rejected by British players on the grounds that it is a Yiddish word used chiefly in the US. As an acronym from *Liquid Oxygen eXplosive,* it would probably be accepted, depending on your house rules about acronyms.)

Here it is worth noting that *Chambers Dictionary* was taken some years ago as the standard word-gamers' dictionary for tournament play, especially in the British National Scrabble Championships. This is because it was the only one to list headwords with large and small initials to indicate whether or not a word should exist only as a name, names being generally unacceptable. Most other dictionaries have since followed suit, and I now prefer the new (1993) *Shorter Oxford English Dictionary* (SOED) in two volumes, though the one-volume *Concise Oxford Dictionary* will do as well. Indeed, any substantial dictionary will do as well – size, nowadays, is more significant than brand. Also useful are two publications by Chambers. *Official Scrabble Words* (1991) lists all words in Chambers of two to nine letters in length. It has the advantage of listing with equal prominence and in strict alphabetical order all grammatical variations of headwords, including comparatives and superlatives, agentives (such as OWER from OWE), and verb forms. A companion volume, *Official Scrabble Lists* (1991), does the same, but classifies words according to length and provides lists of unusual and helpful words, such as those ending in U or containing no vowel but Y. Useful though they are for rapid reference, they are not sufficient in themselves, as they do not provide definitions. If, therefore, a word is not in either book, you may consider it unacceptable, but if it does appear, you will need to refer to a proper dictionary in order to assess whether the claimant has sufficient knowledge of its meaning. Also, of course, they will not in themselves suffice for games that often throw up words of more than nine letters.

Another reason for adopting the Rule of Appeal is that some words may rightly be considered valid although they don't appear in the dictionary, and others deemed invalid even though they do.

English is not merely a list of words: it is also a storehouse of components that may be put together to form words. One of our players recently kicked off with the word UNHOSTED. The rest of us rolled this round our tongues for a while, and decided that if no stone could be left *unturned*, then no TV chat show or children's party could possibly be left *unhosted*, and accordingly allowed it. Subsequent reference to SOED and Chambers revealed that neither lists it. Nor does either list the last word of that venerable Spoonerist joke about the critical music-hall audience who left no turn *unstoned*. Later in the same game I claimed, and was permitted, the unrecorded compound MILDISH, as a possible description of weather by analogy with DAMPISH and DRYISH – both of which are in Chambers. (However, I may have been pushing my luck here, as I've since come to the conclusion that, as the ending -ISH in itself implies a quality exhibited to a *mild* degree, my nonce-word is probably tautological.)

Having demonstrated (I hope) that a word should not be rejected merely because it isn't in a dictionary, let's now turn to words that are in a dictionary but may not be considered acceptable. Possible reasons for disqualifying certain words may be considered under several headings. When is a word not a word? Often, when it falls only under one or more of the following headings.

NAMES

'They are the most economical of all words', declares Sir Alan Gardiner in *The Theory of Proper Names*, 'inasmuch as they make only a very small demand on the eloquence of the speaker, and an equally small demand upon the attention of the listener.'

Really?

If I were listening to a speech in which I was enjoined to show the qualities of a Codrus I should feel that a very great demand was being made upon my attention, and obliged forthwith to consult my *Who's Who in the Ancient World*. Gardiner was evidently no word-gamer; otherwise he would have realized that it is precisely because they make too great a demand on the attention that most players refuse to admit them as words within the meaning of the Act.

In theory, the difference between a proper noun (name) and a common one is that the former is a set containing only one member, while the latter is a generic term for a whole category of similar members. Word-gamers reject names because knowing them is a test of general knowledge, whereas word games are intended to be a test of literacy. It may be reasonable to expect word-gamers to have MOUNTAIN in their vocabulary; but it is not reasonable to expect them to know *Matterhorn* any more than *Makalu* or *Mercedario*.

In practice, of course, many names are not unique. I am not the only David in the street, let alone the world. There could be as many Davids as there are dogs, and it is reasonable to expect literate people to have both words in their vocabulary. Even so, a name is felt to be unique rather than generic, as may be gauged by the incongruous effect produced by assuming the opposite in the following encounter from *The Lost Weekend*:

Hospital orderly:	Name?
Ray Milland:	Birnam.
Hospital orderly:	What kind of Birnam?
Milland:	DON Birnam

Proper names are shared only because there are not enough of them to go around. Dog is generic because it will do for any individual member of a genus of animals which we are all capable of recognizing; we could not look at a person and know for certain that it was a Birnam or a David.

At first sight, English appears to help word-gamers by its convention of writing names with capital initials. Even more advantageously, names which become used as generic drop their capitals. Thus *moll*, originally a proper name (diminutive of Mary), comes to mean a gangster's girlfriend, in which capacity it takes a small M and is acceptable as a generic word or common noun. Similarly, *quisling* (from the Norwegian fascist Vidkun Quisling) is now acceptable as a common-noun synonym for 'traitor', and *boycott* (from the 19th-century Irish land agent Captain Boycott) is a verb.

Unfortunately, this is not always the case. We may refer to a poet as a Shakespeare or a Byron, but not with a small S or B. It all comes down to a question of whether we feel certain names to be 'proper' in any given circumstance. Once again, we trip over the line that can't be drawn.

More serious, because unnoticed by many players, English uses capital initials for words whose status as 'proper' names is highly questionable. What about days of the week and months of the year? You might regard Sunday, January, Monday, February and the rest as generics and favour the French custom of spelling them with small initials. Yet so deeply ingrained is the contrary behaviour of the English that I have even been challenged for spelling the four seasons with small letters instead of capitals!

Again, what about nationals? The French, quite logically, spell their words for Frenchman, Icelander and so on with a small initial. It seems obvious to me that Frenchmen are generic rather than proper. The same applies to languages, though with less force: I can see the argument behind treating French as a proper name, insofar as it denotes a unique language. Less defensible is our habit of spelling adjectives of nationality with a capital initial, except in given phrases. What is the difference between a 'French widow' and a 'french window'? Not just the N in window, but the F in French as well.

Some word-gamers disallow the spelt-out forms of letters of the alphabet, on the grounds that they are names, and therefore, presumably, should be spelt with a capital letter. To my mind, one *aitch* is as generic as another, and I am glad to see that the 1988 revision of the rules of the National Scrabble Championship now permits them. One problem is that there seems to be no universally accepted standard for their actual spellings. Where Chambers recognizes *ef, el* and *es,* SOED prefers *eff, ell* and *ess.* Another concerns non-Roman alphabets. If names of English letters are allowed, what about Greek and Hebrew? Greek *mu* and *pi* are acceptable because, besides being letters, they also denote mathematical quantities. *Iota* also has a meaning, and, one way and another, these would seem to let in all the others for the sake of consistency. How about Hebrew? We surely must accept *aleph* for reasons similar to those justifying *pi,* in that it denotes an order of infinity. Does that then let in all the rest, including the very handy two-letter word *pe*? And if Hebrew, what about Arabic?

Problems of consistency can arise with names of plants and animals. All creatures great and small have scientific names, great and small, taken mostly from Latin. Whereas no one would object to wolf in a word game, neither part of its scientific name, *Canis lupus,* would be accepted, the former if only because it is (by international convention) spelt with a capital, the latter if only because it is Latin and therefore 'foreign'. There is no problem here because we have a so-called popular word (*wolf*), which is quite distinct from the scientific. But problems can arise where no popular word exists. *Dinosaur* has long been a popular word and was never very scientific in the first place, but word-gamers may justifiably baulk at *Stegosaurus* or *Triceratops.* Strictly speaking, or writing, they are spelt with capitals; whether or not they should be spelt so in popular writing is an open question. I pose the question only to be awkward, not to answer it, though I dare say most players would agree to accept them on an equal footing with *dog* and *wolf.*

The gist of this argument, in case it has got lost in the undergrowth, is that proper names should not be allowed in word games because they belong to specialized knowledge rather than to literacy. The task of deciding which names are proper and which generic, or common, is too elaborate for practical play. It is therefore a poor best to prohibit words which in English are only spelt with a capital initial, even if this means throwing out with the specific bathwater such generic babies as *Monday, Zed* and *Tyrannosaurus rex.*

As for brand names and proprietary names, they are (almost literally) a law unto themselves. A bane to teachers and a major threat to literacy, proprietary names are one of the curses of a capitalist society. It's hard to say which are worse – those that already exist as ordinary words, or those that claim a dubious uniqueness by deliberate misspelling. There used to be a removals company called *Dor-to-Dor-Karriers.* I can only hope they've been removed.

I leave this subject with a few names of ponderable propriety. What about *Londoner? Mancunian? Petrine* (epistles)? *Caesar? Mackintosh? Ford? Formica? Spa? Lido? Thermos?*

FOREIGN WORDS

Of all the restrictions commonly followed in word games none is more laudable than the prohibition of foreign words. English speakers rightly take it for granted that the game is to be played in English; if foreign ones are allowed an unfair advantage accrues to the most accomplished linguist playing the game.

Unfortunately, though laudable, the rule is unenforceable. Again there is a line that won't be drawn.

The problem arises because English has a habit of picking up foreign words and gradually absorbing them into its lexicon until a point is reached at which they cease to sound foreign. They are then not foreign but only of foreign origin. By this process, more English words actually turn out to be foreign than native: it has often been pointed out that English is a Germanic language with a vocabulary of which some 75 per cent is Romance (ultimately derived from Latin). It is aggravated by the fact that no two dictionaries, and often no two players, will agree on the extent to which a word in question has become naturalized. Chambers doesn't help in this respect, but SOED follows the useful practice of printing in italics a headword not yet regarded as naturalized.

English easily absorbs foreign words for both phonetic and syntactic reasons. It has a large, rich sound system which can accommodate almost any foreign word with a fair approximation to its original sound – although, in practice, English speakers have a notorious tendency to anglicize beyond recognition. An interesting example of phonetic flexibility is the English speaker's readiness to reproduce passably the sound of CH in *loch* or GH in *Van Gogh*, even though the sound dropped out of English itself several centuries ago. And the fact that English makes minimal use of grammatical modifications such as case-endings means that the absorption of foreign words is not hindered by problems of declension or conjugation.

Being, therefore, in a position to employ foreign words more or less indiscriminately, English readily does so in several different ways:

1. Unlike the Romans, whose pains to translate everything into Latin extended even to the translation of Celtic gods into Mars, Apollo and so on, English speakers quite happily retain native words for things peculiar to their country of origin. Thus, for the price of one *zloty* you may drink *slivovitz* while playing the *crwth* in a *troika*. *Olé*!

2. English-speakers will often not trouble to find equivalents for words denoting things of foreign invention, albeit of international applicability. Hence, the pen of my *ombudsman* is in the *bidet*.

3. Even if there is an English equivalent, a foreign word may be retained for precision or local colour. Both *pueblo* and *kampong* can be replaced by 'village', but English literature would be the poorer without them. *Kampong* is doubly interesting, as it has also been anglicized to *compound* with a somewhat different meaning.

4. Foreign words are often retained when English equivalents may be felt to lose in the translation. The British are particularly fond of French words in cultural contexts, such as *chic, louche, blond(e)*, even *petite*. And *apartheid* was always likelier to lead to *angst* than to *détente*.

5. Many technical terms are straight Greek and Latin, with examples rife in biology and medicine: *rubella, sinus*, the *genus Homo*. Interestingly, Chambers lists *manus* for 'hand' but not *pes* for 'foot', though both may be encountered in the same context (and in SOED, as it happens). Italian musical terms such as *allegro, crescendo,* and *niente* also belong to this category.

All the foreign words quoted above should be acceptable as English in word games. Doubtful cases may be tested by asking the claimant to propose a sentence or context in which the foreign word would be the natural choice of an educated English-speaker. On this basis I'd be surprised to find anyone accepting the German *Gesellschaft* for 'company' (commercial), even though it is listed in Chambers. Even more unacceptable should be individual words abstracted from foreign-language phrases or sayings. Neither *desperandum* from 'nil desperandum', nor *cul* from 'cul-de-sac', nor *sturm* from *Sturm und Drang*, nor *istesso* from *l'istesso tempo*, nor *hoi* from *hoi polloi* has independent existence as a word in English contexts, and for that reason should be disallowed.

DIALECT WORDS

A problem with dialect words is that although everyone knows more or less what they mean by 'dialect', there is no precise linguistic definition of it. The term is often employed patronizingly and in ignorance. I once heard it reported that a WANTED FOR MURDER poster circulated in England appeared not only in English but also in the Indian 'dialects' of Urdu, Punjabi and Gujerati. The writer of the book evidently assumed that different languages, if spoken in the same country, are dialects of one language. Such reasoning would lead to the absurd notion that Welsh and Gaelic are dialects of English.

Dialect is not a strong term amongst the English because regional varieties of the national standard vary little from one another compared with those of more strongly differentiated languages such as Italian. The only English dialect sufficiently well marked to boast literary status is Lallans or Lowlands (Scots). (It is sufficiently marked to be discussed as a language. A Dutch friend of mine once reported that he switched on the radio one Sunday morning to hear what he thought was a church service conducted in Frisian. It turned out to be Lallans.) A good proportion of the words in many English dictionaries are designated 'Scots', and, although I do not necessarily disagree with their acceptance, I am surprised not to have read any questioning of their allowability in books and articles on English word-gaming. Should Sassenach word-gamers be expected to know such words as *kye* – cows, *fley* – frighten, *sark* – shirt, except, perhaps, to show them off in word games? And if you allow these, which appear in Chambers, what about those that don't, such as *mebbies* – perhaps, *throuither* – jumbled up, and *inower,* a compound preposition?

AMERICANISMS

British word-gamers south of the border may be forgiven for their greater knowledge of American English than of Scots. Until 1988, the British National Scrabble Championship rules decreed that words listed in Chambers only as 'US', such as *bronco,* were to be disallowed as 'foreign', which seemed a bit silly when no such prohibition attached to less well-known words of Scots and other dialectal affinities. American words are now admissible since the ban was lifted on words described as foreign. Unfortunately, I think that this has gone too far. Hitherto, British players would generally accept American words as valid (*movie, debunk, racketeer*, etc.), but not American spellings of words common to both languages (*harbor, kilometer, defense*). I'm sorry to see that *Official Scrabble Words* now lists both British and American spellings.

A more sinister aspect of Americanism that British word-gamers are right to resist is that of political correctness. Deliberate omissions from the American equivalent of *OSW* remind one of the deliberate omission of fine old English 'rude' words from the umpteen volumes of the original *Oxford English Dictionary.*

OBSOLETE WORDS AND SPELLINGS

When a word ceases to be current it has started on the road of obsolescence: it becomes first quaint, then old-fashioned, then archaic, and finally obsolete. Many word-gamers are reluctant to accept words that have reached the final stage and are accordingly designated *obsolete* in a dictionary. As to archaic words, such as *thee* and *thou,* surviving only in specialized contexts, lips may be pursed and acceptance grudgingly granted. Fair enough; but then problems arise with the appropriate verb forms. If you permit *thou,* thou canst hardly exclude *hast;* and if *hast,* why not also hath, seeth and wert? Where is the line to be drawn? Well, perhaps I can tell you. In one of our recent games we definitely drew the line at *(thou) faxest!*

It is important not to dismiss words as obsolete or archaic merely because the thing they refer to has vanished from the scene. Groats are obsolete, but *groat* is not. The word remains current to the extent that it has not been replaced by a modern word for the same coin: you may yet dig up one in the garden and will know exactly what to call it. Granted, you are more likely to unearth a *bob* or a *tanner,* but the same principle applies. In similar vein, mermaids and unicorns may not exist, but *mermaid* and *unicorn* undoubtedly do.

The same might be argued of words listed only as Shakespearean or, worse still, Spenserian. Such words may now be accepted by the rules of the British National Scrabble Championship, but I will continue to resist them as obsolete. This may be inconsistent with the argument supporting groats and unicorns; but then, as Emerson said, 'Consistency is the bugaboo of petty minds.'

Obsolete spellings are more easily dealt with – i.e. rejected – on the ground that no literate person would use them in preference to the modern spelling. It should be noted, however, that some words will have equally common variant spellings, such as *(window-)sill* and *cill.* If the main entry in a dictionary quotes alternative spellings they are generally accepted by word-gamers, and there seems nothing wrong in that.

SLANG AND COLLOQUIALISMS

Some word-gamers prohibit slang, presumably on the grounds of propriety. Perhaps a better reason for resisting slang, colloquialisms, and the like, is that they tend to be too ephemeral for inclusion in the dictionary, which is why nearly all dictionary words designated 'slang' seem so quaint and out of date. The reason is only valid if strict adherence to the dictionary is regarded as a rule of the game. I see no reason to prohibit words known to everybody merely because they are too ephemeral to be listed. This is an area where the Rule of Appeal really comes into its own.

ABBREVIATIONS AND ACRONYMS

Many colloquialisms are abbreviations or contractions. I've met word-gamers who object to *bus* and *phone* on the ground that they are abbreviations requiring an apostrophe, and I once argued with a publishing house (not Guinness!) whose copy-editor disinfected my use of *ad* by soaking it in inverted commas. In principle, no objection can be made to abbreviations in every day use. In pract, howev, the princ is ope to abuse. You have no choice but either to put it to the vote or to see how it is listed and described by the dictionary.

It may help to distinguish between spoken contractions and written abbreviations. No objection can reasonably be raised against such natural spoken contractions as *bus, phone, ad* and so on. Their derivation from longer words is only of historical interest. Many words in use today have similar backgrounds which their users are quite unaware of, such as *mob* from the Latin phrase *mobile vulgus.* Written abbreviations, however, are merely orthographic conventions for words which are normally pronounced in full, such as Mr for *mister,* Ms for *manuscript* and St for either *saint* or *street.* No one would accept either these abbreviations, or initialisms such as IOU, OK, VIP and the like.

Inevitably, awkward borderline cases arise where pronunciation follows orthographic abbreviation. I have often tried to claim *viz,* a printer's conventional abbreviation of the Latin *videlicet,* on the ground that that is not only how I read it but also how I use it in speech, albeit in jocular mode. Unfortunately, none of the other members of my word-gaming circle have ever allowed me to count it. It is also not accepted under the 1988 National Scrabble Championship rules and is missing from *Official Scrabble Words* – which, however, accepts *miz* (short for 'misery', according to Chambers, and not as a back-formation from the usual pronunciation of 'Ms' as a style of address for wimmyn). Presumably the difference is that *viz* appears in Chambers with a full stop and *miz* does not. I regard the stop as no more requisite than an apostrophe for *bus.*

We live in an age of acronyms. The anti-smoking lobby in Britain calls itself Action on Smoking and Health, creating the appropriate acronym ASH, perhaps more felicitous a device than SIGMA for the Society of Inventors of Games and Mathematical Attractions, if less imaginative than WATSUP for the Wessex Association for The Study of Unexplained Phenomena. Words that originated as acronyms include *radar, laser, scuba* and *quango.* The safest test for the validity of an acronym as a word is that of being normally written in lower-case letters throughout. This would exclude *Oxfam* unless names are acceptable, and LEM for Lunar Excursion Module, which became outdated before reaching the lower-case status of, for example, *jeep.*

HYPHENATED AND COMPOUND WORDS

A compound word results form sticking together two words to make a whole that is greater than the sum of its parts. A *workshop* is a place where a craft is practised, but is not the right word for a retail outlet where people happen to work. Many word-gamers reject compounds listed in the dictionary with a hyphen, as do the rules of the National Scrabble Championship. The trouble with this is that in English we hyphenate some compounds and not others, and there's little logic to the practice. On the whole, the British are worse than the Americans about keeping compound components a hyphen's length apart. I think American writers would be inclined to make *wordgamer* all one word, and this would be my own practice were it not for the fact that similar experiments I have carried out in the past have always been rehyphenated by fastidious copy-editors. Some hyphens are inserted to aid word recognition and pronunciation. A friend of mine maintains that he can never read the word *cowrote,* in American film guides, without mentally pronouncing it as if it meant *written by a cow.* English writers insert a hyphen in *co-operate* to prevent it, presumably, from sounding like the last three syllables of *recuperate.* This produces the baffling derivative *unco-operative,* which looks like an uncommonly functional Scot. To add to the confusion, hyphens may be omitted or inserted between pairs of words according to context. For example, a *well-known* fact may not be quite as *well known* as it appears.

As Sir Ernest Gowers put it in *The Complete Plain Words,* 'If you take hyphens seriously you will surely go mad'.

In British English we stress the noun rather than the adjective preceding it, as in *red cábbage* and *red ádmiral.* When such pairs become more closely linked, often with metaphorical intent, we may insert a hyphen, as in *red-blóoded* and *red-hánded.* Eventually, we may so far regard the resultant joint venture as a compound as to shift the stress to the first syllable to make the whole thing sound like a single word – as in *réd-belly* and *réd-head.* Eventually, the compound eventually reaches the final stage of complete coalescence into a single word, such as *rédskin* and *rédcurrant.* Similar things happen to other word pairs, such as noun + noun (*typewriter*), noun + verb (*shoplift*), and so on.

This suggests that the presence of a hyphen in a compound marks a stage of evolution from two words into one. Here are some more examples, hyphenated as in *Chambers Dictionary:*

separated	hyphenated	stress-shifted	compounded
long ódds	long-wínded	lóng-hand	lóngbow
under áge	under-prívileged	únder-trick	únderdog
house rúles	house-súrgeon	hóuse-leek	hóusehold
iron lúng	iron-gréy	íron-mine	íronstone
round óff	round-táble	róund-up	róundhead

No self-respecting word-gamer would accept as single words the compounds in the first column or deny those in the fourth column. Most would probably not accept any of the hyphenated forms, but I would be inclined to accept those belonging to the third stage. The blanket prohibition on hyphenated words is only useful as a last resort in case of dispute. Exerting it without question results in the anomalous exclusion of some patently single words that just happen to incorporate a hyphen for other reasons, such as *X-ray, cul-de-sac, forget-me-not,* and others, all of which I would accept on appeal on the grounds that they are spoken and felt to be single words.

A similar blanket rule on the exclusion of words properly spelt with an apostrophe is perhaps desirable in serious competitive play. In home play, I would be inclined to accept single words like *fo'c'sle* but not compounds like *shan't* or *would've.*

INTERJECTIONS

Words like *ah!, oh!, ow!,* and so on, are conventional representations of 'spontaneous utterances', listed as such in SOED and Chambers and so acceptable as words, along with *fy!* and *la!,* which can't have been heard for a long time now. Both dictionaries also recognize *sh!* and *st!,* which some players might feel doubtful about, if only because they don't contain vowels – which, however, can make them very useful in certain crossword games. Surprising omissions from both are the equally useful *mm!* and *zz!,* the former being the only possible representation of a well-known noise expressing agreement, and the latter a frequently encountered conventional way of representing slumber. Even more surprising is the omission of *ee!* as an interjection, though the word does appear as a dialectal variant of *eye.* The sound of dubiety, *h'm!,* is listed, but only with an apostrophe, which disqualifies it under tournament rules. You may, however, wish to make a house rule about any or all of these.

MUSICAL SYLLABLES

Musical syllables may be regarded as specialized forms of interjection and so accepted as words, even in the few instances where they happen also to be listed as words. The Tonic Sol-fa system runs *doh-ray-me-fah-soh-lah-te,* with alternative spellings including *mi, fa, la* and *ti,* and earlier forms *ut* for *doh* and *si* for *ti.* Other forms and systems will be found in the appendix of two-letter words, but it would be scraping the barrel of needless obscurity to accept any not listed in a standard dictionary.

1. SPOKEN WORD GAMES

> *The other project was a scheme for entirely abolishing all words whatsoever; and this was urged as a great advantage in point of health, as well as brevity. For it is plain, that every word we speak is, in some degree, a diminution of our lungs by corrosion; and consequently contributes to the shortening of our lives.*
> *Jonathan Swift*, Gulliver's Travels

ALPHABETICAL ORDURE

> *'This young lady loves you with an H,' the King said, introducing Alice in the hope of turning off the Messenger's attention from himself.*
> *Lewis Carroll*, Through the Looking-Glass

Some of the simplest but most enjoyable games are based on making lists of things with successive letters of the alphabet. An old joke – and I mean old, as it is credited to Samuel Foote, the eighteenth-century comedian – portrays three society ladies engrossed in a game of *I love my love*. Lady Cheere begins 'I love my love with an N, because he is a (k)night'. Lady Fielding follows with 'I love my love with a G, because he is a Giustus' (of the peace, presumably), and Lady Hill caps this with 'I love my love with an F, because he is a Fizician'. *I love my love* represents the sort of memory game where each player in turn repeats a list of things in alphabetical order and adds a new one beginning with the next initial. By changing the subject from love to food to distempers you get such variations as *Alphabet soup* and *Hypochondriac*.

More intelligent alphabet games are based on the idea of conjuring up words from skeletal letter combinations. Dedicated word-players refer to such combinations as 'ghosts'. For example, the letters OWD may be regarded as a ghost of the word HOWDAH. Crosswords are notoriously full of ghosts. What's a word for playhouse, seven letters, T something E something T something E something? Any solver worth their salt will lay this ghost in a THEATRE. Vehicle licence-plates are especially haunted, as any word-gaming driver will be aware.

I LOVE MY LOVE
Any number of players
Good for children and childish adults
More fun than competitive

'I love my love with an A', announces Anna, 'because he is Ambitious. I hate him with an A when he is Anodyne. I took him to Albuquerque and treated him to Apples and Apricots. His name is Arthublaster and he comes from Andromeda'.

'I love my love with a B' begins Byron, 'because she is Barmy. I hate her with a B because she is Bigamous. I took her to Basingstoke and gave her Bluebells and Belladonna. Her name is Bertha and she comes from Bangkok.'

That'll do for now, or there'll be nothing left for your imagination. Each player in turn uses the next letter of the alphabet, following the same formula. You may want to randomize who goes next by having players draw letters from a shuffled pile of letter-cards or tiles, but the results are generally funnier if everybody knows which letter will fall to their lot and can make good use of a bit of thinking time.

Memory variation. The other form of the game sounds like this:

'I love my love with an A because she is Adorable.'

'I love my love with a B because she is Adorable and Beautiful.'

'I love my love with a C because she is Adorable and Beautiful and Cuddly.'

And so on, each player having to repeat the whole of the previous list (under pain of forfeit) before adding a new desirable quality to it. Yet another version has verbs and adverbs – for example 'Because she Dances Delightfully, Excites Enigmatically, Flirts Facetiously … and so on.

I'M OFF
Any number of players
For children and talking gazetteers
More fun than competitive

'I'm going on a journey to Addis Ababa,' says the first, choosing anywhere beginning with A.

'What will you do there?' demand all and sundry.

'I shall Answer Amorous Advertisements,' says the first.

The second player, having declared him- or her-self bound for Belize or Bakersfield, or wherever, and having been interrogated as to intentions, continues 'I shall Beautify Baked Beans', or something equally expressive of the letter B.

This continues until the 26th player (or the fifth, if only seven are playing) has been to Zimbabwe for the purpose of Zincking Zoological Zithers, when it will be time to play something else.

ALPHABET SOUP
Any number of players
Children and people with strong stomachs
More sick-making than fun

'I went to a banquet and ate some Anchovies.'

'I went to that banquet and ate Anchovies and Blackberries.'

'I went to that banquet and ate Anchovies, Blackberries and Chocolate sauce.'

The next player will have eaten Anchovies, Blackberries, Chocolate sauce and Dhal soup; the next might add Eggplant, the fifth Figs, and so on.

Sensitive players may find this game harder to get through than it sounds.

HYPOCHONDRIAC
Any number of players
For children expected by their parents to become doctors
More fun than competitive

'I went into hospital with Appendicitis.'

'I went into hospital because I had Appendicitis and Boils.'

'I went into hospital because I had Appendicitis, Boils, and Cholera.'

I should think this game speaks for itself. The first player to pass out loses.

I PACKED MY BAG
Any number of players
Mainly for children
More fun than competitive

'I went to Alaska and in my bag I packed an Anorak.'

'I went to Barbados and in my bag I packed a Bib.'

'I went to Chile and in my bag I packed a Corset.'

I think you should have got the hang of that. And now for the more amusing …

Memory variation. 'I went away,' says the first, non-committally, and in my bag I packed an Alligator.' The second will have packed an Alligator and a Balloon, the third an Alligator, a Balloon, and a Corkscrew … Need I go on?

ORAL ALPHABENT
Any number of players
Adults and older children
Fun but skill-demanding

An *alphabent* is a sentence or paragraph of 26 words beginning with successive letters of the alphabet. For example:

> *Although banjos can do exceedingly fast gavottes, harps invariably jam. Knowledgeable Lithuanian musicians now openly prohibit quadrilles, rumour suggesting that unimpeachable virgins will xerox your zithers.*

As a written game (see page 67), the composing of alphabents has the advantage of allowing the time necessary for ingenious thought. But to play the game orally, and without malice aforethought, can lead to some rather excruciating entertainment.

Playing in rotation, the first performer opens by announcing a word beginning with A, the second continues with B, the third with C, and so on. Successive words must, of course, follow on grammatically from those immediately preceding, so as to gradually build up a more or less meaningful sentence. If a natural break occurs before the alphabet is completed, the first word of the new sentence must bear some meaningful relation to what has gone before.

It's a good idea to tape the performances, in case brilliant examples emerge that might otherwise be forgotten. Or, at least, write them out as you go along. That way, you can be reminded of the sentence so far in case you have difficulty in thinking of a suitable continuation.

UP THE DICTIONARY
Not too many players
Mainly for adults
Competitive and thought-demanding

This is my title for a game invented by Dave Silverman and originally called Last word – itself an over-used title that has been used for many other games.

Up the dictionary involves 'crashes'. In word gaming, a crash is a letter occurring in one word in the same position as it did in an earlier one. For example, given the word WORD, the word SONG crashes with it by containing an O in second position.

An agreed word length is chosen, let us say five letters. The first player announces such a word beginning with A – for example, ACORN. Thereafter, each player in turn must announce a word which:

● contains at least one crash with the previous word, and

● follows the word in alphabetical order – that is, further up the dictionary.

A player who cannot produce such a word drops out of play, and the winner is the player who made the last word.

A short game might run as follows:

A	C	O	R	**N**
B	L	U	**R**	T
Y	O	U	T	H
Z	**O**	N	E	D
Z	U	L	U	S

Challenged on the ground that it was a proper name *zulus* was shown to be a Scottish two-masted fishing vessel also, and so acceptable as a common noun. As no one could follow without crashing, this was the winning word.

If you find the game becoming predictable after a while, there are ways in which it can be varied. Here are some suggestions:

● Play it backwards, the first word beginning with Z and each subsequent word preceding it in the dictionary.

● Decree that each subsequent word must contain exactly one crash with its predecessor, and must begin either with the same letter (no other crash being allowed) or with the next letter up.

● Award the winner a score of one point for each word he or she contributed to the series. This will encourage players who fancy their chances to advance up the dictionary in small steps, and those who don't to leap as far as possible in one turn.

GHOST

Not too many players
Adults and older children
Requires concentration and good spelling

The first player announces the first letter of a word, without deciding what that word will be. For example, T.

The second then announces a letter that follows the first and is capable of being turned into a word. After T, for example, might come any vowel, or H, R or W. Anyone foolish enough to declare (say) D in this position would promptly be challenged to make a word beginning TD, and would thereby ignominiously lose. Let's say the second player announces A.

After A, the third player (or the first, if only two are playing) might add L, thinking perhaps of TALBOT or TALISMAN, for example.

Play continues in this way, with each in turn adding a new letter to the string. Each new letter must be capable of producing a word in conjunction with all the preceding ones, but the whole point of the game is to avoid being the player who actually completes a valid word of four or more letters. (Words of two or three letters are allowed.) Whoever completes such a word loses the round and begins a new one. Alternatively – by agreement, and if three or more are playing – the losing player drops out (becomes a ghost) for the rest of the round, which ends when only two are left in and one of them wins.

A three-player game might begin as follows:

Jilly:	T ...
Millie:	TA ...
Willie:	TAL ... (thinking of TALC, TALL, etc, but not of TALBOT or TALISMAN, as he would be the one to end the word)
Jilly:	TALO ... (thinking of TALON)
Millie:	TALOR ... (bluffing)
Willie:	Challenge!

In response to Willie's challenge, Millie must now come up with a word beginning TALOR ... or lose the round. If she does find one (which is more than I can do) then Willie will have lost. Yet a third possibility is that Willie might himself bluff by continuing with another letter.

You may only challenge on your turn to play, and instead of adding a letter yourself. You can challenge on either or both of two grounds: one, that the last letter completed a valid word, so the last player loses; or two, that the current sequence of letters cannot produce a valid word. In the first case the onus is on the challenger to prove that such a word exists if no one else claims to have heard of it. In the second, the challenged player must announce and (if necessary) prove the existence of a word that does in fact begin with the current sequence. Whichever player is proved wrong loses the game, or a life, or drops out of play.

SUPERGHOST

Not too many players
Adults and older children
Requires concentration

This is essentially the same as *Ghost* (see above) but with one major difference. Each player in turn adds a letter to either end of the current string. For example:

Barry:	T ...
Carrie:	TA ...
Harry:	PTA ... (thinking of CAPTAIN)
Barry:	PTAG ...
Carrie:	Challenge!
Barry:	HEPTAGON.

In this version the penalty for completing a word does not apply until a fifth letter has been added – words of up to four letters are permissible.

POLTERGEIST
Not too many players
Mainly for adults
Requires even more concentration

You have to be a real fanatic to go in for this extension of the ghostly theme. You may even find yourself having to resort to writing to keep track of it.

In this version, as you might expect from the title, you don't have to add the letters in any particular order, and you may challenge anyone for adding a letter in such a way as to produce an anagram. A short example should make this clear:

Ann:	T.
Ben:	CT.
Con:	CET.
Dan:	CEHT. (thinking of CHEST)
Ann:	CEHRT. (thinking of THRICE)
Ben:	Challenge! Everybody knows CHERT is a compact flinty chalcedony, albeit of dubious etymology.

They didn't, in fact, but were willing to take his word for it.

Poltergeist does not permit short words. After T, for example, Ben would have lost by announcing A or O.

ULTRAGHOST
Not too many players
Mainly for adults
Letter cards or tiles are useful

I was disappointed, but not too surprised, to find a game I thought I had invented (many years ago) popping up in a broadly similar form in a convention of the American National Puzzlers' League. Credited to the pseudonymous 'Ajax', it's a cross between *Ghost* and *Poltergeist*.

Ultraghost derives from the unconscious habit of all word lovers who are also car drivers of making words from the letter groups on vehicle licence-plates. As played at the Convention, cards were held up bearing three-letter sequences, and the object was to see who could come up with the shortest word incorporating those letters in the stated sequence, though not necessarily consecutively. For example:

P   Z   M

yielded PUZZLEMENT quite quickly, but this was soon beaten by the shorter TRAPEZIUM.

produced EXCULPATE, followed by the considerably better OXLIP.

It's convenient to take a set of cards or tiles from a boxed game to play *Ultraghost*. A reasonable distribution would be one each of J, Q, X and Z, and two of everything else. Each player in turn shuffles the cards or jumbles the letters in a bag, and deals or draws them out one by one, placing each in order from left to right. The player whose turn it is, when ready to announce a word, calls out 'One, two, three …', whereupon everybody shouts their word out at once. Those who remain silent score nothing, those who call out the shortest word score one point per letter in the word, the second shortest scores one point less, the third shortest two points less, and so on.

THE NUMBER-PLATE GAME
Best for two to four players
Adults and older children
Letter-cards or tiles are useful

My version of the game described above contains a few further refinements. As before, it's best played with letter-cards or tiles, with one each of J, Q, X, Z and two or three each of the other letters. You also need a grid of three spaces. This represents part of a number plate, and enables you to specify which letter lies in which position, i.e. first, second or third.

Each player in turn becomes the Driver. The Driver shuffles the cards or jumbles the tiles and draws them out one at a time, placing each in a space in the grid. Once placed, a letter may not be moved to a different position, and the next letter may not be drawn until the previous one has been placed. The letter S may not be placed in the third position unless it is the last one drawn. For reasons which will become apparent when you play, you may want to place similar restrictions on D (past-tense ending), G (present-participle ending) and R (agentive suffix).

After a reasonable amount of thinking time – at least ten seconds, and not more than one minute – the Driver announces a word of at least four letters which *begins* with the first letter, *ends* with the last letter, and *includes* the middle letter somewhere between the two. For example:

F   R   C

Let's suppose the Driver calls FORENSIC. Before scoring takes place, each player in turn from the Driver's left has one opportunity to call a word that fulfils the same conditions but is better than the one announced previously. For the purposes of this game 'better' means shorter (but never shorter than four letters), or, if the same length, earlier in alphabetical order. In this case, for instance, the next player to the left might call FORMIC, which is shorter; the next FERRIC, which is the same length but alphabetically earlier; and the next FRANC, which beats them all. The first word called – by the Driver, if he can think of one, or by anyone else if the Driver passes – earns its caller one point, the second (better) word two points, and so on, each subsequent 'better' word gaining an extra point. The Driver, of course, does not get a second bite at the verbal cherry.

The Driver may pass if he thinks that such a word can be made, but cannot himself think of one. He may, however, call 'Impossible', meaning that no such word can possibly be made. For example, J–Z–Q would be a pretty safe bet for such an assertion. In this case, each player in rotation to the left has one opportunity to attempt such a word, and, as before, if anyone does so, any subsequent word must be 'better'. The first such word scores three points, the second (in the unlikely event that it can be beaten) five points, and any subsequent word two more than the preceding one.

If no one can meet the challenge, and all agree that the call of 'impossible' is justified, the Driver removes the cards or tiles and plays again. On this round all scores are doubled. If the same thing happens, scores on the next round are trebled, and so on.

GUESS WHAT?

The underlying theme of the following games is the deduction of words, phrases or ideas by asking questions which are rewarded by clues leading to their identity. *Twenty questions* is the classic example, but there are lots of others too. As usual, we start with simpler games suitable for children and uninhibited adults, and work our way up to more thought-provoking exercises working along similar lines.

I SPY
Any number of players
Not suitable for adults
More fun than competitive

I spy is the ultimate in deductive word games – an exquisite form of intellectual torture for motorists whose families insist on playing it on holiday journeys to the opposite end of the country.

In the unlikely event that you've never heard of it, it is suffice to say that one player becomes the spy, looks around, and makes the ritual announcement 'I spy, with my little eye, something beginning with X' – or whatever other letter may be the initial of the spotted object. The others then try to guess what this is by calling, for example, *xylophone, xebec, xylem, xyster,* and so on. Eventually they give up, and the spy confounds them all by revealing the answer to be *exercise bicycle* or *extremely old person crossing the road.*

Players do not call in turn, or in any other particular order, and the person who guesses correctly becomes the next spy.

BLIND PUGH
At least six players
Any age
Requires paper

I have renamed this game (after a character in *Treasure Island*) as being more descriptive than its original title Key word, a title which I found in a book of language games for primary school children. It can, however, be levelled up to any age and degree of sophistication, and makes a good party game.

One player adopts the role of teacher or umpire, and writes one word on each of several slips of paper – or, better still, prints them neatly on cards large enough to be read by an audience. These are the words the players will be trying to deduce. If you're choosing words for younger children, make sure they're easy words representing common objects, such as *spoon* or *cat* and the like.

Divide the other players into two teams. At each round of play, two members of each team come forward and try to deduce the word on a card selected by the Umpire in the following way:

One of each pair sits with his (or her) back to the umpire, facing the audience of non-participating players. The other stands facing the umpire with her (or his) back to the audience. This done, the Umpire selects a card and holds it up so that it can be seen and read by everyone except the Blind Pughs sitting with their back to it. Let's suppose the word revealed is SPOON.

The standing partner of the left-hand team then gives the Blind Pugh partner a one-word clue to the word on the card – for example, 'Pudding'. Blind Pugh makes a guess at the unknown word – for example, 'Rice'. This being wrong, the turn passes to the right-hand pair. The standing partner might now give the clue 'Metal', so eliciting a guess that might be 'Saucepan'. Play continues, with each standing partner in turn giving a one-word clue and evoking a one-word guess, until one of the Blind Pughs gets it right. That team scores a point, or, if you want to be more sophisticated about it, ten points less the number of clues it took to get the answer. If neither side deduces the word after ten clues (five from each side), the round ends and the next won round scores double.

The two partners are then replaced by other members of their team, and play continues until everyone has had a chance to be Blind Pugh.

TWENTY QUESTIONS
A small group of players
Any age
Competitive but light-hearted

Long successful as a BBC radio game, *Twenty questions* started out as a Victorian parlour game and may be even older.

In the original version, one player, the Caller, writes the name of a picturable object on a card or slip of paper and the others have to deduce what it is. They do this by asking questions about it – preferably in strict rotation, but in no particular order if so agreed – to which the only permissible answers are 'Yes' and 'No'. For example, the opening questions are likely to be along the lines of *Are you more likely to see this indoors than outdoors?, Is it bigger than a car?, Is it something living?,* and so on.

Not all questions count towards the 'twenty' of the title. If the answer to a question is 'Yes', the question is discounted and the questioner can keep asking further questions until one of them gets a *No,* when the turn passes to the next player.

It may come as a surprise to discover how much can be learnt about an object from a series of yeas and nays. For example:

1. Are we looking for one special thing? *No.*
2. Is there one in this room? *No.*
3. Is there one in the street? *No.*
4. In the garden? *Yes.*
   Some kind of plant? *No.*
5. Is it alive? *No.*
6. Was it alive and is now dead? *No.*
7. A bird table? *No.*
8. Does it look as if it ought to be alive? *Yes.*
   Not that horrible stone frog by the pond? *No.*
9. A garden gnome? *Yes.*

If the Caller finds it hard to answer 'Yes' or 'No' to a particular question, perhaps the best thing to do is just pull a face and refuse to answer, in which case the question doesn't count. For example, at question 3, the Caller wondered whether to answer 'No' because the gnome wasn't literally in the street, or 'Yes' because there was at least one garden gnome in an area that could be described as 'in the street' as opposed to 'miles away somewhere else'.

If you want to make a scoring game out of it, the Caller scores one point for each 'No' he gave before the object was guessed, thus gaining a maximum of 20 if it isn't guessed at all.

The game can be extended in scope to include not just things but also people and places. In this case the Caller should start by announcing whether the object of enquiry is a person, a place or a thing.

ANIMAL VEGETABLE MINERAL
A small group of players
Any age
Competitive but light-hearted

I use this title for the more sophisticated version of *Twenty questions* that was devised for radio many years ago. This version goes further still, in that the object of the enquiry can be pretty well anything you can think of, as concrete or abstract and as real or imaginary as you like. Nothing in the rules would prevent such 'objects' as:

- Liquorice Allsorts
- Pandemonium
- The daring young man on the flying trapeze
- A black hole
- The Black Hole of Calcutta
- Boot blacking
- Bootlicking behaviour
- A rose red city, half as old as time
- The North Pole

In this case the Caller conventionally starts by announcing whether the object on the card is animal, vegetable, mineral, or abstract, or some combination of the three. Thus *a stitch in time* might be introduced as 'Abstract, with strong mineral and vegetable connections' – the mineral referring to the needle and the vegetable to the cotton thread. More fun may be had with items that could be one or the other depending on which of several meanings is intended. Sloth, for example, is either animal or abstract, but not both at once. Sometimes the material description can be less than helpful. Anything made of plastic, for example, is, strictly speaking, mineral, assuming that the plastic in question derives from oil. Other descriptions often carry conventional implications. For example, the specification 'vegetable, with strong mineral connections' usually evokes the first question 'Is this paper with printing on it?'

In this version the questioners are not obliged to pose questions of the Yes/No type, and the Caller is usually expected to answer questions of any description. It naturally follows that each player may ask only one question in turn, and that all questions count, regardless of the response. A guess at the object also counts as a question, so in the rare event that 19 questions have been asked and answered there is no option but to make a stab at it on the 20th.

Points can be scored along the following lines. Each plays for him- or her-self and the winner is the first player to reach 100 points. The first Caller is selected at random, and scores one point for each question asked before the object is guessed. Thus if it is guessed on the 20th question the score is 19. If it is not guessed at all the Caller gets a bonus of ten, making 30 in all, and remains the Caller for the next round.

A player who correctly guesses the object scores ten points and becomes the next Caller. Guesses (as opposed to questions) may be made at any time, but a wrong guess made out of turn attracts a penalty of ten points on the guesser. (There is no penalty if the player in turn makes a guess instead of putting a question.)

WHO AM I?
Any number of players
Any age
Light-hearted but requires thought

This game is a cross between *Twenty questions* (above) and *Botticelli* (below). Children should enjoy it.

A first Caller is chosen by any agreed means. He then thinks of a famous person, or historical or fictional character, and announces the initial of their principal name – typically their surname, in the case of real people. The questioners then have to find out who that person is by putting a series of questions which can only be answered by 'Yes' or 'No'. If the character has not been guessed within 20 questions, the Caller has won and calls again, otherwise the correct guesser becomes the next Caller.

BOTTICELLI
Two or more players
More likely to appeal to adults
Competitive but fun

This more elaborate version of *Who am I?* (above) remains one of the most popular of all word games – possibly because it gives general knowledge show-offs an excellent excuse to show off generally and knowledgeably.

As above, the first Caller is chosen by any agreed means. He then thinks of somebody famous, and announces the initial of that person's principal name (usually the surname). The other players then try to find out who the Caller is by asking questions which the Caller must answer in the most appropriate way, as follows:

Caller:	I'm someone beginning with C.
Questioner:	Are you a film comedian?
Caller:	No, I'm not Chaplin.
Questioner:	Did you bring back 'Peace in our time'?
Caller:	No, I'm not Chamberlain.
Questioner:	Were you poisoned by your wife Agrippina?
Caller:	I Claudius? Not likely!
Questioner:	Are you the female author of novels emphasizing family relationships?
Caller:	Er ... Agatha Christie?

At this point the Caller has been caught in ignorance of the Questioner's intended answer, namely, Ivy Compton-Burnett. Now, and whenever the Caller fails to give an answer matching the Questioner's clue, the Questioner is entitled to ask a general knowledge question about the Caller's assumed identity, provided that it is one that can be answered 'Yes' or 'No'. In this case, for instance, the Questioner may ask 'Are you a male character?'

The questioners then revert to their series of questions, to each of which the Caller must give an appropriate response, as before. When caught out again, the Caller might expect further questions seeking clarification:

> Are you American?
> Are you a legendary figure?
> Are you generally regarded as evil?

There's nothing to prohibit successive questioners from choosing a person with the same initial or even the same name, so long as the answer is different on each occasion. For example:

Questioner:	Are you an historical Catherine?
Caller:	No, I'm not Catherine the Great.
Questioner:	Are you another historical Catherine?
Caller:	Nor Catherine of Aragon.
Questioner:	Are you another historical Catherine?
Caller:	Nor Catherine de Medici.
Questioner:	Are you, by any remote chance, yet another historical Catherine?
Caller:	Nor ... er ... Catherine Wheel.

Here the Caller now seems to have run out of real Catherines (though there are still two of Henry VIII's wives to get through) and has to face another general background question.

Theoretically, the round ends when someone has deduced the Caller's identity, and the successful questioner assumes the next alias. But, if it looks as if the round is going on for ever, you may agree to end after a certain amount of time, or when the Caller has successfully denied an agreed number of guesses.

BACKENFORTH
Two or more players
More likely to appeal to adults
Competitive but fun

Briefly, one player reads or announces a word backwards, and the first player to call it out forwards (correctly) scores a point. For an incorrect call, the mistaken caller loses a point and the questioner gains one.

You must allow a certain degree of latitude in deciding exactly how 'backwords' should be pronounced. The word KNIGHT, for example, yields TINE if you reverse it phonetically (sound for sound), but THGINK if you reverse it literally. To keep the players on their toes, it's probably best to allow the Callers to follow their own inclinations in this respect. On the other hand, there's a lot to be said for deliberately not reversing digraphs – that is, combinations in which two letters stand for one sound, such as CH, SH, TH and NG. Thus THUS is better reversed to SUTH than to the unpronounceable SUHT. Similarly, the reverse of CHOP is PO(T)CH, and of SHOP, POSH.

It's reasonable to allow the Caller to write his or her word down as an aid to accurate pronunciation when calling it out. The others, however, should be kept away from writing materials, and be forced to rely entirely on their minds' eye and ear.

CLUE WORDS
Not too many players
Adults and older children
Fun, but requires concentration

The Caller (however chosen) thinks of a word of eight letters, all different, and gives three clues as to its identity.

The first clue is a word of three letters (all different), each of which occurs in the target word. For example, if the target word is HYDROGEN, the first clue might be ROD. Each opponent in turn may have one guess at the target word. Anyone who correctly guesses the answer scores three points and becomes the next Caller.

In the more likely event that no one gets the answer from three letters, the Caller gives a second clue, this time in the form of a word of four letters, all different, and all occurring in the target word – for example, DONE. Again, everyone has a guess, and a correct answer now scores two points.

Assuming no one has yet deduced the target word, the Caller utters a third and last clue in the form of a five-letter word similarly derived from the original, such as HORDE. A correct guess now scores one point.

If the target word remains unguessed, the Caller scores one point and remains the Caller for the next round.

SHAFFE'S GAME

Two players
Adults and older children
Requires some thought

One Samuel A. Shaffe is credited with the invention of this spoken version of the pencil-and-paper game *Jotto*.

One player thinks of a five-letter word and the other has to find out what it is. (You should take it in turns to be the Caller until you get used to the game, after which you can play it simultaneously.) The Guesser proceeds by calling out other words of five letters. To each of these, the Caller responds by stating how many letters of the test word are contained within the target word. For instance, if the target word is SKUNK, the following test words produce the following results:

QUITE	1
BRAND	1
GLOOM	0
SLYLY	1
STICK	2
STUCK	3

and so on. The actual position of the corresponding letters doesn't matter. All that counts is their number. You may agree to a rule that the five letters of the target word must all be different, but no such rule should apply to the test words. Of course, you can use words of any other agreed length.

AESOP'S MISSION

Any number of players
Adults and Victorian children
Fun, but irritating

A good old Victorian game with a good old Victorian name, *Aesop's mission* is introduced in the 1881 *Book of In-Door Amusements, Card Games and Fireside Fun* as follows:

> *One of the gentlemen well acquainted with the game undertakes to represent Aesop. In order to do so more effectually, he may put a cushion or pillow under his coat to imitate a hump, provide himself with a thick stick for a crutch, make a false nose, and put a patch over one eye ...*

I must say this sounds to me more like Long John Silver than Aesop, but it does go to show how thoroughly people entered into games before television came along. No Victorian parlour, it appears, was complete without its thick stick, hump substitute, eye patch and bucket of *papier mâché* for the moulding of an instant false nose.

> *Mama:*   Might one propose a game of Aesop's mission?
> *Papa:*   A splendid notion! – Emily, pray be so kind as to pass the bucket.

No wonder Sherlock Holmes was a master of disguise.

Aesop's mission was to discover which animal had upset the gods by its choice of menu. He would therefore ask each animal in turn to state what it had last dined upon, and to each response would reply either 'Good' or 'Bad', apparently at random. In fact, he would previously have picked upon a common letter of the alphabet as being taboo, and would castigate as 'Bad' any answer containing that letter.

For those who knew the game, the object of play was to discover the taboo letter and to avoid incurring Aesop's censure by choosing answers that did not contain the naughty letter. Those who didn't know the game were left wondering what the whole thing was about, and whether Mama, Papa and Emily were as *compos mentis* as they liked to pretend.

This basic idea may be presented more simply, and quite suitably for children, in the following manner.

Having secretly picked upon a letter of the alphabet as currently taboo, Aesop asks of each player in turn a question requiring a one-word answer. If the answer contains the forbidden letter, the respondent loses a life. The first to lose three lives is the overall loser, and pays a forfeit. (Or loses an overall.)

Supposing T to be the outlawed letter, a sequence might begin:

> *Aesop:*   How old are you?
> *Answer:*   One hundred. (Good)
> *Aesop:*   Who's your favourite author?
> *Answer:*   Dickens. (Good)
> *Aesop:*   Who was that lady I saw you with last night?
> *Answer:*   My sister. (Bad)

And so on.

KOLODNY'S GAME (WORD ELEUSIS)
Two or more players
Mainly for adults
Requires concentration

This game, credited to David Greene Kolodny (but borrowing something from Robert Abbott's card game *Eleusis*), is not so much a deductive game as an inductive one. At least, it's deductive in the sense that, in the long run, your aim is to discover something hidden. What's inductive is the mental process by which you carry this out. In the hope that this is more clear to you than it is to me, let's begin.

One player, the Umpire, invents a rule of play, and the other players seek to discover what it is. To this end, they ask questions designed to elicit Yes/No answers. Each answer, however, refers to the *form* of the question rather than to its content. Exactly how it refers depends upon the rule that has been invented (but not stated) by the current Umpire.

An example should make this less obscure.

The rule of play might be that questions ending in letters A to M are answered 'Yes', while those ending in letters N to Z are answered 'No'. Hence:

> Are you lyinG? – *Yes.*
> Are you telling the trutH? – *Yes.*
> Do you know what you're talking abouT? – *No.*

And so on.

Other rules could relate to whether or not the question contained the word YOU, whether or not it was heralded with a thinking noise such as ERM, whether or not it contained a verb, and so on.

This game is made fun by the fact that questions are framed with a view to testing hypothesized rules as to their form, not for anything to do with their content or factual truthfulness, and may therefore extend over a wide range of facetious subjects. And there are, of course, some questions whose Yes/No answer as required by the logic of the rule may gravely embarrass the respondent.

FOLLOW THAT!

The following games are following games. They're all based on the idea of each player in turn announcing a word that follows on in some way from the one that went before. For example, they may be required to rhyme, or begin with the same letter, or avoid repeating a letter, or continue the sense (or nonsense, as the case may be) of the words preceding them. Many are party games and so can be classified as 'more fun than competitive', though you can easily introduce an element of horror by prescribing forfeits. Be warned, however, that a few call for a little more thought, and at least one is positively intellectual. I've put these at the end in order not to frighten you off too early.

BUZZ
Any number of players
Any age
Fun and competitive

I used to play this at school under the impression that it was a mathematical game, but have since come across it in a book of word games, and what is mathematics if not a language anyway? So here goes.

Players arrange themselves in a theoretical circle and play the game by numbering off one after the other – *one, two,* etc. You may not, however, announce a number which is a multiple of three, or contains a three. Instead, you say *buzz*, otherwise you drop out. Thus the game continues *buzz, four, five, buzz, seven, eight, buzz, ten, eleven, buzz, buzz, fourteen* etc. The number 29 will, of course, be followed by ten *buzz*es. The last player left in is the winner, and presumably gets a score equivalent to the last number stated. You could agree to stop upon reaching 300 if no clear winner has emerged by that time, or when everyone has buzzed themselves to sleep.

Variants. Many people play variations of the game on different rounds in order to keep the players alert. An obvious variation is to change the number and multiple concerned. Another is to introduce a second taboo number running concurrently with the first. Seven is a popular choice. Any number containing or being a multiple of seven is replaced by *bizz*, and any involving both three and seven is announced as *bizz-buzz*.

Then there's the legionary variation, suitable for players who know their Roman numerals. This goes *aye, aye-aye, buzz, aye-vee, vee, buzz,* and so on.

TENNIS ELBOW FOOT
Any number of players
Any age
More fun than competitive

The players sit in a circle or indeed any other arrangement that enables them to see at a glance whose turn it is and how long it will be before their own turn comes round again.

The first player announces a word, which could be TENNIS, but could equally well be one of about 300,000 others. The next player in turn must immediately respond with a word bearing an obvious relation to the first, the third with a word bearing an obvious relation to the second, and so on. Thus TENNIS could be followed by ELBOW, then FOOT, then BALL, then CHAIN ... you catch the drift.

Anyone who fails to respond immediately with a sensibly connected word, or repeats a word that has already occurred, or collapses in uncontrollable hysterics, drops out of play.

The winner is the last player left in, or the first to develop genuine symptoms of tennis elbow or athlete's foot.

FREE ASSOCIATION
Any number of players
Any age
More traumatic than fun

This is an appalling variation on *Tennis elbow foot.* The first player starts with any word, such as PSYCHOANALYSIS, and each succeeding player must promptly respond with the first word that comes to mind as soon as the previous word has been announced. This time it need not be sensibly connected – on the contrary, the whole point of the game lies in discovering what peculiar connections lie within the murky recesses of everybody else's minds. Even more interesting are the mental blocks that sometimes arise when one word or concept completely fails to evoke another in the mind of the next in turn.

The trouble with this game is that it's hard to determine who has won, and why. There are those who credit it with some form of therapeutic value, but I don't believe a word of it.

DISASSOCIATION
Any number of players
Any age
Competitive, funnily enough

Here's the other end of the line from *Tennis elbow foot.* As before, the first player starts with any word and each succeeding player must respond immediately with another. But now the rule is total randomness. Each succeeding word must bear *absolutely no readily discernible connection* with the previous one. Anyone who can spot a connection can challenge the player who said it, and if the others agree that the connection is apparent, the challenged player loses a life. The first player to lose three lives ends the game and pays a forfeit.

Here's how a session might begin:

- Tennis. Ear-drops. Banshee. Mousetrap. Gorge. *Challenge:* Mousetraps contain cheese, which may be Cheddar, as in Gorge. Or, mice may gorge upon the cheese when they find it.

- Gorge. Blacking. Crescent. Hospital. *Challenge:* A hospital might be run by the Red Crescent, Islamic equivalent of the Red Cross.

- Hospital. Pendulum. 43. Haggis. Sex. *Challenge:* Everything reminds me of sex. (*Not upheld.*)

HEADS AND TAILS
Any number of players
Any age
Competitive but fun

A category of names or objects is agreed – let's say towns, for the sake of argument. Each player in turn must then announce the name of a town which (a) begins with the last letter of the previous one, and (b) has not been mentioned before. Such a sequence might begin as follows:

London – Norwich – Hartlepool – Littlehampton ...

and so on. Elimination is the penalty for failing to respond within a few seconds, or failing to match the last letter, or repeating a town already mentioned, or dropping off to sleep.

This makes a good general knowledge quiz for younger players. It can be spiced up in one or two ways. A particularly nasty variation is to penalize a player whose entry begins and ends with the same letter. Another is to play against a timer that sounds an alarm after a predetermined interval. In this version players don't drop out. Instead, the last player to have announced a valid entry when the alarm sounds is the winner.

LIFE SENTENCE
Any number of players
Adults and older children
Fun, but requires concentration

This variation on *Heads and tails* is of my own devising, and is a little harder than its model.

The object is to produce a plausible sentence, or series of consecutive sentences, to which each player contributes one word in turn, and such that each new word begins with the last letter of the preceding one. Anyone unable to continue plausibly drops out, pays a forfeit, or loses six months' remission, as agreed beforehand.

Such a sentence might (conceivably) begin as follows:

When no-one expects sincere explanations, several lies should do ...

This sentence sounds as if it has reached a natural break. The next player must now think of a new sentence that follows on from the first and begins with O.

TRAILERS
Any number of players
Adults and older children
Can give rise to arguments

This is the spoken equivalent of a well-known pencil-and-paper game.

The first player announces a two-word compound. Thereafter, each player in turn must come up with a succeeding compound of which the first half is the same as the second half of its predecessor. For example:

Boathouse
   House-warming
      Warming pan
         Pancake
            Cakestand

Anyone unable to provide a suitable continuation may claim that no continuation is possible. If no one does so, the previous player drops out and the challenger starts a new series. A player whose challenge is met by a valid continuation drops out of play, and the person who provided it continues from there.

CRAMBO
Any number of players
Any age
More fun than competitive

> *In 1706 crambo was explained as 'A term used by schoolboys, when in rhiming, he is to forfeit, who repeats a word that was said before.'*
> *Samuel Pepys was a word-gamer. His entry for 20 May 1660 includes the confession: 'From thence to the Hague again, playing at crambo in the wagon.' (It is just possible that he was using it as a code word for something more nefarious, but perhaps we should give him the benefit of the doubt.)*

This is one of the very few games to take its title from the Latin word for the dish known in Britain as bubble and squeak. The only one, in fact. The phrase *crambe repetita* literally means 'cabbage served up again'. Playful grammarians then came to use it metaphorically in the sense of 'distasteful repetition', applying it in this capacity to prayers repeated in parrot fashion. It then became a natural term for a series of repetitions, not of the same word, but of words that rhyme with it, thus producing the game of *Crambo*. (See also *Dumb crambo* in the Performing Rites section, page 39.) Here's an updated and slightly expanded version of it:

The first player thinks of a rhythmic phrase or short sentence and announces it to the assembled company. Thereafter each player in turn must spontaneously come up with a line of similar length and rhythm (but don't apply this too strictly) that rhymes with those preceding it.

A game might begin as follows:

Never say die.
  Look at the sky.

> Who said pigs can't fly?
>   Wasn't me. Why?
>   Crisps make me cry.
>   Or so you imply.
>   Well, fiddle-de-die ...

A player drops out, or is declared the loser, for drying up, or failing to produce a satisfactory entry (in the unanimous opinion of the other players), or for repeating a rhyme word that has already been used – such as the last line of the above example, as compared with the first.

You might also insist that each new phrase bears some readily observable, or at least explicable, relationship to the previous one. But this does make the game harder, and each player should be then allowed a few seconds' thinking time.

The first player has the awesome responsibility of producing a line end capable of yielding a sequence of rhymes long enough to make the game worthwhile. You could (and I certainly would) devise some sort of scoring system to take this into account. For example, a game might consist of as many rounds as there are players, with each player having one opportunity to start the ball rolling. A round would end when one player contravenes any of the rules stated above. The starter can keep track of the number of lines produced by the whole group. When the round ends, the starter can score as many points as lines produced (including the first), and the defaulter can lose the same number. A starter who also defaults will make only the negative score.

ACRONIMBLE
Any number of players
Adults and older children
Requires concentration

Players arrange themselves in such a way as to be able to play in endless rotation. The first begins a sentence by announcing its subject, which could be a name or a noun not requiring an article (*a* or *the*) as its first word. This is to be taken as the first word of a sentence, which is to be extended by the addition of a new word by each player in turn. The point of the game is that the initial letter of each successive word should spell out a word, which need not be agreed upon at the start of play.

For example, a round might begin:

> John
> Expects
> A
> Nice
> Surprise

thereby spelling out the word JEANS.

If played to the rule of *Ghosts* (see page 14), the real aim of play is to add a letter which forms part of a foreseeable whole word but does not itself end one. A player who completes a word of four or more letters is thereby deemed the loser, and loses a life or pays a forfeit. Or a player may challenge the previous one to prove that the last initial will actually enable a word to be completed. Otherwise, play continues until a player cannot add a word that makes sense or contributes to the spelling of the overall word. That player is the loser, and the preceding player the winner.

Variation. A rather tough variation on this idea resembles the game of *Telegrams* (see page 67). In this one, the whole sentence must produce a sentence which is an acronym of, and relevant to, the first word. For example:

> Trees
> Rarely
> Exceed
> Eighteen
> Stones

It matters not that trees probably weigh more than that – the sentence only has to be meaningful, not necessarily true. In this case, of course, you don't lose by completing the acronym.

PERFORMING RITES

When you get to the punchline of a joke, does your audience laugh? Or does it shuffle its feet and look vaguely embarrassed? When you rise to your feet clutching a sheaf of notes and mumble 'Unaccustomed as I am to public speaking ...', do people readily believe you? When you hail a taxi, does it stop?

In short, are you a good performer?

You never know till you've tried, and the party-ish games gathered below – including the ever popular *Charades* and the cross between it and *Dumb crambo* now known as *Give us a clue* – will give you every opportunity to find out. Whether the answer is an embarrassed apology or a resounding 'NO!', you should find the practice you get from the following exercises serving you in good stead next time you're invited to launch a battleship or read the saucy telegrams.

Several of the games revolve around guessing proverbs from clues provided. You may think it a pity that proverbs no longer enjoy the universal recognition accorded to them up to about the middle of the 20th century, and nowadays have to be replaced by titles of films and television programmes. Still, this won't detract from the games' effectiveness as performance indicators. For, of the various demands they make on you, the one thing they all demand is a bit of quick thinking and glib talking. Not everyone may want to join in (shame!), but those who don't are sure to enjoy the spectacle of everybody else making fools of themselves.

STRIKE A POSE
Any number of players
Any age
More fun than competitive

This fairly simple game is more fun than it sounds in the cold light of print. It won't take up too much of your time before you pass on to more advanced variations of the same idea.

On each of 26 slips of paper, or any other number that takes your fancy, write an adjective, such as angry, bemused, cheerful, downcast, effervescent, grand, hungry, indignant, jaunty, knowing, languorous, moody, overwrought, panicky, querulous, robust, sexy, thoughtful, unhappy, vivacious, wild, (e)xquisite, yearning, or even zestful. Shake them up in a bag. Each player in turn draws a slip from the bag and then strikes a pose expressive of the adjective it specifies. The others, in no particular order, shout out their guesses as to what the adjective might be. If the adjective is not divined within ten guesses, the *poseur* loses a life and chooses who is to pose next. If it is divined, both the *poseur* and the guesser gain a life and the guesser goes next. The game continues until you run out of adjectives.

I wouldn't insist too firmly on having to adopt an absolutely rigid and unmoving pose. For example, ANGRY might be expressed in part by shaking a fist, or PANICKY by quivering like a jelly. But the amount of movement involved shouldn't go so far as to amount to a mimed performance.

YOURS SINCERELY
Any number of players
Any age
More fun than competitive

This is the adverbial version of the adjectival game described above. I'm sure you know what an adverb is. It's a sort of … well, a word that … er … Oh well, perhaps we'd better just describe it.

At each turn one player goes out of the room (or, in my case, switches off his hearing aid) and those left in the room agree on an adverb for the outsider to discover when readmitted to the circle. Returned to circulation, the victim tries to deduce which adverb was agreed on by putting a question to each player in turn. The questioned player must then attempt to give a reply in the manner described by the adverb.

There's no rule about what sort of question you can ask. It may be general or specific, personal or impersonal, or as sensible or silly as you wish. Nor does it matter two hoots (well, three, anyway) whether the answer is true, false or totally meaningless. All that counts is that the way in which the answer is delivered – whether arrogantly, beautifully, cheerfully, declamatorily, elegantly, flippantly, grandiloquently, haltingly, imperiously, judiciously, kindly, laughingly, monotonously, nastily, openly, purringly, quietly, raucously, squeakily, tearfully, unctuously, vivaciously, wheedlingly, (e)xplosively, yearningly, or perhaps even zealously – is in the way referred to by the agreed adverb.

If you want to be a little more formal, you can decree that no single player may be asked more than one question, so that the maximum permissible number of questions is that of the number of players performing the adverb. And you can score a penalty point for each question asked, and another for each wrong guess, so that the ultimate winner is the player with the fewest penalties after an agreed number of rounds have been played.

SPELLING BEE
At least six players, the more the better
Mainly for children and bad spellers
A team game, competitive rather than fun

This is a truly traditional parlour game. 'Why "bee"?', you may ask. Having asked it myself, I actually went to the trouble of looking it up, and found it defined as *a gathering of persons to unite their labour for the benefit of one individual or family, or for some joint amusement, exercise or competition (from the bee's habit of combined labour).*

The benefit to be derived from this game is presumably that of either improving your spelling or being able to show off your own skill at the art. The way to get this game to work well is to divide the company into two teams. Each player is then responsible both for thinking up words to be spelt and for having to spell some words nominated by the other side. It's useful also to appoint an umpire or dictionary consultant – or Queen Bee – to arbitrate as necessary.

Here's one way of organizing the proceedings. Queen Bee tosses a coin to decide which team shall bat first. Each member of the batting team comes to the front and has to defend him- or her-self by correctly spelling a word bowled to him in turn by each member of the fielding team. A 'run' is scored for a correct answer acknowledged by the bowler, or two runs if the bowler challenges it and the spelling is upheld by Queen Bee. Defending successfully against the whole team earns a bonus of six runs and ends the innings. An incorrect spelling puts the batsman 'out' immediately.

When every member of the batting teams has had an innings, the teams reverse roles with the fielding team now batting.

SPELLING ROUND
Any number of players
Mainly for children
Not very competitive

A non-team spelling game more suitable for children may be played as follows:

The players sit in a circle and each in turn becomes the Inquisitor. The Inquisitor sets a word to be spelt – let's say QUESTION – and points to one of the players. Starting with that player, the word must now be spelt letter by letter around the circle of players. That is, the first player says Q, the second U, the third E, and so on. Anyone who makes a mistake or hesitates too long drops out of play, or loses a life.

BANANAS
Any number of players
Mainly for children
More fun than competitive

This is more of a laughing game than a word game.

The first player is chosen by lot (or, if he isn't playing, by Lot's wife) and proceeds to put questions to each other player in turn. Whatever the question, it must be answered with the word 'Bananas'. Anyone who laughs while giving this answer – or in anticipation of giving it, or in hilariously immediate retrospect – loses a life (or an appropriate equivalent) and becomes the next inquisitor.

You may be forgiven for thinking this is a silly game. In fact, you will find it rather more subtle and skilful than Prime Minister's Question Time, as the whole object of the exercise is to frame your question in such a way as to force your respondent to laugh. For example:

> What do you wash your face in each morning? – *Bananas.*
> What do you wear when you go to bed? – *Bananas.*
> What's that you've got up your jumper? – *Bananas.*

Variation. The great thing about this game is its versatility. You may allow the Inquisitor to nominate a different word to be given as the answer for a change. However, *Bananas* does tend to lose its flavour after a while.

TEAPOT
Any number of players
Mainly for children
More fun than competitive

Like *Bananas* (above), *Teapot* is more of a laughing game than a word game, but it has been known to keep children amused.

One player is bundled out of earshot while the others agree on a verb or 'doing-word'. Suppose the verb chosen is *sing*. The victim now returns and aims either to discover the secret verb or to make somebody laugh, whichever is the sooner. This is done by addressing each player in turn and posing a question in which the unknown verb *sing* is replaced by *teapot*. The respondent must reply to the question exactly as if it had contained the hidden verb. In this instance, the inquisition might go as follows:

> *Annie:*   Where do you usually teapot?
> *Benny:*   In the bath.
> *Annie:*   Does Benny teapot nicely?
> *Connie:*   No. He usually shatters the windows.
> *Annie:*   What would you do if I teapotted all over you?
> *Danny:*   I'd probably stuff cotton wool in my ears.

As players tire of this game, they drop out one by one. When only two remain, they are the winners.

TABOO
Any number of players
Any age, but perhaps not too young
More fun than competitive

This word can also be spelt tabu but that is taboo in this book.

Each player in turn becomes the Inquisitor and secretly writes on a slip of paper a word to be considered taboo for their round of inquisition. They then address each other player in turn and pose a question, to which the respondent must give an adequate reply under threat of a forfeit to be agreed by the other players. The Inquisitor scores a point for each answer which does not contain the taboo word, and ends his or her turn upon either scoring ten points or eliciting an answer that does contain it. The overall winner, of course, is the player with the fewest penalty points.

Here's an example. Suppose the taboo word is help. Then suitable questions might include:

- What's an S.O.S. signal?
- Why do you keep blinking? *(Hoping for the reply 'I can't help it').*
- Does your elderly mother do all her own housework?

You would, of course, accept compounds and derivatives, such as HELPS, HELPED, HELPER and so on, as being equally taboo. After a while, it may become obvious which word you are looking for, so try to make your questions as subtle as possible.

You may, if you prefer, prepare this game beforehand by writing taboo words on slips of paper and getting prospective inquisitors to draw them from a bag or box.

QUICK THINKING
Any number of players
Any age
More fun than competitive

Unless you're a quick thinker, you'll need to prepare for this by getting some slips of paper and writing (or drawing) an unlikely object on each one – the funnier, the better.

As the Inquisitor, you address each player in turn, confront her or him with two of these slips drawn at random from a bag or box and then ask a question that may or may not be relevant to the objects so indicated. Relevant or not, the questioned player must now provide an answer to the question that manages to incorporate both objects in the same sentence. For example:

Objects: Bicycle, doughnut
Question: Why did the chicken cross the road?
Answer: Because she was out riding her *bicycle* when she saw a baker's on the other side of the road and suddenly fancied a *doughnut.*

Objects: Hammer, spaghetti
Question: What are your plans for the future?
Answer: As soon as I finish eating this *spaghetti* I'm going to *hammer* you into the ground.

The winner is the player whose answer provokes the greatest laughter.

HOBBY HORSE

Any number of players
Any age
More fun than competitive

I got this from a book of classroom games, but there's no reason why it shouldn't amuse adults of an appropriate disposition. It requires a stock of forenames and surnames, either real or imaginary, so it might be a good idea to make such a collection in advance, unless you're good at thinking up names on the spot.

In each round, one player is appointed Inquisitor. The Inquisitor addresses each other player in turn, putting to them a question beginning 'What's your hobby ...?', followed by a name. The respondent must then come up as quickly as possible with a hobby that begins with the same two initials as the name put to them. So a game might begin:

What's your hobby, Cilla Blackbeard? – *Collecting bonfires.*
What's your hobby, Arthur Daley? – *Acquiring Doodahs.*
What's your hobby, Elizabeth Ragwort? – *Exuding rainbows.*

And so on. Anyone who fails to come up with a correct response within a couple of seconds drops out of play, pays a forfeit or loses a point. You might score a point for an immediate response, plus another point for each other player who laughs at it.

P.S. When I was interviewed on radio about one of my earlier books of games, the interviewer thought it would be a good idea to try some of them out live by way of demonstration, and promptly asked 'What's your hobby, David Parlett?'. Some years later, I came up with the answer 'Deep-sea Pole-vaulting'. Unfortunately, we were no longer on air.

INQUISITION

Any number of players
Probably better for adults
Fun, but can get nasty

This game is not something you can play for ever, as it gets wearing after a while, but it makes a nice party-piece before the novelty begins to wear off. Basically, it's a contest between two players, but it can easily be organized as a team game designed to produce a single winner at the end.

The first player starts by asking the second a question. The second must 'answer a question with a question' – that is, reply with another question that follows on fairly plausibly from the first (in the opinion of the other players). The first player must likewise reply to this with another question, and so on and suchlike, until one of them is eventually careless enough to give a straight answer, or bop the other one on the jaw. The general effect might be:

Zandy:	Why are we playing this game?
Yolande:	What's the matter with it?
Zandy:	Is that supposed to be a reply?
Yolande:	Don't you know a reply when you see one?
Zandy:	Surely you mean 'hear one'?
Yolande:	How do you know what I mean?
Zandy:	Wheeaaaouww …er …er … *(loses game).*

You could try awarding the winner one point for each question answered with a question, but that means someone has to keep count, which is a bit of a bind.

JUST A MINUTE
Four to seven players
Adults and precocious children
Fun, but daunting

As BBC Radio has made this game famous throughout the English-speaking world it needs little introduction. In its raw form it dates back to the Victorian heyday of parlour games. The more formal radio version described here benefits from rules and scoring devised by Ian Messiter. Each player in turn is set a topic and required to speak about it more or less fluently for a whole minute without breaking up or falling into a complete torpor. The radio format pits four players in competition with one another for points awarded by an umpire in accordance with the following rules.

Each in turn embarks upon the quoted topic and tries to keep going for a minute without losing it to someone else. Whoever is speaking when the officially recorded minute is up scores a point, or two points if they started the subject and never lost it.

At any point in the proceedings the speaker can be interrupted by a challenge from another player. The timer is paused while the challenge is argued and the umpire adjudicates.

There are three possible grounds for a challenge, namely:

- *Hesitation*, as when the speaker pauses unduly, speaks unnecessarily slowly or stumbles over words;
- *Deviation*, as when he or she strays from the main subject – or, to stretch a point, deviates from good English usage or general propriety;
- *Repetition*, which should speak for itself, but in practice gives rise to the greatest number of arguments.

If the challenge is upheld, the challenger gains a point and now speaks on the subject for as long as remains of the original minute. If not, the challengee gains the point and carries on from where he or she left off. Points may also be awarded *ex gratia* for clever or witty challenges, even if not upheld. The challenge for repetition ought strictly, I suppose, be allowed only to prevent players from saying essentially the same thing over and over again, whether in the same or different words. In practice, it tends to be used against repetition by the same speaker of almost any word they may have uttered in talking about the same topic, even if the two occurrences have been separated by a period of speech by someone else.

It obviously saves time to have a list of topics planned in advance, though some fun may be had in simply getting everyone to write out two or three suggestions on slips of paper and then drawing them from a hat. It isn't necessary to have the same umpire every time – players can simply take turns to occupy the umpire's chair – but it has to be admitted that some players make better umpires than others, and the ideal umpire could easily prove more successful in that position than as one of the performers.

Here are a few topics to be getting along with:

- The lesser spotted reed-warbler
- Getting lost
- Why my hair always looks like this
- What the butler didn't see
- The Nineteenth Law of Thermodynamics
- Cleopatra's Needle
- How to address royalty
- The effects of inflation on bikinis

HALF A MINUTE
Any number of players
Adults and older children
More fun than competitive

Half a Minute is *Just a Minute*'s kid brother, and has the advantage of being more fun and less cut-throat.

As before, there is an Umpire, who sets the subject and keeps the time. The first player starts talking about the subject and keeps going for about 30 seconds, or less if the time-keeper thinks the speaker is flagging and decides to strike the gong. Come gong-strike, the next in turn (or whoever the current speaker points to) takes the subject over and also keeps going for as long as possible or 30 seconds, whichever is the sooner. This continues until everyone has had a turn at speaking.

Neither any one player nor the company as a whole is obliged to stick to the opening subject, so long as each one broadly continues the drift of the previous speaker, and keeps talking as fluently as possible for as long as they can. Indeed, the chief amusement of this game lies in marvelling at how wide the gulf is between the opening subject and the one completed by the last speaker. In this respect it bears a distinct resemblance to Chinese whispers.

RAILWAY CARRIAGE GAME
Any number of players
Adults and loquacious children
Fun, but quite competitive

This one evidently dates from the days when train passengers sat in transverse compartments and spoke to one another, as opposed to today's longitudinal compartments in which people speak only into mobile telephones.

Two volunteers are dragooned under threat of blackmail and each is given, in secret, a more or less plausible sentence such as might occur in everyday conversation between total strangers. They are then seated in such a way as to approximate a railway carriage set-up and required to launch into conversation. The conversation must proceed, as far as possible, along plausible lines until one player succeeds in getting his or her predetermined sentence *naturally* into the conversation, thereby winning the point. Or losing it, if, in the opinion of the audience, the conversational pretext was less than adequate.

Some constraints and provisos are needed to make the game fair and workable. The conversation should start with an introduction of some neutral topic of conversation, like the weather, in order to prevent the first speaker from establishing a thematic advantage. Then, in accordance with the normal rules of polite conversation in Victorian railway carriages, players should not be allowed excessive licence to interrupt each other's speeches, whether to deflect them from the subject or to seize upon some word of the other's that may be used as a springboard to their own sentence. Finally, it's best not to insist that the winning sentence be produced exactly word for word, so long as it follows the general drift and contains all the key words.

Here's an example of how the conversation might go between two players designated Austen and Byron (for the sake of argument). Byron's hidden sentence is *They do say tennis is good for the elbows*, and Austen's *I've never eaten whelks with a spoon*.

Austen: Looks like rain again.
Byron: Pity. I was rather looking forward to a game this afternoon.
Austen (spotting a possible theme and trying to steer away from it): Well, you can't play anything with puddles around. Except at the seaside, of course.
Byron: Seaside golf course, you say? I prefer tennis myself.
Austen (appealing to the audience): Look, I'm not playing this stupid game if he's going to keep deliberately mishearing … (Cries of 'Shut up!', 'Get on with it', 'It's only a game', etc). Well, anyway, what I like about seaside puddles is the interesting variety of shellfish you find in them. Do you like shellfish?
Byron: No, actually, I prefer tennis myself, because …
Austen: Well *I* prefer eating. I reckon I've had more hot dinners than you've had games of tennis. I'm particularly fond of whelks …
Byron: Whelks aren't hot dinners. And what's more, they're said to be bad for the elbows.
Austen: Whelks haven't got elbows.
Byron: True, but if they had they'd probably love playing tennis, as they say tennis is very good for the elbows.

This cuts short Austen's next remark, which was going to be 'Have you ever played tennis with a spoon?', or, possibly, 'What's your name? Mine's Witherspoon.'

Here are a few secret sentences to keep the party boiling:

- My aunt tried that, but kept falling off in the middle.
- I once had exactly the same experience with a coconut.
- You really ought to get yourself a motorbike.
- As the art mistress said to the gardener.
- Was that supposed to be your sentence?

Here's a piece of useful advice. *Never answer the other player's question*. That way, you're likely to get drawn into a conversational trap leading ineluctably away from your own topic and into theirs. If there's any questions to be asked, make sure it's you that does the asking.

YES AND NO
Any number of players
Any age
Fun, but nerve-racking

Here's another family favourite which at various times has been adapted for radio and television, with the result that most people think – wrongly – that radio and television invented it first. You know the game: it's the one where each contestant is asked a series of quick-fire questions for about half a minute and win a prize if they manage to avoid saying either 'Yes' or 'No' before the gong sounds. The remarkable thing is that it seems to play more on the nerves of the audience than of the contestant, which I suppose is why it was so successful as a form of mass entertainment.

A gong is useful, but not essential – a spoon and saucepan will serve the purpose. What is essential, though, is to have someone expert in asking questions at great speed and fluently. With an inquisitor like this, it's easy to be the victim of a contest that sounds like this, only faster:

Q: So your name's Wright?
A: Right.
Q: Not wrong?
A: Er- er- Correct.
Q: And you come from Edgware?
A: From Edgware I come from, I do.
Q: Not Stanmore?
A: N-n-not quite, just near it.
Q: The 25 bus goes there, doesn't it?
A: I don't think so.
Q: You're sure about that?
A: Positive.
Q: You didn't say 'Yes', did you?
A: No ...
   BONG!

In case you haven't got a brilliant inquisitor, here are two other ways of playing it:

Variation 1. Each player in turn is the contestant and one player is the timekeeper. Everybody else (including the timekeeper, if he or she can concentrate on two things as once) then throws questions at the contestant one by one, or even all at once.

Variation 2. There is no particular contestant or inquisitor. Instead, each player is given five counters, or matchsticks, and then circulate among themselves to engage in conversation as the fancy takes them. Anyone who gets another player to say 'Yes' or 'No' gives them a counter for it. The first player to get rid of all their counters is the winner.

You don't have to play this variation as a formal game. You can have it as a sort of running game played throughout the evening. Just give everyone a pile of counters when they arrive (the later, the fewer, for fairness) and explain the rules. Then they can just give one another counters while indulging in whatever people do at parties, until someone runs out of counters and claims a reward from the host or hostess.

PROVERBS
Any number of players
Adults and older children
More fun than competitive

One player is told to get lost while the others agree among themselves on a proverb or popular saying. Let's suppose it is *Many hands make light work*. The lost player is then returned to the fold and endeavours to discover the agreed phrase by putting a question to each player in turn. The first respondent's reply must include the first word of the hidden phrase, the second reply must include the second, the third the third, and so on. If you didn't start by telling the enquirer how many words are in the phrase, the last respondent should state that no more questions are needed.

For the above example, the questioning might go as follows:

Arthur: What was Napoleon REALLY like?
Bertha: A good MANY people found him hard to get on with.
Arthur: Why did you send me out of the room just now?
Eartha: We wanted to see if your HANDS were likely to go blue with the cold.
Arthur: Who won the Kentucky Derby in 1922?
Luther: Even if I knew, it'd be a bit late to MAKE any money on it.
Arthur: What's a nice girl like you doing in a place like this?
Martha: You wouldn't begrudge me a little LIGHT entertainment now and again, would you?
Arthur: Why did the chicken cross the road?
Yootha: Because it was late for WORK and wanted to get to the other side. No more questions!
Arthur: Your hidden proverb is *People wanted money again because.* Or, failing that, *Many hands make light work.*

In choosing a hidden phrase, players must be careful to avoid one containing such give-away words as HESITATES (*He who ...*), EGGS (*... in one basket*), and so on. When you run out of proverbs, you can start on book or film titles, advertising slogans, and any string of words of topical significance.

If you want to introduce a competitive element by means of scoring, I suggest a basic three points, plus one bonus point for each word remaining if the phrase is correctly guessed before the end is reached, minus one point for a wrong guess.

SHOUTING PROVERBS
Any number of players, the more the merrier
Mainly for children
More fun than competitive

This pastime, as Charles Cotton says in *The Compleat Gamester* of 1674 (though in another connection), cannot be commended for its ingenuity. Nevertheless, it seems to appear in all the word game books from goodness knows when, and may therefore be considered worthy of inclusion on grounds of tradition.

One player is sent to Coventry while the others agree on a proverb, or cliché, or long-winded book title, or something of the sort. It should contain more words rather than fewer, ideally as many words as there are players. One word is assigned to each player, though some players may be allocated two words if there are more words than there are players. The outcast is then returned to the bosom of the family and attempts to discover the proverb. To this end, the others, at a given signal, simultaneously shout out the words individually assigned to them.

It isn't clear to me, from any of the descriptions I've read, whether they all shout out their word once only, in complete unison (like the eminently parodiable 'Slain!' from Walton's *Belshazzar's Feast*, 1931), or instead keep on shouting in an effort to outdo one another in the performance of their individual words. Either way, the guesser is bound to spot such give-away words as HESITATES or EGGS. On the whole, I think the one-off method is preferable, provided you can get everyone to shout in perfect unison. You can then award the victim three points for guessing it immediately, two for requiring a second shout, and one point only for a third.

DUMB CRAMBO

Six or more players
Younger rather than older
More fun than competitive

Dumb crambo– not to be confused with Cram dumbo, the elephant-stuffing game – is the performing version of *Crambo*, the bubble and squeak game (see page 27). I have inserted a scoring system, that being my bent, but there's no need to follow it if you don't see the point(s).

Divide the company into two teams and send one team out to get a Chinese takeaway while the other thinks of a word to be guessed. The agreed word should be one that lends itself to many rhymes. Thus ORANGE would be a very bad word to choose, while BEAR would do admirably.

The other team, which probably hasn't got as far as the front gate yet, is called back into the room and told a word that rhymes with the hidden word. They then have to guess that word in the following way. Any member of the team who has an idea of what the hidden word is must indicate their suggestion by performing a mime. For example, if the hidden word is BEAR, a team member who suspects FAIR might go through the motions of swings and roundabouts and dodgems (the mind boggles!) to get this concept across. Any other member of the team may then guess the word being mimed. If the guess does not match the performance (for example, someone guesses AIR instead of FAIR), the other team scores a point and the performer tries again until someone correctly identifies the mime. If the mime is correctly guessed, but it is not the hidden word, the other team scores another point, and the player who correctly identified it thinks of a new word to try and takes over the miming.

When the word is eventually discovered, the teams swap roles. The winning team, of course, is the one with the greater score when each side has had a previously agreed equal number of turns.

SOLO CHARADES

Four or more players
Adults and older children
Fun or competitive, as preferred

Anyone who has seen a Marx Brothers' film will remember Harpo's distinctive way of explaining current events to his brother Chico. (The best example occurs in the 1946 movie *A Night in Casablanca*.) As it amounts to an extended session of *Solo charades* you can wish for no clearer introduction to the game. But here's a more long-winded explanation for those whose film education is deficient.

One player thinks of a word of two or more syllables and provides clues by performing a mime. If you stick to two syllables it is often possible and always permissible to perform both mimes simultaneously. If you allow three or more, the performer should indicate how many syllables are involved and divide the performance into the same number of distinct sections. Whoever guesses the mimed word first becomes the next performer.

You can make it competitive by giving everyone a number of scoring objects to start with, such as counters or matchsticks. The guessers start by placing one counter each in a pool, which goes to the player who guesses the mime correctly. Each wrong guess requires the guesser to put an extra counter in the pool.

Here are some words and how they might be performed:

TENNIS   Put up ten fingers and hiss like a snake.

CARTOON	Mime driving and hum a tune.
PIANO	Use fingers to mime letter P, then a plus sign for *an(d)*, then an O.
GRANITE	Mime an old lady, and knit (like Harpo in *A Night at the Opera*).
BELLOW	Ring a bell and moo like a cow.

At a pinch, the last example could serve for BELOW. The fun of this game lies as much in its visual punning as anything else. You should decide beforehand whether or not you are going to allow non-verbal noises.

CHARADES
Eight or more players
Any age, but including good organizers
Fun, but elaborate

Unlike Solo charades, this is not a miming game – the mimetic equivalent is *Give us a clue* (below). Charades was the really great game of Victorian family parties, witness this extract from the 1881 edition of *Cassell's Book of In-Door Amusements, Card Games and Fireside Fun*:

'Although the acting of charades is by no means an amusement of very recent invention, it is one which may always be made so thoroughly attractive, according to the amount of originality displayed, that most young people, during an evening's entertainment, hail with glee the announcement that a charade is about to be acted. It is not necessary that anything great be attempted in the way of dressing, scenery or similar preparations, such as are almost indispensable to the performance of private theatricals. Nothing is needed beyond a few old clothes, shawls and hats, and a good few actors, or rather, a few clever, bright, intelligent young people, all willing to employ their best energies in contributing to the amusement of their friends. What ability they may possess as actors will soon become evident by the success or failure of the charade.

The word charade derives its name from the Italian word *schiarare* – *to unravel* or *clear up*. Suitable as the word may be in some instances, we cannot help thinking that in the majority of cases the acting of a charade has the effect of making the word chosen anything but clear; indeed, the object of the players generally is to make it as ambiguous as possible. As all players of round games know how charades are got up it would be superfluous to give any elaborate instructions regarding them ...'

It is still played with enthusiasm in certain circles, although, dating as it does from the years long before television, it requires more cleverness, time and thought than most people are nowadays able or willing to devote to making their own amusements. But it's worth while planning such an event if you know you're going to get enough intelligent people together on a forthcoming occasion.

Divide the players into two teams, and separate them into different rooms to get on with their planning. Each team thinks of a word of three syllables – or more or fewer, by prior agreement – each of which can stand on its own as a separate word. The preparation consists in planning a number of scenes to be acted out by the players, more or less ad lib. The first scene must include a word sounding like the first syllable of the chosen word, the second and third scenes likewise for the second and third syllables, and the fourth scene must contain the whole word. The four scenes need not bear any relation to one another – never mind the classical unities of time, place and action. The teams then come together and each of them performs its set of playlets for the other to guess their hidden word.

To take a simple example, let's suppose the hidden word is COPYRIGHT. The first scene could involve two motorists arguing over parking spaces and yellow lines, and one of them calling a policeman, ensuring that the word COP gets into the conversation.

The second could be a performance of the following joke, which I will condense to its essentials. It concerns the preparation of a headstone for a recently deceased pillar of a parish church in Lancashire. The Parish Council eventually decided on just her name and dates, and the all-embracing inscription *She was thine*. When the local monumental mason presented his work for approval it read *She was thin*. 'Idiot!', they said, 'You've missed out the E.' 'Don't worry', he said, 'I can fit that in very quickly.' Next day he presented his work again. This time, it read *'Ee, she was thin'*. (Now you see why it has to be a Lancashire joke.)

The third could be almost anything attaching prominence to the word RIGHT or, preferably, and since punning is allowed, WRITE. As for the fourth, there's no need to set it in a publisher's office. It would be sufficient for one of the actors to make a witty aside and for one of the others to ask if there was any copyright on it.

Expert players are well able to bluff in this game by making a double entry. That is, they choose another word containing the same number of syllables, and ensure that it, too, is incorporated bit by bit in every playlet except one. Their hope is that those who are guessing will latch on to the wrong word.

GIVE US A CLUE

At least eight players
Any age, but including good organizers
Fun, if you like dogmatically applied ritual

This is the dumb (mimed) version of *Charades* (above) that achieved such popularity on television a few years ago, giving the old parlour game a new lease of life and a new title to boot. Much of the fun consisted in following set rituals of mimed explanation that could just as well have been given verbally, but which encouraged people to yell things out together as if at a pantomime.

As befits an organized game, it's best to play this on a fairly formal basis. The host or organizer should previously have thought up titles of books, plays and films, written each one on a slip of paper, and put them into a bag or box. The company is divided into two or more teams. Each team plays in turn, while the others look on and laugh (or cry, depending on the performances). One member of the team draws a slip from the bag or box, and, after a little time for thought, tries to indicate that title to the rest of his or her team, which has one minute after the performance in which to deduce the title. During that period, the performer is not allowed to say anything, but may encourage or discourage guesses by appropriate signs and actions, or repeat any part of the performance, or even change an element of performance if there's time enough to do so.

The performance must be enacted in accordance with certain conventions, as follows. First, indicate the medium or art form in the following way:

Book Place hands in clapping or praying position and open them out from the top to mime opening a book.
Play Make a grand bow or curtsey.
Film Encircle thumb and forefinger before one eye to indicate a camera lens and turn an imaginary camera handle.
Television programme Draw a rectangular screen in the air.
Song Mime an opera singer in full flood.

If the title has been used in more than one form, mime them all, so long as they have exactly the same title. It is conventional for the onlookers to shout 'Book!', 'Film!' or whatever to show that they have grasped the subtleties of the semiotics, and for the performer to nod agreement, or, in the unlikely event that no one has understood, to do the mime again.

Next, indicate the number of words in the title by holding up the same number of fingers. If the title is to be mimed as a whole instead of word by word, then use both hands to outline the shape of a large circle in the air.

Having established the overall format, the performer continues by miming each word, one at a time. Show the number of the word by displaying the same number of fingers. If the word is to be subdivided into syllables, show the number of the syllable about to be performed by placing the same number of fingers against the forearm.

- If the word to be indicated is THE, make a capital T with both forefingers;
- If it is A or AN, indicate a little word by making a small C or unclosed circle with the forefinger and thumb of one hand;
- If the mime is to be a pun, or a slightly inaccurate rendering of the intended word, waggle your ears (if you can) or cup one of them with your hand to show that it will only sound vaguely similar.

It goes without saying that titles with give-away words should be avoided. You may also want to avoid titles that can be split into syllables of dubious propriety, depending on the company, but this loses half the fun of the game. In this connection I can only say that the last time we played, no one guessed the title *Lord of the Flies* from an imaginative performance that might not have gone down well on television. The nearest suggestion was *Much Ado About Nothing*.

PUN IS FROM HEAVEN

A distinguishing mark of the snark, according to Lewis Carroll, is that 'it always looks grave at a pun'. Not surprising, when you consider that another of the creature's cardinal deficiencies is 'its slowness in taking a jest'. In other words, it has no sense of humour. So now you know what to call people who groan at puns or in other ways affect to despise them. They're snarks. For non-snarks, here's a collection of punning activities that are not so much games as rituals. They only become games, in the competitive sense of the word, if you can be bothered to think of a way of deciding who has won.

KNOCK KNOCK

> 'Knock knock'
> 'Who's there?'
> 'Don Giovanni'
> 'Don Giovanni who?'
> 'Don Giovann' any ice cream today?'

Knock-knock jokes are an example of ritual punning activities that seem to go in phases and crazes. This particular one seems to have been going on for ever, but I dare say it will eventually play itself out. Anyway, the above example shows you exactly what's involved. All you have to do is take it in turns to think them up or scrape them from the bottom of your memory barrel.

> 'Knock knock'
> 'Who's there?'
> 'Mary'
> 'Mary who?'
> 'Mary Christmas and a Happy New Year'

'Knock knock'
'Who's there?'
'Statue'
'Statue who?'
'Statue? I thought it was somebody else.'

If you want to make it a bit more difficult, you can insist on using topical names. Politicians, for example:

'Knock knock'
'Who's there?'
'Major'
'Major who?'
'Major laugh, didn't I?'

Or you can go for those in which the punch lines involve launching into song:

'Knock knock'
'Who's there?'
'M. A. B. – It's a big horse.
'M. A. B. – It's a big horse who?
'M. A. B. – It's a big horse I'm a Londoner / That I love London town ...'

'Knock knock'
'Who's there?'
'Dolores'
'Dolores who?'
'Dolores be an England / And England shall be free ...'

My all-time favourite, albeit not sung, is:

'Knock knock'
'Who's there?'
'Sutton.'
'Sutton who?'
'Burial Chamber.'

But enough of this madness ...

WHAT SORT OF GAME AM I?

My family used to play this as an in-car game.

It drove me to distraction.

And here's why:

Arthur	I'm a key, I'm a key – what sort of key am I?
Bertha	A don-key? *(No.)*
Carla	A tur-key? *(No.)*
Dorla	A door key? *(No.)*
Ern	A flunky? *(No.)*
Fern	A Russ-ki?...

And so on. Eventually, Arthur (or whoever asked such a silly question in the first place) will run out of alternatives and have to stop saying 'No' because he can't think of any alternatives that haven't yet been tried. And, as there's no reason why the punning element shouldn't come at the start of the word instead of the end, he can finally fool them all by declaring himself to be a 'key-schlorain' (normally spelt *quiche Lorraine*).

You may want to introduce a rule requiring the questioner to state at which end of the word it appears.

Be careful when playing this with young children who haven't yet got the hang of punning. My son, at his first attempt, declared himself to be some kind of bus. We tried all sorts of buses, including some he'd never heard of, like *rebus* and *arquebus*, but to no avail. Finally, we gave up. Proudly, he announced himself to be a 137 bus. For him, this had the double advantage of being a route number he was acquainted with, and also of being a high enough number not to be easily reached by the logical process of starting at route 1 and counting upwards.

What sort of game am I? has a regrettable tendency to get silly as time passes. You don't believe me? Then try this:

Annie:	I'm a bit, I'm a bit – What sort of bit am I?
Bennie:	A rab-bit? *(No.)*
Connie:	A bit-tern? *(No.)*
Denny:	A gam-bit? *(No.)*
All:	Give up.
Annie:	I'm a bit fed up with this game – let's play something else.

AWFUL AUTHORS

Knock-knock jokes are one form of name game. Even older, *Awful authors* involves matching invented authors with punning names to appropriate book titles. Here are some classic examples:

The Importance of being Earnest	by August Demeanour
Puddings I have Known	by Charlotte Russe
Exciting Tales	by Cliff Hanger
Not very Exciting Tales	by Luke Warm
A Fraction Too Soon	by Lois Carmen Denominator
Eaten in Africa	by Lionel Gettcha
Medieval Romances	by Mort Darthur
Great Stories from Opera	by Barbara Seville
French Songs	by Sonny Les Matines

More will be found under the entry *Name* in the Playing with Words section (page 154).

Rather more difficult, but worth while if you come up with anything good, is the task of devising questions to which the answer is a single name. For example:

What's a good name for a grate? Alexander.
What's a good name for an eel? Achilles.
What do you call a man in a hole? Doug.
How do you greet a flower called Cynthia? Hyacinth.

NICHOLAS MONICAS ...

(or Nickerless Monickers) is a title I couldn't resist ascribing to a game inspired by a paragraph in *The Guinness Book of Names* by Leslie Dunkling (page 162). He quotes the Canadian author W. P. Kinsella as introducing Span, the Society for the Prevention and Annihilation of Nicknames. Its members make a point of addressing one another by their names in full and themselves object to being familiarly abbreviated. Indeed, they go as far as to avoid all words containing pet names, and say things like *I'll be totally francis with you – I cannot pay the william.* As non-sexists, they give one another patricks or patricias on the back. It will come as no surprise to learn that the society was founded by an Oxford donald. The game simply consists of inventing more examples in a given space of time, say five minutes. For example:

● *Visiting Canada? Don't miss a visit to Lake Winifredmargaret.*
● *My favourite flowers are chrisantheadoramothers.*
● *Don't sniff – use a henry-a-jeffrey.*
● *If you don't know the spelling, check it in the richardtionhenry.*
● *Who washed that spider down the overflorence?*
● *He died without projennifer.*

DAFT DEFINITIONS

The most basic punning game consists in thinking up alternative definitions for words you thought you already knew the meaning of, such as:

> *Aldermen* – every male here present
> *Battery* – place where bats live
> *Centimetre* – what you get when your kid sister's late coming out of school
> *Dehydrate* – the way tax is calculated on concealed earnings
> *Equipment* – he was only joking
> *Favourable* – prefer the male of the species
> *Gladiator* – how the cannibal felt about the lady missionary
> *Homespun* – domestic joke

And so on. One way of turning this into a game is to assign each player a letter of the alphabet and get them to think up a daft definition for a word beginning with that letter. The first to do so scores as many points as there are players, the second one point fewer, the third two fewer, and so on. Keep playing until you have run out of letters.

'ORRIBLE ORIGINS

A game popularized by BBC Radio's *My Word!* programme involves giving players a well-known phrase, saying or book title and inviting them to invent a preposterous origin for it. The idea is supposed to be that the original phrase was actually quite different and has become corrupted with the passage of time, but, of course, the whole thing is an excuse for devising a complicated series of puns. Frank Muir, for example – or was it Dennis Norden? – launched into a story about an Eskimo with bad circulation who came to a nasty end through trying to warm his boat with a paraffin stove, thereby proving that *You can't have your kayak and heat it*. Probably one of theirs, though recounted verbally to me as a joke, is the story about the commercial traveller who asked for a cup of tea in a Liverpool café and was invited to try a popular local product called Koala. He found it so full of fluffy fur as to be undrinkable, and asked for it to be poured through a tea-strainer. 'Oh no,' came the shocked reply, 'The Koala tea of Mersey is not strained.'

To make a workable game of this, you need some really dedicated punsters and a reliable source of phrases and saying, such as *The Concise Oxford Dictionary of Proverbs*. You can either give everyone the same proverb, or a different proverb for each one. Here are a few picked more or less at random, with some suggestions for how they might be perverted into punning punch lines. You'll have to invent the preceding stories for yourself.

One good turn deserves another – *One could earn desserts for mother*
The hand that rocks the cradle rules the world – *The ham that rots the crate'll fool the ward*

No man is a hero to his valet – *Snowman eases hair oil to the valley*
A nod's as good as a wink to a blind horse – *An otter's goods are (a) wig, (2) a blind, or (c).*

SILLY-ME'S

This is my title for a punning game inspired by a line from Peter Sellers's pastiche travelogue *Balham – Gateway to the South*. The line in question is a delightful parody of Dean Burgon's *A rose-red city, 'half as old as Time'* (from *Petra*, 1845), which is transmuted by Sellers into *A rose-red city, half as gold as green …*, thereby punning on a well-off suburb of North London better known as Golders Green. A friend and I soon came up with similar similes, such as:

> *as full as earth*
> *as right as cramp*
> *as bodily as salt*

Need I go on? Once you've got the idea, you can set it as a task for a group of players, allowing them one point for each new discovery and a second for devising one that nobody else in the group has thought of. Having set this as a magazine competition on two occasions I can assure you that at least sixty can be found. More, even, if you allow some really atrocious word-manglings, such as:

> *as saucy as apprentice*
> *as wily as telegraphy*
> *as mad as an avenue*

RHYMING SILLY-ME'S

A variation on the above. In this case the comparison is made with something that rhymes, such as:

> *as daft as rafters*
> *as glad as adders*
> *as merry as terriers*
> *as pale as gaolers*

If you play this competitively, award an extra point for particularly appropriate examples, such as:

> *as brash as flashers*
> *as damp as campers*
> *as fleet as cheetahs*
> *as glib as fibbers*

or even contradictory ones:

> *as dull as colours.*

VULTURE UP TO?

For this game you need to come prepared with a list of animal names at least two syllables in length. The aim is to use each one as the start of a colloquial phrase by treating it as a pun. The title itself is an example. Others include:

> Ostrich – *in time saves nine*
> Aardvark – *and no play makes Jack a dull boy*
> Butterfly – *or I'll be late for dinner*

Sea anemone – *shoot on sight*
Woodpecker – *if she'd only let me*

A quicker way of playing it is to work out all your definitions beforehand and then get players to deduce what animal is represented by each one. For example:

Marsupial fond of fizzy drinks? – Coca koala
Sea bird that always repays favours? – One good tern
Cat that beats its young with open paws? – Cuff lynx

TONTO

This excruciating game is credited to Pat McCormick and was said to have been first played at a convention of the American National Puzzlers' League.

One player stands up and tries to respond as quickly as possible to questions set by the others. Each question is one that the questioner has arrived at by thinking of the name of a prominent person or historical character and then turning it into a clue by means of a pun. Here are some sample questions and answer:

Is Austrian composer ready to come out of the closet? No – Josef Haydn.
Does Italian portrait-sitter own her own house? No – Mona Lisa.
Who owned a cake-burning fireplace? Alfred the Great.

The respondent scores a point for each correct answer. Whoever poses a question that fails to get answered stands up and takes over as the new victim. If you want to be fair about it, you can insist that a player who has already had a turn as respondent shouldn't get another turn but should choose someone who has yet to have a go. The round ends when everyone has had a turn, and the winner, of course, is the player with the highest score.

TOM SWIFTIES

The origin of this series of puns is described in the Playing with Words section (see page 164). A Tom Swifty may be defined as an adverb that puns on its verbal antecedent, but the best way of getting across what this actually means is to give a few examples, thus:

'I've eaten your brother William,' said the cannibal, wilfully.
'I seem to have lost my buttonhole,' he declared, lackadaisically.
'I'm just sharpening my ballpoint on the cheese-grater,' he explained, pensively.

All you can do with this, to turn it into a game, is to give the company long enough to see who can come up with (a) the most and (b) the funniest examples.

DEFECTIVE DETECTIVE

Speaking as the proud possessor of every one of Erle Stanley Gardner's Perry Mason novels published on this side of the Atlantic (and several that weren't) I can confirm that the title of every one of them begins *The Case of the ...*, from *Amorous Aunt* to *Worried Waitress*. This useless piece of information serves as the springboard to a game based on rhyming rather than punning, though the effect is much the same.

One player thinks of a Case of ... in which the two parts rhyme or pun, and gives a clue to it. Whoever guesses correctly scores a point and sets the next one, and so on until you run out of ideas. For example:

Incompetent investigator? *The Case of the Defective Detective*

Timid representative? *The Case of the Delicate Delegate*
Belgian Wart? *The Case of the Flemish Blemish*

WORDBURGERS

Two or more players
Any age
A miscellany of silly lists

Folk etymology is a wondrous thing. Remember how HAMBURGER, named from its presumed origin in Hamburg, gave rise to a multitude of comparable delicacies with such names as BEEFBURGER and even VEGGIEBURGER? Folk etymology – not necessarily unthinkingly or unawares – took the original name to have something to do with HAM, and simply changed that element to whatever other foodstuff could be bashed into the same shape and stuck between a pair of buns. By the same process, the political embarrassment of WATERGATE gave journalists the invaluable device of attaching -GATE to the end of any political scandal in order to produce snappy headlines of immediate intelligibility 'by association'. By this process, such a concoction as MORTARGATE will immediately suggest a scandal in the building trade, and I suppose a scandal in the groves of Academe would soon produce the headline EDUGATE. And a split in the Cabinet, BIFURGATE.

Or take BOUTIQUE. A friend of mine living in Chesterfield reports a shoe-shop called BOOTIQUE. A shop selling fossilized insects would be an ANTIQUE, one selling cheap and nasty kitchenware a PLASTIQUE, any old iron a RUSTIQUE. And a dental surgery would undoubtedly be a TOOTHIQUE.

What about some more wordburgers along these lines?

> ## Answer to Beheadments problem (pages 52–3)
>
> The original American list is: ATYPICAL, BRIGHTNESS, CHASTEN, DEVOLUTION, EVALUATION, FRIGHTFULLY, GASTRONOMICALLY, HARBOR, ISLANDER, JUNCTION, KNIGHTLY, LITERATE, MEAGERNESS, NEVERMORE, OROTUND, PRESIDENTIAL, REVOLUTIONARY, SPECULATION, TREASONABLE, UPRAISE, VINDICATION, WHEREABOUTS, YOURSELVES, ZONE. These score 199 in total, or 200 with the British spelling HARBOUR. When MEAGERNESS is respelt the British way it fails to produce a valid word after beheadal. But an acceptable alternative of the same length would be MATHEMATIC.

2. WRITTEN WORD GAMES

The Moving Finger writes, and, having writ,
Moves on; nor all thy Piety nor Wit
Shall lure it back to cancel half a Line,
Nor all thy Tears wash out a Word of it.
Edward Fitzgerald, The Rubáiyát of Omar Khayyám

LISTOMANIA

For people who just like playing around with words, whether for sound or sense or both, nothing could be easier or more addictive than compiling lists of words that have some peculiar or amusing feature in common. And nothing could be simpler than to turn such a compilation into a competitive game. Just state the requirement, give everyone ten minutes to make a list, then read them out and see whose list is longest or contains the most bizarre entries. Here are a few ideas to be getting on with. You can easily invent more for yourself.

DIGRAMS
Two or more players: best for more
Any age
Lettered cards or tiles useful but not essential

A digram is a two-letter combination. For example, the word WORD contains three digrams: WO, OR, and RD. (Some digrams are also *digraphs,* where the two letters stand for a single sound, like TH and NG in THING.)

In this game, all you have to do is to pick a digram and see who can make the longest list of words which include the two letter combination. A good way of choosing the digram is to take two cards or tiles at random from a shuffled pack of lettered cards or bag of tiles. For example, if the selected letters are NX, the word ANXIOUS and its relatives will readily spring to mind, though if they're XN you'll have more of a problem.

A slight drawback of this game is its unevenness. Some digrams are so common, such as ST, TH, and any involving a consonant and a vowel, that you could be up all night writing lists, while others are so obscure, like XN, that you'll spend most of your allotted time just twiddling your thumbs. One way of overcoming this is to keep choosing digrams until you get everyone's agreement on one that seems neither too easy nor too hard. Another is to prohibit all words beginning or ending with the stated digram, as this will avoid making the game too easy. You should also, in any case, prohibit mere grammatical variations on the same word. For example, given SK, you would allow only one of ASK, ASKS, ASKED, ASKING, ASKER, and so on – but not, of course, ASKANCE, which has nothing to do with asking.

A good scoring system is to award two points for a word found only by one player and one point for all others. Another, which is only practicable if the digram is such that no one can find more than about ten words, is to score for each word as many points as it contains letters. You might also want to award a bonus of ten to the player who comes up with the longest list, or who finds the word that would come first if all found words were listed in alphabetical order.

Tip. An obvious wrinkle of this game is to attack awkward combinations by thinking of compound words. For example, given HP, you will immediately cast around for words like TOOTHPASTE, CATCHPOLE and the like.

TRIGRAMS

Two or more players: best for more
Any age
Lettered cards or tiles useful but not essential

The same as *Digrams*, above, but involving combinations of three consecutive letters. You won't be surprised to find it harder to think of workable combinations, so here are a few to be getting on with:

ASM — CAU — CTR — HIG — IVI — LLO — NQU — RGE — TTL — UST

PREFIXES

Two or more players: best for more
Adults and older children
No special requirements

See who can think of the most words beginning with a stated prefix, such as:

BE-	as in BECALM (but not as in BEDSOCKS)
CON-	as in CONSPIRE (but not as in CONKER)
DIS-	as in DISGRACE (but not as in DISHCLOTH)
EN-	as in ENGULF (but not as in ENOUGH)
FOR-	as in FORBID (but not as in FORESEE)
FORE-	as in FORESEE (but not as in FOREIGN)
MIS-	as in MISTRUST (but not as in MISTLETOE)
PRE-	as in PRECAUTION (but not as in PREEN)
SUB-	as in SUBMARINE (but not as in SUBEROSE)
TRI-	as in TRIANGLE (but not as in TRIPWIRE)

I think this is a silly game, but there's no accounting for taste. Don't play it if you don't understand why some words listed above are allowable and others not. The best prefixes are FOR- and FORE-, as these throw up the players who don't know the difference between FORBEAR and FOREBEAR, or FORGO and FOREGO. As for FORSEE, if any such word existed it would have to mean something like 'prevent from seeing'.

SUFFIXES

Two or more players: best for more
Adults and older children
No special requirements

This is the same as *Prefixes* (above), except that it goes to the other extreme. Players are now invited to compile a list of words sharing the same final element. English suffixes include -MENT, -SHIP, -LESS, -NESS, and even -LESSNESS. The only trouble is that there are so many possibilities, many of which can be made up on the spur of the moment, that you'll need to introduce some restriction on what may be allowed. For example, you might insist that they all begin with the same letter, or, conversely, that no two in one list should begin with the same letter. To prevent outlandish concoctions like CONTRARILESSNESS you might also award points only for the shortest words found beginning with each letter.

Incidentally, it might be fun to pretend that -CEDE is a suffix (it isn't really) as in INTERCEDE and PRECEDE. You can then deduct 1000 points from anyone who comes up with the non-existent SUPERCEDE – a pseudo-word that has become one of the greatest misspellings of our time.

FORE AND AFT
Two or more, best for more
Any age, but must be evenly matched
No special requirements

Compile as long a list as you can of words that each begin and end with the same letter. In case this sounds too easy, try adding the following restrictions:

1. Only one word is required for each letter.
2. For each letter, whoever finds the longest word scores two points.
3. Or, the length of each word is the score for that word.

Variant. Try compiling a list of words of which the first begins with A and ends with B, the second begins with B and ends with C, and so on as far as zebra. Then work backwards, finding a word for Z–Y, Y–X, and so on.

BACRONYMS
Two or more players, best for more
Adults and older children
No special equipment needed

A palindrome (see page 158) is a word that reads the same backwards and forwards, such as MADAM. A homonym is a word-form that has two different and unrelated meanings, such as STICK which can mean either 'rod' or 'adhere'. So what do you call a word-form that is not a palindrome and produces a valid but entirely different word when read backwards, such as LIVED and DEVIL. I have decided to call them 'bacronyms'. And, having done that, I have little to offer beyond inviting your group of players to see who can compile the longest list of bacronyms, or the 'best' list by whatever restrictions you choose to impose. For example, you might specify that no two bacronym pairs in any one person's list should have both the same initial and contain the same number of letters.

ALL IN A ROW
Two or more players, best for more
Adults and older children
A one-off exercise

List as many words as you can think of which contain:

1. Two consecutive letters (as in ALPHABET, AFGHAN, etc)
2. Three consecutive letters (as in DEFY)
3. Four consecutive letters …

Well, I can't think of any, so I should hesitate to go to five.

Variation. When you've done this one to death, try listing as many words as you can whose component letters are taken entirely from a specified range of the alphabet, such as A to G. (CABBAGE springs to mind.)

STAIRWAY

Two or more players, best for more
Any age, but evenly matched
Lettered cards or tiles useful but not vital

Choose a letter at random. Then see who can compile the longest list of words beginning with this letter. The first word in the list must be of two letters, the second of three, then four, five, six, and so on. Oh yes, and you're not allowed to skip a tread in the stairway, so if you can't think of a 12-letter word your list ends there, even if you can think of words from 13 to 130 letters in length thereafter.

I suggest a score of one point per word, and two for each word which, for its length, comes earliest in alphabetical order. With half a dozen players or more, you could also give a bonus for the word of any given length that comes last in alphabetical order.

CHARITY

Two or more players
Adults and older children

A charitable word is one that can give up a letter without ceasing to be a word. For example, CHARITABLE is charitable, because it remains CHARTABLE after losing an I, and PEAR even more charitable, because whatever letter is removed leaves a word (EAR, PER, PAR, PEA).

In this game, players are required to compile a list of charitable words, the first beginning with A, the second with B, and so on. After an agreed length of time, which may be from ten to twenty minutes depending on the players' skill and patience, read out the contributions for each letter and score for them.

The simple score is one point for each letter that can be given up. By this reckoning, PEAR scores four points, because four letters can be removed, and CHARITABLE earns only one point.

If you want a more sophisticated system that also takes into account the length of the charitable word, then multiply the number of removable letters by the length of the word. By this reckoning, PEAR scores $4 \times 4 = 16$ and CHARITABLE $1 \times 10 = 10$. But a ten-letter word capable of losing either of two letters would score 20. (I can't think of one. Can you?)

BEHEADMENTS

Two or more players
Adults and older children
Not so easy

You can't play this game very often, as there is always a best possible result and someone is bound to remember what it is. But it makes a nice little exercise for people who haven't come across it before.

Each player's object is to list 26 words, beginning with successive letters of the alphabet, so that when each word is 'beheaded' – i.e. deprived of its initial – the remainder still forms another valid word. For example, you might start with ARID – RID, BLOOM – LOOM, etc, and finish with YEARNING and ZANY. To make it more competitive, you can change the scoring from one point per word to one point per letter in each word (not counting the chopped initial), thereby placing a premium on finding the longest words possible of their type.

According to the American National Puzzlers' League, the highest possible score by this method is 199, using only words appearing as main entries in the *Merriam-Webster Pocket Dictionary*. The highest score recorded in actual competition was 129. The 24 words producing this score – two initials proving impossible – are listed on page 48. Spelling differences on opposite sides of the Atlantic make 200 the equivalent highest score for words of British spelling. One of the words on the American list doesn't work when transposed into British spelling, but I have replaced it with a British equivalent of the same length.

Variants. You can vary the scoring in several ways to alter the strategy of the game. One way is to score for the shortest possible beheaded words instead of the longest. In this case you score ten for failing to find a word for a given initial, and the winner, of course, is the player with the *lowest* score. Another is to end the game as soon as one player calls 'Stop!' and then to award a bonus of 20 to whoever compiled the longest list. A more intricate variation is to accept only words that end in a given letter, such as E, N, or something equally common; or only words that contain a given letter; or only words of an agreed length.

NUMWORDS
Two or more players
Adults and older children
Pocket calculators permissible

Being of a somewhat mathematical bent I've devised several games and puzzles based on the idea of considering words as numbers, hence 'numwords'. The simplest way of doing so is to count A as 1, B as 2, and so on up to Z as 26. By this method, a numword of any given value – say 58 – is defined as a word whose constituent letters yield that total. The value itself may be called a 'wordnum'. Thus the wordnum of the numword thing would be 58, i.e. 20 + 8 + 9 + 14 + 7. If you get on with the following game, you might also enjoy Centurion (page 77) and Inflation (page 78).

The listing game is quite simple. There are as many rounds as there are players. At each round, the next player in turn calls a random number, perhaps lying between 50 and 100 to start with and until you get used to the game. Everyone then has five or ten minutes in which to compile as long a list as possible of words whose letters total exactly that number. Additional credit may be accorded for having the longest or the shortest such word possible in one's list.

Variant. For a given length of word, or for a given initial letter, see who can find (a) the lowest and (b) the highest valued numword meeting the specification. For example, given three letters, the numword of lowest value is BAA, worth 4, and the highest WRY, worth 66. (If sheep words are not accepted, the lowest is ABB for 5.)

CATEGORIES (GUGGENHEIM)
Two or more players
Any age, but evenly matched
An old favourite

This old favourite certainly goes back to Victorian times and probably beyond. Its perennial popularity probably has something to do with the opportunity it affords of showing off one's general knowledge in a competitive context.

Players agree on a set of category headings, about 20 in number, and everybody writes this list down the left-hand side of their sheet of paper. Typical category headings at elementary level might include Town, Bird, Actor, Item of clothing, and so on.

The next thing to do is to decide which letter of the alphabet should appear in the initial position. This should exclude X and Z. Letters J, K and Q are often easier than you think, and N more difficult. You might want to choose such a letter at random by drawing from a pack of lettered cards or bag of lettered tiles.

You then have an agreed length of time, say five or ten minutes, in which to find an example of each category beginning with the stated letter. For example, initial A might produce a list beginning:

Town	Aberdeen
Bird	Albatross
Actor	Andrews
Clothing	Anorak

Names of people should be those of their main or surname, so it doesn't matter whether the Andrews in question is Julie or Harry or Dana.

When the time is up, everyone passes their list to their left-hand neighbour for marking. The examples collected for each category are read out loud and a point scored for each. I further recommend scoring two for an entry that no one else has got, unless everyone has something different, and three for an entry in a category which no one else has been able to fill at all. Queries and challenges may be made at this stage. For example, as a game beginning with 'A' would one accept American football? Probably so among British players, for whom it differs from the game they know simply as football, but not among American players, for whom the qualification 'American' is unnecessary. Such queries should be put to the players, and I favour the rule that an entry is acceptable if accepted by at least one player other than the one whose idea it was.

Not surprisingly, the winner is the player with the highest score. Even less surprisingly, you can then draw another column, choose another letter, and go round once again. And again and again, until you're sick of the whole thing.

The fairest way of deciding on the 20 categories is to let each player in turn nominate one and to forbid it if everyone else objects. If it is rejected, the proposer must wait until his turn comes round again before making another suggestion. This should overcome the irritation of being forced into esoteric subjects. For example, I only accept Footballer if I am allowed to have Language, and Rock Group if I can have Heavenly Body. (Astronomical object, that is.)

Here are some categories that may set your mind running along suitable tracks. For a circle of mixed ages or abilities, each main heading may be taken to include any of the subdivisions that follow it. More advanced players may prefer to ignore the main heading and take one or more of the subdivisions as main categories.

People by name
Actor – *Film star, TV performer*
Artist – *Painter, Sculptor, Photographer, Cartoonist …*
Fictitious character – *Legendary, Mythological*
Historical character – *Monarch, Head of State, Inventor …*
Musician – *Composer, Conductor, Performer, Band, Group …*
Sportsperson – *Footballer, Swimmer, Commentator …*
Author – *Novelist, Poet, Playwright, Journalist …*
Politician

Saint
Scientist

Personal matters
Something to wear – *Clothing, Adornment ...*
Something to eat
Something to drink
Nationality
Occupation
Illness or Disease

Natural world
Animal – *Mammal, Reptile/Amphibian, Dinosaur ...*
Bird
Fish, or other sea creature
Insect, or other invertebrate
Plant – *Flower, Shrub, Tree, Fruit, Vegetable ...*

Geographical
Country, State, Region, County ...
Mountain
River
Town or City
Sea – *Lake, Loch ...*
Feature (e.g. desert, moraine, glacier, etc)

Miscellaneous
Game (for playing, not bagging)
Heavenly body (by type or name, e.g. star, Betelgeuse)
Language (excluding body, foul, etc)
Means of transport (excluding transports of delight)
Subway or underground station
Title of book, play, film, opera etc (argue among yourselves)
Tool or implement
Unit of measurement (or currency)
Weapon (so intended, thus excluding umbrella, etc)

Guggenheim. In this frequently listed variant, each player draws a grid of (say) 5 × 5 squares. Down the left side for five agreed categories, and along the top, five agreed initials. The rest is as before. In effect, you're playing five short games at once.

WORD LADDERS
Two or more players
Any age
Fun rather than competitive

Another perennial favourite. Players agree on two words of the same length, and each then attempts to compose a chain of words linking one to the other by changing only one letter at a time. For example, using only words listed in my nearest dictionary, I can get from ABBA to ZOON in 16 steps: ABBA, ABBE, ABLE, ABLY, ALLY, ILLY, INLY, ONLY, OILY, WILY, WILE, BILE, BOLE, BORE, BORN, BOON, ZOON. Can you do better?

The winner is either the player who finishes first, or the one who links the two words in the shortest chain.

HANG AROUND ...

Hangman is the best-known and most popular example of a series of games in which you have to deduce a word from a basic amount of given material by asking questions to elicit clues. If you like *Hangman*, you'll love some of the more refined and ingenious derivatives that follow.

HANGMAN

Best for two, more possible
Mainly for children

One player, whom I shall refrain from calling the Hangperson, thinks of a word and draws a row of dots or dashes, one for each letter of that word. The task of the others is to prevent the execution by deducing the key word before the Hangman manages to construct a gallows and finish suspending the victim, a process taking exactly 13 steps.

Each of the rescuers in turn calls out a letter of the alphabet. If the word contains it, the Hangman writes it in to the appropriate space, or spaces if it occurs more than once. If not, he draws one part of the gruesome picture shown here. The numbers indicate what order the various components are usually drawn in. Details of the drawing vary from player to player. Some, for example, show the victim's eyes instead of feet. Of course, it doesn't really matter what you include or the order in which you draw the components, so long as there are exactly thirteen of them.

Anyone at any time may call out the suspected word. If it's right, the Hangman has lost his victim. If not, he adds another segment to the drawing. (Or, according to some players, wins the game outright and completes the drawing.)

Variation. If agreed, you may prefer that a guessed letter be written only once even if it occurs more often, but this isn't usual practice. Some players insist that the hangman write his word down on a hidden piece of paper before the questioning begins. This prevents a very clever hangman from cheating by changing the word as he goes along. On the other hand, if you're all a bunch of very clever players, you may prefer to encourage this nefarious practice.

Scoring. If you want to keep scores, try this method. A player who correctly announces the hidden word before the drawing is complete scores one point for each part of the drawing not yet completed – in other words, 13 minus the number of components so far drawn. For a wrong guess, the hangman gets a part-score of one point per component so far completed, and play continues. For completing the drawing without having his word deduced, the hangman scores 13, plus whatever part-scores he may already have made for wrong guesses.

Comments. Hangman makes a good classroom game and can help with developing young children's literacy. Younger players tend at first to choose letters haphazardly, but after a while begin to discover that many letter combinations follow regular patterns. For example, something ending in G–T will often have an H in between, and a U in second position may easily be preceded by a Q. They will also soon discover that shorter words are harder to discover than longer ones because there are so many possibilities. Think of all the three-letter words ending in Y, for instance.

JOTTO
Two players
Adults and older children

Jotto, also spelt Giotto and sometimes called Word Mastermind, is a form of deduction which can be played with words or numbers or even little coloured pegs in a board full of holes. I used to play the number version under the title *Bull and Cow*, a cow being scored when you get a number right, and a bull when you get it in the right position.

Each player secretly writes down a key word of an agreed length – let's say five letters. You may prefer more or fewer, the only important thing being that both have the same number. Each player's aim is to deduce the other's key word first, playing as follows.

Each in turn calls out a five-letter test word, and the other announces how many letters of the test word appear in the key word, regardless of position. The caller, for reference, will write the test word down together with the number of correspondences or 'hits' it produces. For example:

Key word	O	B	O	E	S	*Letters in common*
Test words	T	R	A	M	P	0
	C	H	O	M	P	1
	B	O	T	C	H	2
	B	O	O	S	T	4

From this example you will note that the position of the letters is of no account to the number of hits announced, and that hits are calculated on a one-to-one basis. That is, although there are two O's in OBOES, the test word BOTCH contains only one O and so scores only one hit in respect of that letter, whereas BOOST counts two for containing both.

Ending and scoring. The strict rule of play about announcing your opponent's word is that you may only do so on your turn to play and instead of calling a test word. If you're right, the game ends and you score ten minus the number of test words you have called. (Ten shots should be enough for a five-letter word, but you may prefer to make it 20.) For a wrong guess, you're merely barred from calling a test word on that turn.

Strategy. This example also illustrates an element of strategy – not to mention luck. The lucky break is getting zero for the first test word. Now you know for certain five letters that *don't* appear, so that the single hit you get for your second, CHOMP, must be one of C, H and O. The extra hit on turn three establishes B as certain, as you have already eliminated T. On the whole, the best number of hits to get is either zero, which gives you five definite negatives to use as blanks in future shots, or 4 or 5, for obvious reasons. Any other number at start of play is pretty useless, as you have no idea what the hits are until you have established some blanks to measure them by.

Strategy can also be applied to thinking up good key words in the first place. The ideal word is not an obscure one containing rare letters, like QUAKY or HYRAX, but one containing common letters that yield many anagrams, like STONE (NOTES, TONES, ONSET) or LARGE (LAGER, REGAL, GLARE). It can cost your opponent up to three turns to find out which of several five-letter words is the real McCoy. (For this reason, by the way, each player is required to write the true word down before play begins, so it can't be changed when this situation arises. But see also *Wild Jotto*, below.)

Problem. Can you find five test words that between them use up all 25 letters of the alphabet? (Answer at the end of this section, page 96.)

DOUBLE JEOPARDY
Two players
Adults and older children

This clever variation on the game of *Jotto* was suggested by Don Laycock, an Australian games enthusiast.

In *Double jeopardy*, each time you call out a test word you must also announce how many hits it makes with your own key word. For example, in the game illustrated above, your own word might be CRAZE. On calling your first word, TRAMP, you would announce 'Two' besides hearing how many hits it makes on your opponent's word. Of course, two is a deliberately unhelpful number of hits for your opponent to make, which is precisely why you chose it. Later, however, you may find that the word you want to use as a test yields such useful information as 'No hits' or 'Five', in which case you must weigh up whether it is worth giving away such useful information in order to get the information you need yourself.

CRASH
Two players
Adults and older children

This extension of *Jotto* isn't really harder, just more drawn-out and diabolical. Play as before, only this time, instead of calling out the number of hits scored by the other player's test word, you call out the number of crashes. A crash is a correct letter but only *in its correct position.* So, in the sample game above, you would still score no hits and one, respectively, for TRAMP and CHOMP, but zero for BOTCH and only one for BOOST. The latter's anagram BOOTS, however, would have netted you two, for the middle O and final S.

WILD JOTTO, WILD CRASH
Two players
A game for real experts at Jotto or Crash

Both *Jotto* and its derivative *Crash* may be played 'wild' as follows. You are allowed to change your key word as often as you like, provided that whatever it is at any stage in the game is entirely consistent with the information you have already given.

An eccentric feature of this game is that you needn't start off with any word at all! For example, your opponent calls TRAMP, and you declare 'One' as a matter of principle, as it's an unhelpful number. This means that whatever word you finally acknowledge as 'correct' must contain one of those five letters (in *Wild Jotto*), or one of them in that specific position (*Wild Crash*). You can see from this that you have to keep very careful track of the information you're providing.

FAIRY JOTTO, FAIRY CRASH
Two players
Experts only!

Just as Fairy Chess is Chess played with pieces that don't exist in the real game, so Fairy word games are those played with letter combinations that don't form real words. In effect, *Fairy Jotto* and *Fairy Crash* amount to abstract games like the numerical *Bull and Cow* or the colourful *Mastermind*, except that they are complicated by the increased number of possibilities – namely, 26 letters instead of only ten digits or eight colours.

Fairy Jotto is played exactly like *Jotto*, except that your key word and all test words must be five-letter combinations that do *not* form genuine words. Anyone whose key word is a real one automatically loses the game, and any test word that turns out to be real (by reference to the dictionary) need not be answered and loses its caller a turn.

Of course, it's easy to avoid real words by simply ensuring that any given letter combination contains no vowel. This doesn't matter – but, for fun, you may want to introduce the additional rule that a 'fairy' word is one which *could* exist according to the rules of English orthography, but *doesn't*. This would prevent you from using such letter combinations as CRUNJ or XLYMH, but force you into essaying such pronounceable combinations as CRUNK or GLYPH. You would then be challenged, and rightly so, for both of these words do exist, and so are not true fairies within the meaning of the Act.

Fairy Crash can be left to squeak for itself.

CASTAWORDS
Two players
Adults and older children

This elaboration of *Jotto* comes from a copy of the American magazine *World Games Review,* but as my copy was incomplete I don't know whom to credit.

Each player writes out 24 different letters of the alphabet in four rows of six. The letters of each row should be entered in alphabetical order. It is not essential for any six-letter row to constitute a real word, and unlikely that any will do so. The aim is to be the first to reconstruct the other's four rows by the following method.

Each in turn calls out a genuine word consisting of four different letters. The other player responds by stating how those four letters are distributed between the rows of his grid. For example, the response '1–1–1–1' indicates that the four called letters appear one in each row, '2–1–1' (the commonest response) that two appear in one row and one each in two others, and so on. A response that totals only 3 or 2 instead of 4 shows that (respectively) one or two letters of the called word do not appear in the grid.

A one-sided example of play will illustrate the procedure. The missing letters are H and N.

A G I K S W	CRAM = 2 1 1	PERT = 4
B C F L M X	CHAP = 1 1 1	PORT = 3 1
D J O U Y Z	HOLE = 1 1 1	SLOT = 1 1 1 1
E P Q R T V	PIKE = 2 2	SWOT = 2 1 1
	RIPE = 3 1	... and so on.

CONVERGENCE
Adults and older children
A game of concurrent sentences

I can't remember where I found this verbal expansion of *Jotto*, but I wish whoever invented it had given it a more exciting title, as it's really much more fun than it sounds from the heading.

Each player writes down a sentence containing any agreed number of words, typically four until you get used to it. The aim is to be the first to deduce the other player's sentence by the following means.

Each in turn calls out a test sentence of four words. For each word of the test sentence, the other states whether that word of the key sentence comes before or after it in alphabetical order. For example:

> *Key sentence*   WILL YOU BE MINE
> *Test sentence*   ONLY WHEN I LAUGH
> The information given in response is *after after before before* since WILL comes alphabetically after ONLY, YOU after WHEN, BE before I, and MINE after LAUGH.

Play continues until someone wins by calling a test sentence that happens to be identical to the one sought. In case this goes on too long, you may agree to impose a limit on the total number of calls that can be made, say 20 or 25. If no one has it by then, the setter has won.

You may find it more convenient to say *up* and *down* instead of the more long-winded *after, before.* You may also prefer to shorten the game by concentrating only on the first letter of each word rather than the whole one. By this method, you would say 'Same' when it has the same initial. So, in the above example, the test sentence WE DON'T CARE, SEE? would get the response 'After, same, before, before'.

QUIZL
Two players (more possible)
Adults and older children
A deductive game of bluff

This game of my invention could be described as Battleship with Words. We'll assume two players for ease of description.

Each player draws two 25-square grids of five rows and five columns. Think of a key word of five letters, all different, and write it across one of the five rows or down one of the five columns. Fill the remaining squares with 20 of the 21 remaining letters of the alphabet, no letter being duplicated. (We usually omit the Q for practical reasons, but there's no rule about it.) The columns run from one to five from left to right along the top of the grid, and the rows from 6 to 0 down the left-hand side. This enables you to identify any grid by means of a numerical cross-reference. For example, the central square is designated '38'.

The aim of the game is to deduce your opponent's key word before he or she deduces yours.

Each of you in turn 'bombs' a square in the other player's grid by calling out its number, and the other states what letter occupies that square. Suppose you start by calling '38'. If the reply you get is 'T', then you will record 'T' in the central square of your second grid, and the turn passes to your opponent. The second grid, of course, is used to keep a record of the results you get.

On any of your turns to play, you may declare what you think your opponent's word is instead of bombing a square. If you're right, the game ends and you score one point for each square you have not yet bombed – or, to put it another way, 25 less the number of shots you have had, which gives you a higher score for an earlier correct guess. If you're wrong, the only penalty is that you must wait till your next turn before bombing another square (or making another guess).

At end of play both grids are revealed to ensure that one player has scored correctly without contravention of any of the following special rules.

Special rule 1. Your grid must contain only one true word. If it is found to contain more, the other player wins and scores 25.

Special rule 2. If you discover your opponent's key word as the result of uncovering all five letters, instead of by means of a guess before it is fully revealed, you cannot win. Play then continues until your opponent either scores for guessing your word, or draws by accidentally uncovering it.

Strategy. There are two main points of strategy. The first consists in choosing a key word that's hard to guess when three or even four of its letters are revealed. Would you, for instance, persist in bombing a line that so far shows such a combination as -IVA-, or P-O-H, or ZI-KY? The second consists in filling the other squares with letters in combinations that look as if they might produce words when three or four letters are revealed. This is where the bluffing skill really comes in to its own. Here's an effective grid containing the key word PSALM:

	1	2	3	4	5
6	F	T	J	U	P
7	C	R	O	N	S
8	Z	B	W	K	A
9	E	X	V	I	L
0	D	Y	H	G	M

After a few shots, the second row might easily suggest a word like CROPS or CRONE, and the first column perhaps FAZED or ACHED. All the letters along the bottom row are good word-enders, and both EXVIL and UNKIG are at least pronounceable.

Variation 1. Instead of calling out grid references and being told what letters occupy them, you could instead agree to call out letters and be told which squares they occupy. This merely adds a bit of variety without altering the essence of play or making it any easier or harder.

Variation 2. In the anagram version, the key-word may be inserted as an anagram, with its letters in any order. This makes for a much harder game, especially since you must now be certain that no other row or column contains an unsuspected real word.

Version for three or more players. Each player draws as many grids as there are players, one containing the camouflaged key word and the others for recording the results of shots on other players' grids. Each player calls in turn, and everyone except that player then in turn states what letter occupies that square of their own grid. Inevitably, this will sometimes mean that a square is called of which the contents are already known in one or two cases. For example, if you start a three-player game by calling '38', the others will reveal their central squares but you will not. Later, one opponent may be desperate to know what's in your own 38, and will call it, despite knowing what's in that of the other player.

Any player when in turn to play may guess an opponent's word instead of bombing a square. If correct, that player scores in the usual way and may then continue by either calling another player's word or bombing a square. If not correct, his turn ends without bombing.

GET THE MESSAGE (PHRASE MAZE)

Two players (more possible but unwieldy)
Adults and older children

This game of my invention, a close relative of *Quizl* (above), first appeared in *Games & Puzzles* magazine (first series) and was later described under the name Phrase Maze by somebody else.

Each player draws two 25-square grids of five rows and five columns. Number the columns from one to five from left to right along the top of the grid, and the rows from 6 to 0 down the left-hand side. This enables you to identify any grid by means of a numerical cross-reference. For example, the central square is designated '38'.

Now think of a well-known phrase or saying, or film or book title, of up to 25 letters. Starting anywhere in the grid, write it in in such a way that each subsequent letter lies adjacent to the previous one, thus forming a maze of straight lines and right angles. For example, you might insert HE WHO HESITATES IS LOST starting at square 58 and producing the following effect:

	1	2	3	4	5
6	E	H	O		
7	S	I	H	W	
8		T		E	H
9	T	A	S	L	T
0	E	S	I	O	S

As before, you each in turn 'bomb' an enemy square by calling its grid reference, are told what letter occupies it, and enter this into your second square in order to build up a picture of the other's message. Upon any turn to play, you may announce the message instead of bombing a square, but cannot bomb until your next turn if you failed to get the message right.

Every time you hit a blank square, you score one point. This scoring is designed to encourage players to think of messages that fill up as many squares as possible, preferably all 25. For correctly deducing the other's message, you score, in addition to any blanks you may have scored already, one point for each letter of the message that has been deduced instead of bombed.

You can, of course, play on a larger grid to incorporate longer messages. And you may, if you like, allow the message to be written with diagonal leaps as well as orthogonal ones – or even, if it comes to that, write in each succeeding letter a knight's move away from its predecessor.

FOREHEADS

Four to six players
Adults and older children

This deductive invention of Dave Silverman makes a nice party game, though it belongs technically in this section because it involves writing.

Each player writes a four-letter word neatly and largely on a self-adhesive label, about 4 cm by 2 cm, and sticks it on the forehead of the player on his or her right, without showing them what the word is. The aim is to be the first to discover what your own word is.

Each player in turn announces a word. It must be exactly four letters in length, and each letter must be one that's visible on another player's forehead. Repeated letters are allowed, both on the forehead words and in the called words. But a called word itself may not be called again, whether by the same or another player. A player who cannot think of an unused word to call within a reasonable time must pass. If anyone happens by sheer fluke to call the word on their own forehead without knowing it, the other players should try not to let on, as any comment or laughter will enable them to guess their word on their next turn. (On the other hand, however, you might bluff by trying to kid someone that they have called their own word.)

You may, upon your turn to play, guess at the word on your own forehead. You win the game, and play ceases, if you call either the right word or an anagram of it. In other words, your aim is to deduce the letters on your forehead – you don't have to guess what order they appear in. If you're wrong, you keep playing (to enable the others to deduce information from your called words), but cannot have another shot at your own and therefore cannot win.

Variation. The overall winner is the first to score three points. If you guess right, and have zero or a plus number of points, you score a point; but if you have a negative number, they are cancelled out and your score is reset to zero. If you guess wrong, and currently have zero or a negative number, you lose another point; but if you have a plus number, it is reduced to zero.

IN-WORD LOOKING

The most straightforward of all word games are those in which you try to construct as many words as possible from a given set of letters, usually in the form of a single word of nine or more letters. There seems to be no technical term for this type of word-play. It isn't exactly *anagram,* which implies rearranging all the letters of the given word rather than a selection of any length. Perhaps *apogram* would pass muster, coming from Greek roots meaning *away from* and *letters.*

WORD HUNT
Two or more players, four or five best
Any age but evenly matched in vocabulary

Agree on a word of about ten letters (more or fewer according to taste). Ideally, it should contain no duplicate letters and no S. Allow players ten minutes in which to write down as many words as they can that use only letters taken from the key word. Found words must be at least three letters in length, and no letter may appear more often in a found word than it appears in the source. If the source does contain S, it is not permissible to claim two for the same word written with and without S. Obviously, THING and THINGS are the same word singular and plural, and HEAR and HEARS the same verb in different forms. Less obviously, it would cause unnecessary argument to claim both DOE as the singular animal and DOES as the verb form of DO, and it is for this reason that S ought not to appear.

Score. The simplest scoring system is one point per found word. You may agree to score two points for a word that no one else has found. Or you may carry refinement even further, scoring none for each word found by everyone, one for a word found by all but one player, two if found by all but two players, and so on.

Comment. Some years ago my group of players became so hooked on this game that we went to the trouble of agreeing a long word at one session, taking it home and working on it for a week, then comparing results and scoring at our next. This may be carrying the whole thing too far.

TARGET
Two or more players, four or five best
Any age but players should be evenly matched in vocabulary
Come prepared

A refinement of *Word hunt*, published for many years in *The Daily Express* as a rival to the crossword, and since adopted by many other British newspapers and magazines. In this version the key word is nine letters in length, and these are written into a grid of 3 × 3 squares. Players then have to find words of at least three letters, all deriving from the letters of the grid and all including the central letter, and including the nine-letter word itself.

To make a home game of this, you need each player to come prepared by having constructed such a grid based on a nine-letter word. Either each player in turn sits out while the others work on that player's grid, or all the grids are put on simultaneous display and everyone works on all other grids except their own.

NAME IN VAIN (NAMAGRAMS)
Two or more players
Adults and precocious adolescents
No preparation required

Announce the name of a well-known character from history or present-day celebrity, then see who can make the best and most apt anagram from the letters of that name. The press is full of examples of this potentially scurrilous game, it being a much-favoured pastime and one that is helped considerably by the availability of computer anagram programs. Here are some classic examples of anagrams derived from historical figures and cultural celebrities. In case you can't work out who they are from the clues provided, the answers appear at the end of this section.

A weakish speller, am I? *(playwright)*
Flit on, cheering angel *(nurse)*
Greatest born idealist *(poet)*
Hated for ill *(dictator)*
I paint modern *(painter)*
Old West action *(actor)*
Thelma *(dramatic protagonist)*
Won half the New World's glory *(poet)*

ACROSTIC-HUNT
Two or more players, four or five best
Any age but evenly matched in vocabulary

This is my name for an ingenious refinement of *Word hunt* originally described under the rather undistinctive title Dictionary.

First, agree on a key word of ten letters, preferably without too many duplications of any given letter. Suppose it is PERSIFLAGE, since that's the word of which I retain genuine examples of play. Each player's object is then to compile a list of ten words, of which the first begins with P, the second with E, the third with R, and so on throughout the letters of the key word. Only one word is needed for each initial, but if a given letter is duplicated (such as E in this case), the two words must be different. No word in the list may consist of a string of letters taken entire and unchanged from the key. This applies particularly to the first word. For example, if the key word is PROTRACTOR, you may not claim for PROTRACT, TRACTOR, or ACTOR. The best part of the game is that you score according to the length of each word you find – the longer, the better.

There are several ways of finishing. We just stop when everyone agrees they can't find any more. Alternatively, you might fix a definite time limit of, say 15 minutes, or – and this is the more competitively vicious version – you must all stop when one player says 'Stop!'.

Score. Players then announce, compare and score for their first word, then their second, and so on. Each acceptable word scores one point per letter it contains. The highest possible score is 100, but as this requires ten different anagrams of the ten-letter key word you won't expect to reach it very often. A good score is one between 50 and 70.

Here are the words four of us came up with for PERSIFLAGE:

First player ...		*Second ...*		*Third ...*		*Fourth ...*	
PRESAGE	7	PLEASE	6	PILFERS	7	PRAISE	6
ELAPSE	6	EARS	4	EAGLES	6	EAGLES	6
RELAPSE	7	RIFLES	6	REGALES	7	REPLIES	7
SERIF	5	SPIRAL	6	SPIRAL	6	SILAGE	6
IRE	3	ISLE	4	IFS	3	ISLE	4
FRAIL	5	FLARES	6	FRAGILE	7	FRAGILE	7
LARGE	5	LAGERS	6	LAGERS	6	LAHERS	6
ARISE	5	AGREES	6	AGILE	5	ASPIRE	6
GRAPES	6	GRAPES	6	GRAPES	6	GRAILS	6
EAGLES	6	ERASE	5	ERASE	5	ERASE	5
Totals	**55**		**55**		**58**		**59**

Problem. Can you match the target scores for these three 10-letter words?
CUSTOMABLE – target 65   PNEUMATICS – target 67   CENTRALITY – target 74.

STRINGS

Two to four players
Any age

A single sheet of paper is needed for this traditional game, which can be played at almost any level of sophistication.

Turn the paper sideways so the long edge is along the top. The first player writes a single letter of the alphabet at the middle of the top edge in order to start a string of letters. It may as well be A or I, as all words made in play score according to their length, and this will yield a point to the first player. Each player in turn thereafter may do *either* or *both* of the following:

1. Add a new letter to the left or right end of the existing string.

2. Make a word by underlining one or more consecutive letters in the string that form a valid word, provided that the same word has not already been made and scored. Only one such word may be made in a turn.

If you do both, the word you make must incorporate the letter you added. You may not score for a word entirely contained within another that has already been scored, such as KIN if ASKING has already been used. Nor may you score for simply adding an S to the right of the row and making a plural or third person verb form of a word that has already been scored. Some players count any single vowel as a nominal word for one point, which has the effect of encouraging their addition and so opening up more possibilities.

Here's how a simple game might go. Instead of underlining the words made, I've written them beneath the row, with the second player's entries in italics:

TAXIFANYETIS

        a ------------------- 1
       an --------------- 2
      fan --------------- 3
      any ------------- 3
      if ------------------- 2
    x i ------------------- 2
    a ------------------------ 1   ('ax' was not accepted)
  t a x i --------------------- 4
            ye ------------ 2
           yet ----------- 3
           yeti ---------- 4
               is ------- 2

So far, the first player has 13 to the second's 16. Keep playing up to an agreed target score, such as 50.

You can boost the scores to produce more significant margins of victory by squaring the individual scores, yielding 4 for a word of two letters, 9 for three, 16 for four, and so on. In this case I suggest that, rather than score 1 for adding a vowel and failing to make a longer word of it, you may immediately add a consonant to the other end of the row and score for that, if possible. (By my rules, Y is always a vowel.)

SPELL 'EM OUT
Two players
Adults and older children
A spoken and written game

Each player in turn becomes the Caller, the other player being the Stopper. The Caller mentally runs through the alphabet in order from A to Z, not too fast, announcing 'A' out loud to indicate the start, but going through the rest in silence. At any desired time, the Stopper calls 'Stop!', and the Caller announces the letter just reached. The Stopper writes this letter down, and may then either go for a word (see below) or else call upon the Caller to repeat the process. If called upon to do so, the Caller again announces 'A' out loud and continues silently through the alphabet until the Stopper says 'Stop!' The letter just reached is announced again, and the Stopper writes it to the right of the previous letter.

This whole process is repeated until the Stopper, having just written in the latest letter, decides to go for a word. This is done by announcing a word of three or more letters which begins with the first letter in the row and incorporates all the others in the same order in which they appear. The score for this is 5 points for each called letter, minus the total word length. For example, suppose the first letter is C. The Stopper could stop here and announce CAP for 2 points (5 for C less 3 for length), or continue. If the next letter is M, the Stopper could announce CAM for 7 points. If play continues, and the next letter is F, the Stopper could attempt COMFY for 10, or, if this colloquialism is disallowed, COMFORT for 8 points.

Obviously, the Stopper will want to get as long a word as possible, and will keep going so long as the letters are fairly usable. But let's suppose the next letter is X, giving the row CMFX. Being unable to make anything of this, the Stopper must make a word using as many letters as possible – in this case COMFY or COMFORT, whichever is allowed – and scores only one point per called letter, in this case three.

STORY TIME

Most word games are about finding and manipulating individual words. But some involve arranging words into meaningful (in the nonsensical sense of the term) phrases and sentences. This section is entirely devoted to them.

TELEGRAMS

Any number of players
Adults and older children
Fun rather than competitive

Choose a word at random and spell it out. Everyone then has to compose a telegram whose initial letters form the chosen word. For example, if the random word is MESSAGE, telegrams might read:

MICE EATEN SAUSAGES. SEVERAL ARE GETTING ECZEMA.

MEET ETHEL STATION SATURDAY AND GET EARWIGS

MUM'S ELBOW STUCK. SEND A GREASED EGG-CUP

This is hardly a competitive game, and doesn't lend itself to scoring; but it's great fun.

ACRONYMOUS BOSH

Any number of players
Adults and older children
Fun rather than competitive

In this more challenging version of *Telegrams* (above), the given word is the main name of a celebrity or historical character, and the required telegrams should relate in some way to their character or achievements. For example:

Napoleon: NEED ARMY. PREPARING OFFENSIVE. LEFT ELBA OTHER NIGHT.
Groucho: GET REALLY OLD UNDERWEAR. COMEDY HOUSE ORDERS.
Madonna: MAKE A DIN. OUR NEW NEIGHBOUR'S AWFUL.

In the business game version, one player announces the name of a real-life company, which may be a set of initials, though the game is funnier if it isn't. The name is then treated as an acronym, and players compete as to who can devise the best acronymous phrase describing the activity or perceived character of the company in question. For example:

British Telecom (BT)   BAN TALKING (or BLITHERING TWITS)
W. H. Smith   WE HAVE SOLD MANY ILLITERATE TOMES HERE
Tesco   TRY EATING SLUGS COOKED OUTDOORS

ALPHABENT

Any number of players
Adults and older children
Fun rather than competitive

I thought I had invented this game, but later discovered the American National Puzzlers' League had already done so. Related to *Telegrams*, it requires the players to concoct an intelligible (if not necessarily intelligent) sentence, paragraph, or even short story, consisting of 26 words beginning with successive letters of the alphabet. Only the first example is mine; the rest emanate from the pen of my brother, who turned out to be extraordinarily adept at this strangely compulsive exercise.

1. *As belligerent conductors deftly exercised finger groups, horn-players joined knees lovingly – meanwhile, neophyte oboists played Rachmaninov, seeming to undergo variations where xylophonists yielded zigzags.*

2. *A brilliant Cockney doctor emerged from Gynaecology, having incautiously just knocked long-suffering matron's neurologist out – protesting (quite rightly so) that untrained veterinarians wouldn't've X-rayed your zygoma.*

3. *As birds can dive even from great heights, I just know larks must nest on pinnacles, quietly recollecting shattered thoughts, until violent winds xenomorphosize yon zones.*

4. *A born coward, Darius eventually found great happiness in judicially kicking loud-mouthed neopotists on picking quarrels, rightly saying that unkindness vitiated warring Xerxes' youthful zeal.*

He then capped the whole thing with this 51-word poetic *tour de force*, in which, having arrived at Z, he works his way back through the alphabet to A.

> *A brilliant crystal, descending earthwards from*
> *glowering heavens,*
> *introducing jewel-like, kaleidoscopic*
> *luminescence, moved noiselessly over*
> *palatial quadrangles,*
> *reflecting silent transformations under*
> *vaulted windows,*
> *xanthisizing yellowing zones, yew-lined xysts,*
> *winding vagrantly upwards towards*
> *sequestered rooftops –*
> *quiescent posterns of neglected mansions,*
> *lonely knolls, joyless, inhospitable houses –*
> *gliding,*
> *falling ever downwards*
> *cascading*
> *brightly*
> *away ...*

TRY-POE

Any number of players
Any literate age
Preparation desirable

This is my title for a traditional game that turns out to be more amusing than it looks. If possible, get everyone to come prepared with a list of words in alphabetical order, which they have compiled by taking a verse or stanza from a poem. Or provide them all yourself, though it's still better to do this in advance than to lose everyone's interest while you rearrange them. You will be not surprised to learn that the aim of the game is to be the first to reconstruct the verse from its alphabetized components. Try this one:

A	GONE	MY	SHOES
AND	HAS	MY	SINGING
AND	HEAR	MY	THE
ARE	I	OF	THE
BITS	IT'S	OVER	TO
FALLEN	LONG	ROAD	WAY
FOLK	MOUNTAIN	SAYING	WITS

You should agree in advance which of two ways to play *Try-poe*. By one method, the selected stanza should be cast in a regular mould of rhyme and metre, and the aim is to reconstruct the original with word-for-word precision. By the other, the passage may follow the modern practice of eschewing all formal discipline, and the winner is the player who produces the most amusing concoction of poetic pseudery.

CONSEQUENCES

The more players, the better
Any age
No preparation needed

This is no exception to the rule that the best games were mostly invented long ago. It was described as 'old fashioned' even in *Cassell's Book of In-Door Amusements and Fireside Fun* in 1881. Up to about the middle of the 20th century, much of its charm consisted in the scope it provided for indulging in a sort of titillating suggestiveness that has since been rendered pointless by the frankness of the times.

Each player is given a sheet of writing paper long enough to be folded over ten times. On the top line they write down an adjective or descriptive phrase that might apply to a man – for example, *debonair, irascible, long-in-the-tooth, devious,* etc. Everyone then folds the top line over so that it is concealed from view, and passes the sheet to their left-hand neighbour.

On the second line, immediately below the fold, that neighbour writes in the name of a man, chap, guy, bloke, or other male person. He may be living or dead or fictitious, but living celebrities are usually preferred, or even the name of someone taking part in the game, though this can prove somewhat risky, especially if he is big and has no sense of humour.

This, too, is folded over and passed to the next on the left, who writes in the word MET, followed by an adjective or phrase that might describe a woman. The same procedure occurs ten times in all, the various components occurring in the following order (as dictated by whoever is leading the game):

1. *Male description*
2. *Man's name*
3. MET + *female description*
4. *Woman's name*
5. *Place where they met*
6. *What he gave her*
7. *What he said to her*
8. *What she said to him*
9. *The consequence*
10. *What the world said about it*

or, as a concession to the march of progress, what the media said about it.

When all have been written, the sheets of paper are passed round for the last time and unfolded by their various recipients. The players conclude by reading out the resultant stories one by one.

Here's a completed sheet, just to give you a flavour of the thing.

Shy and retiring ...
Erich von Thunderbold ...
met the amazingly hairy

Mata Hari
in the back of a burnt-out tank.
He gave her a pint of crème de menthe
and said 'Fancy a quick one?'
She said to him 'Who's that at the door?'
The consequence was, they both entered for the Derby
And the world said 'So that's how Mafeking was relieved'.

HEADLINES
Any number of players
Adults and older children
No preparation needed

I once invented a variant of *Consequences* involving a special pack of cards. It can be adapted for pencil and paper by playing as follows.

Each player writes the next in succession of the following words or phrases, folds it over, and passes it to the left for continuation, as before. In this game there are five components, and they are to be written in such a way as to produce the sort of startling but nugatory headline beloved of certain types of tabloid.

The five components are:

1. *Description of person*
2. *Type of person by habit or occupation*
3. *Verb in present tense*
4. *Object of verb*
5. *Place of occurrence.*

The result, if properly done, produces headlines of the following sort:

Happy-Go-Lucky Mother Of Six Blames Fifth Columnist In Graveyard

Hounded Dog-Trainer Urges Viola Lessons Up A Gum-Tree

Mystified Fishmonger Demands Lobotomy Underneath The Arches

Out-Of-Work Vicar Seeks White-Collar Job In Coal Mine

Self-Confessed Shrink Eats Digital Watch On Top Of Old Smoky

PASS IT ON
Any number of players
Any age
No preparation needed

This is my title for a game that must be as old as the hills.

It's the one where each person has a piece of writing paper – the longer, the better – and starts by writing along the top the first line of a story, of such a length that one or two words will go over on to the second line. The top line is then folded over in such a way as to conceal itself but leave the few words of continuation exposed. The papers are then all passed to the left, and each again writes a second line that carries on intelligibly (if not intelligently) from the few words exposed by the previous player. Keep doing this until one player has room for only one more line and so calls a halt to the affair. You then unfold the papers you finished with, and each in turn reads out the story thereon inscribed, hoping it's a good deal funnier than this one, or at least more grammatical. The slanting dashes indicate where the next player took over.

Once upon a time there were three out-of-work bears,
each of whom / was loved in succession by Marie Antoinette, a French queen
famous for / about half an hour. Caesar, however, the gates of the camp
having been fortified / with a glass of tonic wine. Suddenly,
everyone wanted / to know if it was true that Goldilocks
was wearing / a décolleté mackintosh, when Mme de Pompadour
promptly started / up a four-horsepower chariot. The Gauls
soon declared themselves / bankrupt and wondered how long
it would be before / they returned from chopping trees in the woods.
'Oh!', cried / the queen, 'I do hope I haven't interrupted anything.' To this,
Louis replied / '5000 javelins, a brace of elephant and a packet of pins'.
But this / seems as good a place as any to boil my shoes,
so I'll just / remind you of what Mamma Bear said. 'Young lady,'
she began, / 'I must say this is better than the game we played last week.'

If parts of this seem strangely coherent, like a dream in retrospect, a little analysis will show the reason why. It is because the specimen was written by four players, three of whom were concentrating on a definite theme inevitably unrelated to that of anyone else – in this case, respectively, Goldilocks and the three bears, courtesans, and either Julius Caesar's *De Bellico Gallico* or Asterix the Gaul.

NEWSCASTER'S NIGHTMARE

Any number of players
Any age
No preparation needed

In this variation of *Pass it on*, the underlying assumption is that a radio broadcaster's script for the news has got into a muddle. The method of play is the same, each in turn writing a line of script and folding it over, leaving a few words dangling for the next to continue from. The newsy theme, however, imposes a unity of style designed to add to the fun. Thus one such bulletin might begin:

The Bolivian Minister of Nuts and Bolts
has arrived in Chile / wearing a shortie nightie
with the words / 'No to privatization'.
In spite of / protests by workers in the treacle industry,
their purpose is / thought to be sabotage, but
the President is / unlikely to make a statement
before ...

And so on. I dare say you get the idea. It is as nothing to the story of the radio announcer who could never get the hang of pronouncing 'Rimsky-Korsakov' and always tried to avoid it. Eventually the dreaded moment came. Taking it very slowly, he declared 'And now for a work by Rim-sky-Kor-sa-kov – it's that old favourite, the Bum of the Flightle-Bee'.

McGONAGALLESE

(*or* Love me, love my doggerel)
Any number of players
Any age
No preparation needed

A yet more ingenious version of *Pass it on* has everyone cooperating in the production of rhyming couplets which, with any luck, will end up sounding like an epic by William McGonagall out of *Monty Python's Flying Circus*.

Given the usual long sheet of writing paper, each player on the first turn writes a line of verse to establish a metre and rhythm, and passes it on to the next without folding it over. On the second turn, each player writes a line of the same length as the first and rhyming with it, then folds it over to conceal both lines, and finally writes a third line of the same length and metre but starting a new rhyme-ending. Play continues in this way, with each player writing a line that rhymes with the one that's visible, then concealing it and starting a new line. When all are agreed that no more lines can be supported by the paper available, the last player writes only the rhyming line and then stops. When the resultant poems are read out, they may be found to resemble the following example:

> *I'll tell you an epic that never began:*
> *It started, I ween, at the Siege of Sedan –*
> *There was a young lady who watched from afar*
> *Albeit from the comparative safety of her car.*
> *It was, so they say, a decrepit saloon*
> *Propelled by the gas from a hot-air balloon.*
> *She sailed through the air with the greatest of ease*
> *To finish at rest on the points of her knees.*
> *It can't be described as a graceful descent*
> *And always leaves one of your handlebars bent.*
> *But enough of this twaddle. The Siege of Sedan*
> *Is said to have ended before it began.*

ALL IN A ROW

The following games have to do with making rows or sequences of words. The general idea is that each in turn adds a new word to a list in such a way as to match or continue the theme of those that have gone before. In some, your further aim is to reduce the number of options open to the next player. On the whole, these games tend to be of the more challenging and thought-provoking variety.

UNCRASH

Two to four players
Adults and older children
Fast and fun

This game can be played with words of any length, but four makes a good start. Basically, each player in turn adds a word to a list of four-letter words until one player can't go without 'crashing'. A 'crash' occurs when you write a word of which at least one letter has already appeared in the same position higher up the list. For example, if the first word is POST, it can be followed by any word of four different letters, or by OPTS or STOP, but not by TOPS, which crashes the O, nor by POTS, which crashes both P and O.

There are several ways of arranging the game. You can have one piece of paper and pass it round for each subsequent word to be added. Or you can have a piece each, and all compile the same list as each player in turn calls a new word out. Or you can play as many simultaneous games as there are players in the following way: each player writes a start word at the top of a sheet of paper, then passes it to the left and writes the second word on the sheet passed from the right, and so on.

Here's a sample four-player game with three-letter words:

1	S	A	Y
2	N	O	T
3	A	H	A
4	O	N	E
1	P	U	B
2	F	I	X
3	Y	E	W
4	G	Y	P
1	E	G	G
2	I	R	K
3	T	W	O
4	?		

The fourth player loses, being unable to find a continuation that does not contain a letter crashing with one higher up the same column of letters (even if you can). One scoring system is to award a point to the player who wrote the last word and to deduct one from the player who would have been forced to crash. Another would be to award four points (the number of players) to the player who entered the last word (TWO), then progressively one point less to each preceding player other than the loser, who scores zero.

Uncrash is a great game for post mortems. Player 4 evidently lost by entering GYP. Was there a winning alternative, or, at least, one that could have prevented the loss?

You can, of course, play with words of any agreed length. The longer the words, the longer the game will usually last before somebody crashes out, though no game can last longer then 26 moves. One way of increasing the scope without getting too complicated is to use longer words but ban only crashes made in a central block of letters, odd for odd and even for even. For example, you could use seven-letter words and prohibit crashes only in the central three, or words of eight letters and prohibit them only in the central four.

WORD PING-PONG
Two or more players
Adults and older children
Fun, but rather long

This game was invented by P. Perkins and first appeared in *Games & Puzzles* (1st series). Unusually for a word game, it is based on a game of an entirely different sort, as the name itself indicates. Just in case you don't know, Table tennis or ping-pong is played up to 21 points, with each player serving (i.e. going first) five times in succession before passing the lead to the other player. The winner is the first to reach 21, but if the score gets to 20–20 then the service alternates until one player scores two points in succession. A 'rally' is a period of play starting with a service and continuing with alternate moves until one player scores a point.

Toss a coin, or something, to decide who goes first. Each service is made by writing down a four-letter word. This starts a list which is to be continued by each player in turn in accordance with the following rules:

● Each new word must be formed by changing just one letter of the previous word. The server may change only the first or second letter, and the opponent only the third or fourth. (This, rather cleverly, represents the two sides of the table separated by a 'net'.)

● The serving word (the first in any rally) must be capable of taking a change in its third or fourth letter. If the opponent cannot respond, and the server cannot show how a response could have been made, the service is a fault and the second player scores the point.

● You may not make a word that has already appeared in the same rally, nor use the same serving word twice in the same game.

● A rally ends when one player cannot make a valid response, and the other player thereupon scores a point.

● You may not use the same letter in the same position more than three times in the same rally.

The inventor illustrates a rally between Odd and Even as follows:

1	L	A	S	T
2	L	A	S	*H*
3	*C*	A	S	H
4	C	A	S	*T*
5	*P*	A	S	T
6	P	A	*N*	T
7	P	*I*	N	T
8	P	I	N	*E*
9	*W*	I	N	E
10	W	I	*S*	E
11	*R*	I	S	E
12	R	I	*C*	E
13	?			

Now the server is stuck. Having used both A and I three times in the same rally, he is obliged to change the vowel in second position, and there is no such word as RECE, ROCE, or RYCE. Even therefore scores, and Odd serves again.

Doubles. *Word ping-pong* can be played by four in doubles. The rules are exactly as above, except that the two members of each partnership play alternately. They are not allowed to confer.

Threesome. Three-handed ping-pong may sound daft, but here are my suggested rules for adapting the word game for play by three.

● Each in turn enters a four-letter word differing from the previous word by one letter.

● No player may change either of the two letters changed in the two preceding turns.

● No letter may appear more than five times in the same position.

● When a player cannot continue, he drops out and the next player tries to continue.

● When two players have dropped out, the third scores the point and the turn to serve passes to the left of the previous server.

NYMPHABET
Two players
Adults and older children
Fun or serious, as preferred

This game of my invention takes its name from *nim*, an old English word meaning 'take' and also denoting any game in which two players alternately remove a restricted number of objects from a row or array until one player wins by taking the last one. I used to play this at school with each player taking one, two or three matches away from a row of thirteen. Something similar features in that still controversial film *Last Year at Marienbad*.

The basic game. On a single sheet of paper write the letters of the alphabet in a row from

A to Z. Each player in turn writes a word. The first word must begin with A, and its writer crosses off the A of the communal alphabet. If it also contains a B, the B is also deleted. If a C follows somewhere after the B, that letter is also deleted, as also is a D if it follows the C, and so on. For example, the first word might be ACE, deleting only A, or ABLE, deleting A and B. The word ABDICATE would similarly dispose of A, B and C, but not of D, as it precedes the C instead of following it. However, ABDICATED would delete the D too, though not the E, as it doesn't follow the qualifying D.

The second player then writes a word beginning with the next undeleted letter of the alphabet, thereby deleting it and any other successive letters that may follow it in the correct order. This continues until one player loses by being forced to use the Z. (It would seem more logical to win by using the Z, but you'll find in practice that this gives the second player a winning advantage.)

Thus a game might run as follows:

First player	*Second player*
ABaCk	DEFyinG
HIJacK	LaMiNatiOn
PiQue	ReSTaUrant
VoW	XYlophone
Zip *(loses)*	

After a while you will discover that whoever deletes the letter U wins the game – unless, that is, the other can find a word beginning with V that also eliminates W and X, otherwise the word WAXY wins. Further backtracking shows that whoever writes the letter P wins, for whatever comes next enables the P writer to cancel all letters up to U – unless, that is, the other can find a Q-word that also eliminates R, S, T and U.

If and when you eventually convince yourself that either the first or the second player is bound to win, assuming best possible play, you'll be ready to open the game up in any of the following ways,

Variation 1. Start with Z and work backwards.

Variation 2. The first player announces what letter he proposes to start with, and the second then specifies whether the game is to be played forwards (A–Z) or backwards (Z–A). The alphabet is considered as circular, with A and Z consecutive. The winner now is certainly the player who uses the 26th and last letter. Here's a game in which the starter began in the middle with N and the follower decreed backward play.

First player	*Second player*
NaMeLy	KneeJerk
IncHinG	FED
CaBAl	ZYgoma
Xi	WeeVil
UTiliSeR	QuiPO *(wins)*

Variation 3. This is played like the last variation, but with an important difference that considerably alters the strategy. Here the winner is the player finishing with the higher score when all letters have been used, and it makes no difference who writes the last word. Each word counts one point for each letter it uses up, and each player's final score is that of all these individual scores multiplied together. For example:

First player	*Second player*
QueeReST = 4	UVula = 2
WaXY = 3	ZABaglione = 3
CeDE = 3	FiGHtIng = 4
JacKaL = 3	MiNOrshiP = 4

Here the first player wins by $4 \times 3 \times 3 \times 3 = 108$ as against $2 \times 3 \times 4 \times 4 = 96$. If instead of UVULA the second player had tried UNVOWED, and found it supported by the dictionary, the latter might have won with a score of 192.

ARROW OF LETTERS (WORDSPROUTS)
Two players
Adults and older children
Needs a lot of space

If you know the pencil-and-paper game of Sprouts you will recognize the origin of this verbal adaptation made by Michael Grendon. It can get complicated, and it's advisable to allow plenty of space on the paper for it to expand into.

A word of four letters, all different, is agreed upon, and these four letters are written in a row, each enclosed by a circle, along the approximate middle of the sheet of paper. Each successive letter is connected by an arrow from left to right to show the direction of reading.

From now on, each player in turn adds a new encircled letter, and connects it by means of an arrow to one or more existing letters. The new letter must differ from any that has gone before (unless you want the game to go on for ever). That player then scores, at the rate of one point per letter, for each and every word that can be made which uses the letter just entered and correctly follows the line of arrows indicating the direction of reading.

For example, to the above diagram the first player might add the letter H:

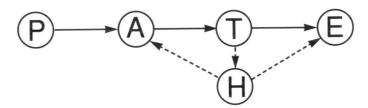

With the addition of appropriate arrows, this yields a score of 4 for PATH, 4 for HATE, and 3 for THE, total 11 points.

The next player might add an S:

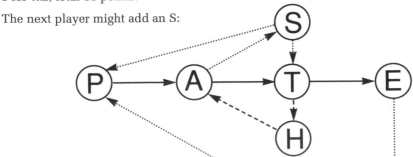

Suitably connected arrows now produce 5 for PASTE, 5 for HASTE, 4 for HASP, and 4 for STEP, making 18 in all.

Play continues in the same way until neither player can add a letter without breaking a rule. If one player passes and the other can add a letter, the game ends when that last letter has been added and all possible scores made for that turn. The remaining rules are:

● Words may only be made by following the arrows in the direction of reading.

● In following that direction, no letter may be omitted or jumped over.

● No arrow may cross another or cross over an encircled letter.

● No encircled letter may have more than four arrows attached to it, whether by head or tail, but this does not prevent four-arrowed letters from being used in subsequent words.

● No given pair of letters may be connected by more than one arrow, and that arrow may point in one direction only.

● No score attaches to a shorter word that is entirely contained within a longer. Thus, in the example illustrated, the score of five for PASTE precludes that of four for PAST.

The inventor points out that the rule requiring each scorable word to incorporate the letter just added prevents one player from profiting from any score the opponent might have made but missed. To counter this, you may want to introduce a rule equivalent to huffing in Draughts or Muggins in Crib, whereby, before adding your new letter, you may declare and score for anything your opponent might have scored but didn't.

Also, it isn't clear to me whether the prohibition on scoring shorter words contained within longer applies to words of equal length but starting from different positions. For example, if you score 4 for LANE, can you not also score 4 for ELAN? I think this adds a further element of skill and ought to be allowed.

CENTURION

Two or more players
Adults and older children
Requires enthusiasm for adding up

If you have no head for figures and don't like adding up, try this game of my invention. It will do you good.

The main game is for two.

The letters of the alphabet are assigned numerical values according to their position, from A = 1 to Z = 26. The first player writes down a three-letter word whose combined letter value totals 10 or less – for example

A C E = 9 (1 + 3 + 5)

The second writes beneath it a three-letter word beginning with the last letter of the first, and beside it notes the cumulative total of letters written so far. For example:

E N D = 32 (5 + 14 + 4 + 9 for ACE)

Play continues with each adding a three-letter word and noting the combined total so far. No word may appear more than once in the list. The player who causes the cumulative total to reach three figures (100 or more) is the loser. Thus the game started above might continue as follows:

D A B adds 7 for 39

B U G adds 30 for 69

D A Y adds 30 for 99 *and wins.*

Double centurion is played by three or more players and goes up to 200. Four may play in partnerships. Partners play alternately and may not consult.

INFLATION
Two or more players
Adults and older children
More adding up

A close relative of *Centurion, Inflation* is based on the same principle of assigning values to the letters of the alphabet from A = 1 to Z = 26.

The starter writes a word of three letters together with its total value, which may not be more than ten, for example:

A C E = 9

This begins a list to which each player in turn appends a new three-letter word, together with its value. Each new word must start with a letter used in the preceding word, and no word may appear more than once in the same list. Furthermore – and this is the point of the game – each new word must also be higher in value than the last. The first player unable to add a higher-valued word is the loser, and the writer of the preceding word is the winner.

The shortest possible game lasts for three moves, with several possibilities for the first two words:

A B B = 5

B U Y = 48

W R Y = 64

Since WRY is the highest-counting three-letter word acceptable under my rules of play, anyone who enters a word containing one of those three letters is giving the game away.

If this gets too easy, change the rules so that whoever writes the last word loses. Now it becomes incumbent upon everyone to have in mind a valid word to follow the one they add themselves.

OILERS
Two players
Adults and older children
A game of logic

This game, first described in the magazine *Word Ways* by Dave Silverman, takes its name from that of the mathematician Euler. So you may not be surprised to discover that it's not so much a word game as a mathematical game that happens to make use of words.

Basic game. Oilers is played with a stockpile of nine four-letter words. At each turn, a player In effect 'captures' a word. This may be done by starting with a list of the words concerned and crossing one off the list at each turn, or by writing them on nine separate slips of paper and removing one at each turn. The nine words are:

F	I	S	H		S	O	U	P		S	W	A	N
G	I	R	L		H	O	R	N		A	R	M	Y
K	N	I	T		V	O	T	E		C	H	A	T

Each player in turn deletes or removes a word, and the winner is the first player to capture three words containing one letter in common. If neither player does so, the result is a draw. For example:

Adam:	HORN	
Eve:	SOUP	
Adam:	KNIT	
Eve:	SWAN	*(Otherwise Adam has three N's)*
Adam:	FISH	*(Otherwise Eve has three S's)*
Eve:	GIRL	
Adam:	CHAT	*(Wins)*

Adam now has three words containing H. Had Eve tried to counter this by taking CHAT, Adam would have taken GIRL and got three I's.

You will quickly realize that *Oilers* is the verbal equivalent of Noughts and Crosses, or Tic Tac Toe. If you look at the grid of nine words above, arranged in the traditional three rows of three, you will note that each row, column and long diagonal of three in a line contains exactly three occurrences of one letter – for example, the top row contains three S's, the third column three A's, and the top left diagonal three H's. It follows, therefore, that taking a word is equivalent to placing a nought or a cross in one of the nine spaces. That being so, Adam's opening move was equivalent to playing in the centre square, a well-known strong move, and Eve's to playing in a central edge square, a well-known weak move. Once you discover this, Basic Oilers will always end in a draw. That's the time to progress to …

Advanced Oilers. The advanced game is played with a stock of 16 three-letter words and with a slightly different objective. The words are:

A	P	E		D	A	Y		C	A	N		R	A	T
L	I	P		D	I	E		T	I	N		R	I	G
H	O	P		D	O	T		O	N	E		R	O	W
P	U	T		B	U	D		S	U	N		R	U	E

As before, each player takes a word in turn. The first to move – the 'Toiler' – wins if *either* player collects four words having one letter in common. The second to move – the 'Spoiler' – wins if *neither* has four such words by the time all sixteen have been captured.

Four-square *Oilers* obviously cannot end in a draw, and anyone keen on recreational mathematics will soon discover that one player can always win with perfect play.

MANY A CROSS WORD ...

Many word games are based on the same idea as the crossword puzzle, that of writing letters into a squared grid in such a way as to form words that go from left to right across and link with words written vertically from top to bottom.

LYNX
Two players
Adults and older children
Printed crossword grid needed

The simplest way of turning ordinary crosswords into a competitive game is as follows. Using the printed crossword grid from a newspaper or magazine, and ignoring the clues provided, each in turn enters a word in such a way as to fill one light exactly. The score for the first word is the number of letters it contains. Each subsequent word must also fill one light exactly and must connect with at least one word already in place. The score for each new word entered is 'length times links' – that is, the length of the new word entered, multiplied by the number of its letters already in position from words running in the opposite direction. For example, you would score 5 points for writing START as the first word, or into a light containing just one letter already in position, but you would get 10 for writing START into a light showing – T-R-, and 15 for filling out S-A-T.

DOUBLE CROSS
Two players
Adults and older children
Squared paper needed

The simplest way of playing competitive crosswords on blank squared paper, as distinct from existing crossword grids as above, is as follows. Take some squared paper and draw a square frame of any agreed size – say 15 × 15. Better still, take two sheets and draw two frames of the same size. This enables you to play two games at once so that neither has to sit around twiddling thumbs while the other juggles with words.

Each player starts by entering a word of at least seven letters across the frame in such a way as to cover the central square (or one of the four central squares in an even-numbered grid), and passes it across to the other. Play continues with each in turn writing in a word that either extends an existing word, or crosses an existing word by using an existing letter at the joint, or both. Do not black in any squares to mark the limit of a word at either end, in case it can be legitimately extended. Do, however, insert a thick black line wherever a word you enter abuts against an existing word without extending it. This is called a bar line. For example:

	L					T
	A					H
	S	T	A	R	T	O
	T					U
B	E	N	D	I	N	G
	D					H

The first word was START, and the fourth entry THOUGH, necessitating the insertion of a bar after START because there is no such word as STARTO.

All the letters you enter in one turn must be in the same line and must create or form part of at least one new word. Each turn produces a score made up as follows: one point for each letter in every new word made in that turn, minus one point for each bar line you have to add to separate it from an adjacent incompatible word. The word THOUGH, in the above example, consequently scores five instead of six points.

Keep going until one player cannot add another word. The player with the higher score wins.

ALPHACROSS
Two or more players
Adults and older children
Cleverer version of previous game

If you find *Double cross* rather lacking in point and direction, try this more challenging variety.

On squared paper, draw a frame outlining a grid of (say) 11 × 11 squares. If more than two play, increase the number on each side by two for each additional player.

Each player starts by writing out a complete alphabet from A to Z, either on a separate slip or on the squared sheet and headed by their name. Each in turn then writes one word into the grid. The first entry must cross the centre square and each subsequent word must cross at least one other word going in the opposite direction. The same word may not appear more than once in the same grid, either in whole or in part. As before, use a thick bar line to separate two adjacent letters if they don't form part of the same word, only this time there is no scoring penalty for doing so. Or, if you prefer, block in whole squares at either end of a word that doesn't touch the edge of the grid, though this tends to make the game a little too cramped.

Each time you write a word in, you cross off your alphabet every letter you have just written down if you haven't already used it. Needless to say, the winner is the first player to use up their entire alphabet.

For example, the first player might start with QUIZZICAL, deleting seven different letters from their alphabet including two or three difficult ones (Q, U, Z) that might be hard to fit in later. The next player could not then cross it with QUIZ or QUIZZES, as this would contravene the 'same word' rule, but might, for instance, cross the C with QUACKING, thereby deleting seven different letters (excluding the C itself, which was already there).

You may find it desirable to limit the maximum permitted word length to six or seven letters.

SCRAMBLE
Two or more players, more better
Adults and older children
Takes time

The title may not tell you much about the subject of the game, but it well describes the sort of panic that ensues as players race to be the first to complete their task of crossword composition.

Each player takes a piece of squared paper and frames a grid of an agreed crossword size, say 11 × 11. A subject or theme is agreed, and everyone enters this as the first word along the top row from the left corner. From now on it's everyone for themselves, the aim being to fill your grid with a crossword in which every entry relates to the theme.

Keep going until the cleverest player completes their grid and calls 'Stop!' The finished crosswords are then passed to each person's left-hand neighbour for checking and scoring. Score one point for each letter of each acceptable and correctly spelt word or phrase. This means that every checked letter counts twice, once in each direction. Any word that a checker feels may not be acceptable is put to the vote, and is deemed acceptable if supported by at least one player other than the player who used it. If an entry is misspelt or deemed unacceptable, it scores nothing, but this has no effect on the score of any valid words that may run across it. The player who finished first and called an end to the game gets a bonus of 20 for finishing with the highest score. But anyone and everyone who scores more points than the stopper gets the 20-point bonus instead.

Here's a sample crossword based on the word and theme KITCHEN:

The player checking this grid queried EMETICS, UNSET, POTIONS and COCO. The compiler argued for one of these on the grounds that if no stone could be left unturned, then, by the same grammatical token, no jelly could be left UNSET. As for EMETICS, she thought the contents of this particular kitchen could be left to speak for themselves. These were upheld, but COCO was shown to be the name of a tree and not of a fruit, nut or bean, and POTIONS was disallowed on the grounds that such things should be kept in the bathroom, if not the poisons cupboard. This crossword finally scored 54 across and 58 down, making 112 in all.

Tip. The longer your words, the more they score. It's therefore a good idea to start off by entering three or four long words, not necessarily crossing each other, but providing easy connecting letters for subsequent shorter words to latch on to.

BLACK SQUARES
Two players
Adults and older children
A concentrated game of bluff

This excellent game comes from a collection of inventions by Harry Woollerton published in the first series of *Games & Puzzles* magazine under the general heading 'Games you haven't played before'. It takes a lot of time and thought, but well rewards the effort. I should add that I found it necessary to tighten up and modify some of the rules, as the existing ones didn't seem to cover every situation that arose when we first played.

You need a sheet of paper ruled into a grid of 12×12 squares each at least 1 cm^2 in size. You need both ink and pencil, and a rubber for erasing appropriate pencilled entries. The grid must be inked in, as you don't want to keep erasing bits.

Black squares is a crossword game in that all the letters eventually written in must form a proper crossword, with horizontal and vertical words crossing at letters common to both. Each word will have a 'black square' (filled in solid) in front of its first letter and following its last, unless either of these comes at the edge of the grid. No part of the finished crossword may be entirely cut off from the rest of it by black squares. It is for the players to decide whether to allow proper names and multi-word phrases, but I recommend sticking to basic rules: single words only, no names, and acceptable only if listed in the dictionary and not classified as foreign.

Scores are made not for filling in words as such, but for correctly identifying squares in which it is impossible to enter a letter which will complete a word in conjunction with any other letter previously written in. Such a square is called 'black', and is filled in when acknowledged as such by both players.

On your turn to play, you may pencil in any number of letters, one to a square. They must all be in line with one another, either horizontally or vertically. They need not form words, but they must be *capable* of being formed into words that *all* connect with one another in legal crossword fashion. Also, at least one of them must form a word in conjunction with at least one letter that has been inked in on a previous turn. Although there is no limit on the number of letters you may pencil in, you may find that more than four or five will threaten to make the game unbearably complicated and long-winded.

Let's suppose your opponent started and it's now your turn to consider the position left by the letters that have just been pencilled in. If you can see how they all connect, or at least believe that they can properly connect, you ink them in, and then end your turn by pencilling in some more letters for your opponent to consider in the same way.

If, however, you think they won't properly connect, or won't make valid words if they do, then you may challenge, and your opponent must seek to pencil in all the connected words resulting from the previous turn. If this attempt is successful, you must ink in all the resultant words, and your false challenge ends your turn. If it isn't, your challenge is correct. You therefore erase all the letters concerned, and continue your turn by pencilling in more letters for your opponent to consider.

There is no score for completing words nor penalty for pencilling in letters that have to be erased. Instead, scores derive from correctly identifying 'black squares' as follows.

If on your turn to play you cannot challenge your opponent, and accept the validity of the pencilled letters by inking them in, then you may claim a black square instead of writing more letters in. A black square is one which cannot be filled with a letter that forms a valid word and properly fits the crossword. For example, suppose one corner of the grid contains the following letters:

You can't claim a black square in front of the J, as the top line can be formed into MAJOR, nor between the X and the N, as the bottom line will produce VIXEN, nor immediately above the I, since, assuming MAJOR, the down word could be one of many words such as SARI, OKAPI, and so on. If the square below O is to be filled, the word it forms part of will have to connect in some way with the N in the corner, as it is not legal to leave a letter unconnected from the rest of the crossword. No problem here – assuming VIXEN, you could fill that square with an N, making ONE or a word so ending. Nor would the square to its right be black, as the N of ONE could make NO across, and there are plenty of words ending in -RON to complete the last word down. In this position, there is only one black square to be claimed, and that is the one between J and X. So you claim it.

When either player claims a black square, the other will seek to disprove it by showing how it can be filled with a valid letter. If the claimant is successful, and the square cannot be filled, it is inked in as a black square. The claimant then scores one point, and continues play by pencilling more letters in, as before. If not, and it is shown that a valid letter can be put in place, then the valid letter and all the words it creates are inked in. The opponent thereby scores two points, and continues play by pencilling more letters in. When you are trying to prove that a claimed black square can in fact be filled, you should do so by writing it and its adjoining words in pencil, so that they can be erased in the event that you are wrong.

Play continues until every square is either black or contains a letter.

RAGAMAN
Two or more players
Adults and older children
A game of concentration

This game was invented by Richard Sharp and, as its name implies, has something to do with anagrams. It works best for two.

Start with the inevitable grid of squares, with an odd number along each side. The minimum 5 × 5 is suitable for a short game, and suitable to start with. It's advisable not to expand it until you're fairly sure you're going to get addicted.

Each player in turn writes a letter in a square. The first letter goes in the central square. If it happens to be a one-letter word, such as A or I, the player cannot claim a score for it. Each subsequent letter must be placed in a square next to a previously entered letter, whether horizontally, vertically or diagonally. For each new letter entered, its writer may score for any word it makes in conjunction with any line of successive letter, whether horizontally, vertically or diagonally. Only one word may be counted in each direction, making a possible maximum of four (down, across, and two diagonals).

For example, in the following game the first player entered Y and the second added M to make MY for a score of two points, i.e. the length of the word. The first then entered A, scoring two for AM (or MA) and two for AY. The second then entered the E above Y, scoring a total of six for ME, YE and AE. Next followed the E below Y, gaining two for AE and three for EYE.

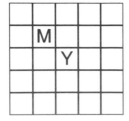
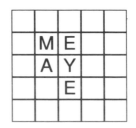

The completed grid is shown below, together with the remaining words and scores.

A	T	A	O	M
U	M	E	T	M
S	A	Y	W	O
N	H	E	S	A
O	S	Y	R	R

First player

Y = 0

AM, AY = 4

EYE, EA = 5

WET, MAT = 6

YEA, AM, AT = 7

MUTE, THY, AT = 9

MATHS, SEWN = 9

HEN, NAE, SUN = 9

ONUS, SO, HOY = 9

WORST, ARE = 8

MOAT, MOTHY = 9

MOAN, ASHEN, AWE = 12

MANOR, SORRY = 10

Second player

MY = 2

YE, AY, ME = 6

WE, WE, WAY = 7

EMU, EAU, UT = 8

MATH, HE = 6

UNMET, NEW = 8

SH, US, YAWS = 8

OAT, NO, TOW, OE = 10

SWOT, HENS = 8

ON, OAT, SO, OW = 9

ROSY, SOY, SHY, YE = 12

ANUS, AT, YAMS = 10

You might argue about the acceptability of some of these entries, but the main point is to show how the game works. In this example the first player wins by 97 to 94. If you prefer a more clear-cut margin of victory, try any of the following:

● In Sharp's suggested 'advanced' version, you score also for anagrams of any words made. By this method, the first player's score of 8 for WORST and ARE would increase to 29 in all for WORST, STROW, WORTS, TROWS (if accepted), ARE, EAR and ERA.

● This is just the sort of game in which I prefer the 'triangular' scoring system of 3 for a word of two letters, 6 for three, 10 for four, and 15 for five.

● Or you can follow the scoring system of the related game of *Last word* (below), by multiplying the score of individual words instead of adding them. For example, the first player's WORST and ARE would score not 5 + 3 = 8 but 5 × 3 = 15. By this method the win would go to the second player, with a total of 259 to 235.

Another scoring rule worth considering is that of prohibiting the score of a word that has already been made.

LAST WORD

Two or more players
Adults and older children
A more elaborate form of the above

Last word was invented by Sid Sackson, one of the world's leading games inventors. Its similarity to *Ragaman* is coincidence probably due to the fact that great minds think alike. As Sackson is American and Sharp British, you won't be surprised to find that *Last word* is bigger and lasts longer.

Start with a grid of 11 × 11 squares, or even 13 × 13 if you think you can face it. Then fill the nine centre squares with nine random letters, for example by opening a book anywhere and taking the first nine letters at the top of the page. For example, suppose the beginning of this paragraph were at the top of the page. Then you would 'seed' the grid like this:

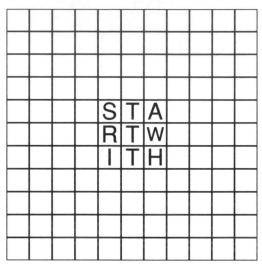

Each player in turn now adds one letter to the grid in such a way as to adjoin at least one letter already in place, whether horizontally, vertically or diagonally. The player entering the letter then scores for every word it can make in conjunction with any line of successive letters in a row, column or diagonal. The letters need not be in the correct order, but they must be successive – that is, not interrupted by any letter not used in the word claimed. The score for a turn is that of the length of the word if only one is made, or, if more than one, those of the individual lengths multiplied together.

For example, the first player might enter an O below the last T. This would yield the words OI (if acceptable), OH, and TOT, for a score of $2 \times 2 \times 3 = 12$. If the second then entered an A immediately before RTW, the resultant words AI, WART, AS would score $2 \times 4 \times 2 = 16$.

Sackson's professionalism as an inventor is exhibited in the following elegant rule for determining the end of the game. Play ends as soon as a letter has been placed in at least one square along each of the four edges of the overall grid. (A corner square does not count for two.) The effect of this rule is to encourage the player in the lead to go off in all directions as soon as possible in order to reach all edges and so end the game while still ahead. The other players (assuming more than two) may cooperate in trying to prevent it by encouraging the growth of a central cluster and not branching out any further than necessary. This attempt is encouraged by an additional rule of play, namely, that you may not enter a letter unless it makes a valid scoring word in two or more directions.

WORDSWORTH
Two to six players, ideal for three
Any age
A family favourite

You can tell this is a classic and popular game from the variety of names under which it appears, including Crossword, Scorewords, Wordsquares, and several others. I used to play it at school, and always enjoy its occasional revival.

Each player draws a grid of 5 × 5 squares. Each player in turn calls out a letter, and everyone enters that letter in their own grid, in whatever position they think is best for making words. This continues until 24 squares have been filled. Everyone may fill the last square with whatever letter they like.

Finally, everyone passes their completed grid to their left-hand neighbour, who 'marks' it as follows. For each row and each column (ten lines in all) score 3 for a three-letter word, 4 for a four-letter word, and 5 for a five-letter word. The letters must be consecutive and read in the right order from left to right in a row or top to bottom in a column. Only one word may be scored in each line, though some players permit two three-letter words with the central letter of the line being common to both – so that, for example, BEDEW would better score 6 for BED, DEW than a straight 5 for the whole word. Diagonal words don't count. A marker who doubts the validity of a word may put it to the vote, unless players prefer to put it strictly to the test of being in the dictionary. The highest possible score is 50, or 60 if you allow overlapping three-letter words.

Advanced scoring. In our circle we prefer to adopt a boosted scoring system which gives more credit to overlapping words. Under these rules, a line may contain two or even three distinct words, with as many overlapping letters as necessary, provided only that where a shorter word is entirely contained within a longer word, only the longer word counts. The score for a five-letter word is doubled to 10. Lines may therefore produce any of the following possible scores:

3	for a three-letter word
4	for a four-letter word
6	for two threes (e.g. HOTAP = HOT + TAP)
7	for a three and a four (e.g. CARCH = CAR + ARCH, but not ARC)
8	for two fours (e.g. CARTY = CART + ARTY)
9	for three threes (e.g. BAGET = BAG + AGE + GET)
10	for five (so BEDEW scores 10 rather than 6 for BED + DEW)

This gives a possible maximum of 100.

Here are two Wordsworthian squares compiled from the same game. The last, 'free', letter was the S of SUMO in the first grid and the R of ERA in the second.

Comments. The most obvious skill required for this game is a good knowledge of short words, especially those involving awkward letters. It also helps to know whether a given letter is likely to be more useful at or near the beginning of a word, and so best placed near the top or to the left, or at or near the end, and so better placed to the right or near the bottom edge. For this purpose, you may like to look at the table of letter position frequencies on page 185.

When starting, take account of the number of players. Note that, the more players there are, the fewer chances you get of choosing letters most convenient to your grid. Counting your final free entry, you get 13 choices in a two-player game, 9 with three players, 7 with four, 6 with five and only 5 with six. The greater the number of players, therefore, the less you will try for five-letter words scoring 10, and the more for overlapping short words.

By the time you have entered about five or six letters, you will be thinking not only about the position of new letters in relation to the beginning and end of lines, but also about their combination into useful bigrams with letters already in position. For example, good opening bigrams are BL, BR, CH, CL, CR, FL, FR, GL, GR, PL, PR, SC, SH, SL, SP, ST, TH, WH, while good enders include CH, CAT, FT, GHQ, RT, SH, ST, TH.

With about half the grid filled you may already have formed one five-letter word, and have four letters in position for conversion into a fiver on your final free turn. It can be helpful, especially with a large number of players, to keep one line available as a rubbish dump for letters that will not combine well with the skeletal words you already have. But don't overdo it. Filling it up early suggests you are not making the most of your opportunities.

Stronger players can take great advantage of weaker ones by planning word patterns involving tricky letters like K and V. They then call these letters themselves and wait for weaker or more nervous players to come up with the E's and S's necessary to dig themselves out of a hole. This is the point at which gamesmanship begins to overtake wordmanship. An alert and sensitive player can often divine which word one or more opponents are trying to make, and either cash in on it as well or else throw in a monkey-wrench in the shape of a J, Q, X or Z to make it impossible.

Since everyone needs vowels, everyone tends to leave it to everyone else to call them. You'd be surprised how long it can take someone to break down and call the first E or A. Sometimes neither of these invaluable letters gets called at all. This increases the urgency to make your consonants combine well. As a matter of principle it is usually wise to call the most obscure letters of all those that will actually enable you to form a word in your own grid, even if only one of three letters.

If you play the overlapping word version, don't be mesmerised by the score of 10 for a five-letter word. It isn't worth getting your statutory two fivers (in the three- or four-player game) if your other 16 squares are full of junk. Remember that three three-letter words count only one less than one five.

SINKO
Two players
Adults and older children
Short and sweet

This brief but outstandingly brilliant game was first described by Dave Silverman in the American magazine *Word Ways*.

Draw a grid of 5 × 5 squares. Each plays in turn, and the winner is the last player to write in a valid five-letter word. The first player enters any five-letter word into any one of the five rows or columns. The second does likewise, entering a word into any other row or column. It may cross the first word by means of a shared letter, or run parallel to it. Play continues in this way, with each player entering a five-letter word in any row or column. Wherever words cross one another they must, of course, incorporate a letter already in position from a previous entry. It is not necessary, however – and it can be dangerous – to ensure that adjacent letters are combinable.

Whoever enters the last word wins. This may be because the grid is full up, or because the other player cannot enter a word that can be made from the letter combinations already in place in any row or column, or simply because, foreseeing defeat, the other resigns. Here's an illustrative game from actual play.

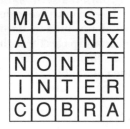

The order of play was COBRA, EXTRA, MANIC, INTER, SNEER, NONET, MANSE. There being seven words in place, the winner was the player who went first. The second was unable to find a word fitting any of the patterns A--NX, A-ONO, or N-NTR.

Optional scoring. For *Sinko*, I suggest a score of one point for each letter written in the grid in excess of 10. (It is easy to show that 10 is the smallest number of letters a grid must take before play becomes impossible – just write JUJUS along the bottom row and AFFIX immediately above it.) Scoring actually increases the skill of the game by allowing a player with good foresight to resign before the winner's score gets too high. In the above game, for example, the winner scored 13, but would have scored only 9 had the second player resigned instead of entering the losing word NONET.

Comments. Any game consisting of a small number of moves, but whose opening moves entail millions of possibilities, lends itself to fascinating analyses and post mortems. *Sinko* is no exception. For example, if, in the above game, we can safely declare NONET to be a losing move, because it allows the winning entry MANSE in the top row, we can ask whether the second player should have resigned, or whether there might have been a winning alternative. Indeed there is. Since NONET is the only word that will fit the middle row, and since nothing ends in -TB (middle column) or -NX (second row), the game can be saved by entering something like PIANO or GUANO in the second column, thereby also rendering the first and third rows impossible. The second player would then have won for 12 points.

But if either of these will win for the second player, it must follow that the first player's previous entry, SNEER, was itself a mistake. Was there a better entry at that point in the game? I believe there was. In fact, I have backtracked through this game far enough to convince myself that, after the opening COBRA on the first turn and EXTRA on the second, the first player ineluctably lost by adding MANIC as the third word! But, of course, it's always easier to identify losing moves and winning alternatives with the benefit of hindsight than it is to calculate them in advance.

You will observe that the first player has a very slight theoretical advantage, in that, if each succeeding word is written in parallel with the first, the first player will enter the fifth and last word. The second player should therefore hesitate to write a word in parallel with the first, as the first will almost certainly find a third word that will kill off all the columns. A second word in parallel with the first is only good if it produces promising two-letter combinations in all five columns.

The critical position always occurs when entering a new word in one direction kills off all possibilities in the other. You should avoid making the killer word unless you can calculate a certain win from it.

CALL YOUR OWN BLUFF

Fictionary dictionary is the best name I know for a game that became popular on British TV under the title *Call my Bluff*. It's the one where a chairman or word-setter announces an obscure word and the players have to decide which of several possible definitions is the true one and which invented by the other players. Since then it has become the stock in trade of word puzzle pages throughout the printed world. Several variations may be played upon this theme, as demonstrated by the other games that follow. Most can be played off the cuff, but one or two require advance preparation, and nearly all work best if you come prepared.

FICTIONARY DICTIONARY
Four to six players
Adults and older children
Requires a substantial dictionary or book of obscure words

jargoon *means ...*

1. a brilliant colourless or pale zircon
2. a military flag or standard
3. a small bay, usually icebound
4. deliberately adopted speech mannerism like that of Eccles, Bluebottle *et al*

outsucken *means ...*

1. a body washed up on the shore
2. a tenant's freedom from thirlage to a mill
3. lost from view in the distance
4. to extract venom from a snake-bite

romboyled *means ...*

1. discovered to be secretly Irish
2. heated up in a cauldron
3. punished by being drawn up and over the rigging (less harsh than *keelhauled*)
4. sought after with a warrant

(Answers on page 96.)

A good source of words for *Fictionary dictionary* is Chambers *Dictionary Game Dictionary,* by James Cochrane, as it is specifically designed for this game.

Each player in turn becomes the word-setter. A round is complete when everyone has had their turn, and a game consists of any number of rounds.

The word-setter takes the dictionary, finds an obscure word, or a word with a bizarre alternative meaning, announces it clearly and spells it if necessary.

He then writes on a slip of paper its true definition, or whichever he prefers of several possible definitions – shortening if need be, but not rewording. At the same time, everyone else contrives a fictitious but plausible definition and writes it on his or her own slip. The word-setter takes these slips as they are completed. When all are ready, he arranges the true and fictitious definitions in alphabetical order of their first words and then reads them out one by one.

Now the voting begins. Each in turn, starting with the player to the word-setter's left, votes for one of the definitions as being authentic. The word-setter does not vote, of course, but when everyone has finished he reveals the true definition.

My recommended scoring is as follows, and it applies to all other games of the family too.

Each player scores one point for having spotted the true definition, and one for each opponent whom he fooled into nominating his own. The word-setter scores nothing, except in the event that no-one gets the true definition, in which case he scores one per voter.

The turn to be word-setter then passes to the left.

Comments. It can save browsing time to arrange in advance that players will come equipped with the words they intend to spring on the rest of the company. To this idea you might object that the danger then exists of one or more players' genuinely knowing the definition of someone else's word. However, this can be overcome in the same way as the unprepared game – that is, by requiring anyone who does know the real meaning to own up in advance so that the word-setter can choose another. Preplanning helps here, since all you need to overcome this problem is to come with more words than you need for the game. There's plenty more in the dictionary.

Various optional rules can be applied by agreement. For example, some players don't insist that the word-setter write the definition 'as is' but allow him to rewrite it in his own words. The only difference this makes is that the other players must now guess the true definition by recognizing the style of the word-setter rather than the style of the dictionary.

In case it doesn't go without saying, you are allowed to vote for your own definition. This ploy is pure bluff and is only worth trying when you are the first to call, or perhaps the second in a large group. The idea, of course, is that you may thereby persuade others to vote for your definition. It takes a lot of nerve to play it this way.

Strategy. *Fictionary dictionary* is an ideal game for word-lovers who revel in etymology – who just love grubbing around in the roots of words to see how they all connect. Given such players, there's no point in looking at a word of such obvious Germanic roots as *thrutch* and then trying to persuade anyone that it means a Polynesian sea-going vessel. Or again, since a *xylometer* obviously has something to do with wood and with measuring, you won't get far by defining it as an Eskimo nose-flute. A common habit to avoid is that of assuming every word to be a noun. Don't forget to include a fair proportion of verbs and adjectives in your definitions.

Another careless habit is to base definitions on your own well-known field of expertise or obsessive interest. If you're a keen gardener, keep off the lawn, or your topic will grass on you. Conversely, if you know your opponents well enough, you can often guess who will have gone for a definition relating to photography or field sports or whatever. Suppose the word is *birefringent* and the most remarkable definition is 'doubly refracting, like Iceland spar'. Who's bluffing whom? Has the word-setter given the game away by choosing a definition nobody else is technical enough to have thought of? Or has somebody else had the cheek to run a technological bluff? Actually, that *is* the true definition. But then, suppose it had been 'inversely refracting, like pentine crystal'. That would have been me, running a bluff with a bit of pure invention.

The word-setter can have as much bluffing fun as anyone. Your main aim in this position is to choose a word whose true definition baffles credibility. One way of doing this is to choose a definition that sounds as though it were written in the style of another player. Another is to choose a definition that sounds too obvious to be true. Take *proleg,* for example. An alert and imaginative player might try to palm this off as 'a pre-Bolshevik term for a member of the lowest class of serfdom', or, possibly, 'a false premiss assumed for the sake of logical argument'. I'm sure I should have voted for either of these in preference to the true definition, namely 'an insect larva's abdominal leg, distinguished from a thoracic or "true" leg'. Frankly, it sounds too bad to be true, and suspect it to have been a joke perpetrated by the compilers of *Chambers*.

FABULARY VOCABULARY
Four to six players
Adults and older children
Requires fictitious words invented in advance

Fictionary dictionary doesn't have to be played with real words. If you start with purely imaginary words in the first instance then you have an imaginative variation that can hardly be called other than *Fabulary vocabulary*.

As before, the word-setter announces a word and everyone (including the setter) writes a definition for it on a slip of paper. When all have been passed to the setter, he reads them out and everyone votes for their preferred definition, which in this case may not be their own. The difference here is that votes must be made simultaneously and without collusion, which is best done by writing them down and then revealing them when all are ready.

In this version everyone scores on the same basis, including the word-setter. You get one point for each player who voted for your definition. You may prefer to scale the scores up in order to make them more interesting. A good way of doing this is to score one for attracting one vote, 3 (1 + 2) for two votes, 6 (1 + 2 + 3) for three, 10 (1 + 2 + 3 + 4) for four, and so on.

I invented this variation in order to exploit a word-inventing computer program of my own devising. Here are 26 of them – one for each week of the first (or second) half of the year – together with my suggested definitions.

antipavello	*a tessellation of clay tiles in herringbone pattern*
binoctode	*a poem recited twice nightly (or, erroneously, once every two nights)*
coges	*a bout of hard thinking ('Don't upset him – he's got the coges')*
dogeer	*a Venetian sycophant*
elylamper	*pejorative term for a Cardiff nightwatchman*
focery	*an unsavoury Irish practice*
gantiform	*glove-shaped*
hodero	*a Mexican bricklayer*
isagron	*a soap substitute derived from seals' intestines*
juminoce	*smelling sweet and sickly, like hyacinths past their prime*
kaipe	*a Greek delicacy of sardines cooked in sponge cake*
landop	*where you might, if you're not careful*
miserafin	*a cheap and dangerous substitute for paraffin*
nowit	*in Yorkshire, an idiot ('not wit'); in Lancashire, a know-all ('know it')*
ovase	*almost egg-shaped, but not quite*
pethod	*a group of five, especially sheep (Cumbrian)*
quisato	*one who does not know where he is going (usu. operatic hero)*
ravimen	*a diet of pasta and mineral water*
sinsuan	*having feet shaped like those of a monkey*
transamontist	*member of a Basque splinter group opposed to everything on principle*
untutic	*describing behaviour unworthy of a scholar and a gentleman*
vollex	*emotion leading to untutic behaviour*
wilyn	*wily, but poor at spelling*

xonk	*conglomerate of matted hair etc. removed from waste trap of bathroom sink*
yeldon	*nodley (backslang)*
zimon	*a West Country pieman (as in Zimple Ziman)*

ENCYCLOPEDIA FICTANNICA
Four to six players
Adults and older children
Requires advance preparation with a concise encyclopedia

The most mind-boggling variant of *Fictionary dictionary* is undoubtedly that in which the dictionary is replaced by an encyclopedia, or at least the General Information section of what Messrs Pears have been calling a *Cyclopedia* since 1897. Just imagine – you have a whole ten minutes in which to think up and write down a plausible explanation of *the Tarpeian Rock, the Plug Riots, the Marprelate Tracts*, or even something you *have* (vaguely) heard of, like the Northern Lights, or the Black Hole of Calcutta!

The rules of play are the same as for *Fictionary dictionary*, with the obvious additional requirement that players need to come well prepared with entries culled from their own favourite encyclopedic sources. Some idea of the ingenuity it calls forth may be had from the following example, which came up the first time we played it. The entry heading requiring explanation was French, namely *levant et couchant*, and the interesting thing about the four definitions given below is that each one attracted just one vote. So which is the genuine odd one out? (Answer at the end of this section, page 96.)

1. French equivalent of 'bed and breakfast'. Now obsolete in the literal sense since employed by Parisian anarchists of the 1860s to describe those of their number who had been seized and held without trial, and hence become a general term for imprisonment in such circumstances.

2. Picturesque term coined in the Napoleonic French Republic to denote the Mediterranean Sea, presumably inspired by the sight of the sun *levant* at its eastern and *couchant* at its western extremity.

3. The right to distrain cattle, which, having strayed on to one's land, have remained there long enough to have *risen* to graze and *settled* to rest at least once – in effect, for one whole day.

4. A type of comedic 'double-act' once popular in French music halls. It was characterized by knockabout routines (typically one comedian falling down while the other was rising to his feet), and often led to free-for-all *apache* dancing.

WHOSE WHO'S WHO?
Four to six players
Adults and older children
Requires some sort of 'Who's Who?'

If you haven't got access to the *Dictionary of National Biography,* or the original *Who's Who*, you can make do with the Prominent People section of good old *Pears Cyclopedia* to play this logical derivative of *Fictionary dictionary*. The word-setter now becomes the name-dropper, and each player's aim is to compose a convincing potted autobiography of the prominent person notified by the name-dropper. As before, everyone scores a point for spotting the correct life history and a point for each vote attracted by their own composition. What makes this version more amusing is the fact that the names dropped may well be those of figures of whom everyone has heard. This tends to make the entries very similar and so increases the difficulty of identifying the true one. Players should agree beforehand whether or not the character's years of birth and death should be cited by the name-dropper.

Which of the following entries correctly describes Rosa Bonheur? (Answer at the end of this section, page 96.)

1. (1822–99) A native of Bordeaux, and one of the most noted animal painters of the nineteenth century.
2. (1840–99) A follower of Florence Nightingale, whose nursing service she adopted and modified during the Franco-Prussian War. The award bearing her name was last presented in 1958.
3. (1884–1914) Belgian soprano associated with a revival of interest in French folk songs. Died in mysterious circumstances following rumours of a liaison with the composer Claude Debussy.
4. (1903–) Viennese film actress famed for historical roles but who failed to make a successful transition to talking pictures.

WHERE THE HECK?
Four to six players
Adults and older children
Requires an atlas or world gazetteer

This game invites you to invent exotic locations and identify real ones. I use an ancient volume entitled *The Penguin Encyclopedia of Places* by W. G. Moore, which I think is no longer in print. But you'll probably find a suitable gazetteer for the purpose.

As you can imagine, everyone has to concoct an authentic-sounding encyclopedic description of a place, and then identify the correct one when all are read out. For example, which of the following correctly identifies Jubaland? (For answer see page 96.)

1. A barren, mountainous peninsula forming part of the British Antarctic Territory, but with sovereignty claimed also by Chile and Argentina.
2. Former province of Kenya incorporated in Italian Somaliland in 1926. Main occupation cattle and camel rearing.
3. Name originally applied to the South Island of New Zealand by its discoverer, Tasman, in 1642.
4. An area of Germany bordering on the Sudetenland. Its distinctive Slavic culture and dialect, moribund in Bismarck's day, was subsequently wiped out and its people dispersed.

CAPTIONS COURAGEOUS
Four to six players
Adults and older children
Requires advance preparation.

The title will be recognized as a pun on Kipling's novel *Captains Courageous,* which became a much admired film of the 1930s. It was perpetrated in the 1950s by Bob Reisner for a series of books consisting of reproductions of famous paintings to which he had attached outrageous captions. For example, Hilliard's portrait miniature of an unknown Elizabethan romantic leaning against a tree in springtime is headed 'I refuse to read my sonnets to jazz', while Millet's *The Gleaners* gives rise to 'On your marks – get set – GO!.' Rubens's *Judgement of Paris* (though anyone else's would have done just as well) yields 'I have the right to cancel my membership after making six club choices'; and I have never been able to see any of these pictures since without mentally attaching Reisner's amazingly apt enhancements to them.

To turn this into a domestic game of the Fictionary family does not require the assistance of books of art reproductions. All you need do is come prepared in the following way. From newspapers and magazines cut out any captioned pictures that either are amusing in themselves or have amusing or incongruous captions attached to them. Separate caption from picture, paste each picture on to a standard sheet of paper, such as A4, and number it for identification. Paste all the captions together on another sheet, and number them in correct relation to their pictures.

Each player in turn presents a picture and declares the name of the periodical it is taken from. He then writes the true caption on a slip of paper while everyone else composes a suitable caption of their own, so far as possible in a style appropriate to the stated source. The slips are then passed to the setter, who reads them out, calls for votes on the correct one, and records the scores. Follow either the basic scoring of *Fictionary dictionary* or the expanded scoring of *Fabulary vocabulary* (see pages 90–92).

Captions courageous gives perhaps greater rein to the imagination than any other game of this family. As with the others, much of the skill lies in adopting a style of writing suited to the source. Provided you don't look too closely at the quality of the paper, the same picture could have come from *Time* magazine, *The Times* newspaper, or *Radio Times*, or equally well from a satirical magazine like *Private Eye* or a fish-and-chip tabloid like the *Sun*. Then again, what exactly does the picture show? Why was it selected for inclusion? If it's a couple, is either one of them the true subject and the other the stooge? If both, are they divorcing, or announcing their engagement? Or were they both involved in an armed robbery? If so, from which end of the gun?

Best of all is the opportunity afforded for deviously choosing obviously mistaken captions. In one of our games, for instance, the picture was purportedly that of a well-camouflaged butterfly in suitable surroundings. The true caption was 'The butterfly is the patch of lighter orange near the bottom left corner.' This gave everyone much food for thought, chiefly because the picture was printed in glorious black and white. Which was more likely – that the original caption-writer had made a mistake or been double-crossed at production stage, or that one of the players was either absent-minded or colour-blind, or that someone was running an ingenious bluff?

A similar bluff was perpetrated when one of our players produced a still from the Marx Brothers' film *A Day at the Races*, which was due to be shown on BBC television. One of the captions on offer gave the date of the film as 1938. In fact, the true date was 1937, and everyone thought everyone else knew it. Had one player made a mistake? Could such an error appear in so august a publication as *Radio Times*? Or was somebody trying to make us think it most likely that the second explanation was the true one? A pretty problem! The mistake finally proved to be that of the august journal.

SUSPENDED SENTENCES
Four to six players
Adults and incredibly old children
Requires slips of paper and source books

This Fictionary variant of my invention was first published in *Games & Puzzles* magazine (original series) and later given its better title by Ross Eckler in the same publication. It's much harder than the others and certainly not as easy at it looks. On the other hand, it's a natural extension of the foregoing word games and far too good an idea to pass up without a struggle. So, here goes …

One player, whom I shall dub the Bookie, selects a single sentence from any book he may have to hand, from *Moll Flanders* to *Lolita*, and announces the initial letters of the words that compose it. You won't be surprised to learn that everyone else then composes a sentence starting with the same initial letters, hands them in, listens to them all including the true one, and votes and scores accordingly.

A built-in problem of this game is that few sentences in works of literature contain as few as ten words, which is about the maximum length acceptable for a playable game. For this reason, you are allowed to extract from a very long sentence any shorter one that can reasonably stand alone. Take, for instance, this passage from Dickens's *Our Mutual Friend*:

> *The Secretary thought, as he glanced at the schoolmaster's face, that he had opened a channel here indeed, and that it was an unexpectedly dark and deep and stormy one, and difficult to sound.*

From this it would be legitimate to extract H.G.A.T.S.F. from 'He glanced at the schoolmaster's face', or H.H.O.A.C.H.I. from 'He had opened a channel here indeed', or perhaps I.W.A.U.D.A.D.A.S.O. from 'It was an unexpectedly dark and deep and stormy one'.

The only generally useful tip I can pass on for the production of sentences is to start at the end and work backwards. Obviously, you will also latch on to words beginning with T to produce such useful particles as THE, THIS, THAT, THEY, THESE, THOSE, and so on.

To give you a flavour of the game in practice, here's a short sentence from a P. D. James novel *(Unnatural Causes,* chapter 6): O.D.T.E.T.O.M. Which of the following sentences genuinely produced it? (Answer below.)

> **1.** Our doctors think everything turns on medicine.
> **2.** Olive declined to entertain tiresome old men.
> **3.** One doesn't tell everything to one's maid.
> **4.** One day they even talked of marriage.
> **5.** Only dilettantes take exception to old masters.

Ross Eckler proposed a variation on *Suspended sentences*, in which you are given the lengths of the words comprising it rather than their initial letters. So, for example, the sentences presented above as H.G.A.T.S.F. would be presented as 2.7.2.3.13.3. I haven't played this, but it looks even harder than the original.

3. BOXED WORD GAMES

Boxed word games involving lettered dice, cards or tiles come and go with bewildering rapidity. While some are duds and deservedly fail to attract a following, many other excellent games also disappear within a year or two. Those deserving of a better fate include Ad-Lib, On-Words, Lexicon, Kan-U-Go, My Word, Blockwords, and an outstandingly original crossword game called Montage, in which the players built a crossword using coloured tiles that had no letters marked on them at all! In this section I describe some half a dozen games that either are already classics or could well become so. All are available at time of writing, Lexicon having been relaunched (1995) after an absence of several years. Many other currently boxed games are omitted here on one of two grounds. Some are merely boxed versions of well-known traditional games in which pencil and paper have been replaced by a modicum of equipment, but nothing of any noteworthy originality has been added to the basic idea, while others are not so much word games as general knowledge or quiz games of the 'trivia' family.

SCRABBLE
The classic word game
Developed by Alfred Butts and James Brunot, published in UK by J. W. Spear &
Sons plc
For 2–4 players aged ten to adult

Scrabble is the Chess of word games – a fact attested to by its status as a game played at national tournament level in the UK, US and Australia, and by the number of books, magazine articles and puzzles devoted to it or based upon it. How it reached this position is a fascinating story, which we'll come to in a minute.

Scrabble works best for two, though up to four can play. Each starts with seven letter-tiles drawn at random from a bag of 100 tiles. Of these, 98 are marked with a letter and a point-value, as shown in the upper row of the table, and two are blanks. A blank has no point-value but can be used to represent any desired letter. The lower row shows the quantity of each letter in the set.

1	1	1	1	1	1	1	1	1	1	2	2	3	3	4	4	3	3	4	4	4	8	5	10	8	10
E	A	I	O	N	R	T	L	S	U	D	G	B	C	F	H	M	P	V	W	Y	J	K	Q	X	Z
9	8	8	8	6	6	6	4	4	4	4	3	2	2	2	2	2	2	2	2	2	1	1	1	1	1

Each player in turn places one or more tiles on the board and draws a like number from the bag so long as there are some left. The board on which they are played consists of $15 \times 15 = 125$ squares, and the letter tiles must be so played as to create or extend a word reading horizontally from left to right or vertically downwards. All words must be properly interlocking; that is, any two adjacent tiles must form part of a valid word. The first word must cover the central square. All letters placed in a single turn must be placed in alignment with one another, but any and all new words thereby created in either direction count to the player's credit.

The basic value of a word is the total point-value of its constituent letters, with a letter which forms part of a word in two directions counting once in each direction. The clever feature of the game, and that from which most of its positional strategy derives, is that certain squares, designated premium squares, increase the value of a word in any of four ways. The premium squares, coloured light and dark blue respectively, double and triple the value of any individual letter placed on them. Those coloured light and dark red respectively double and triple the value of the whole word placed across them, after first taking into account the enhanced value of any premium letter square that may be simultaneously involved. These bonuses only apply on the turn upon which the appropriate square is actually covered.

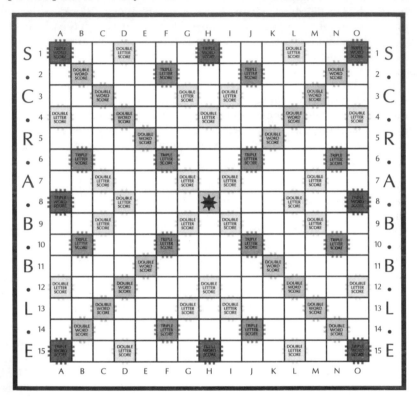

Given that the opening word must cover the central square, it is evident that the arrangement is designed to favour the gradual expansion of words in all directions outwards, with the more valuable squares tending to lie at the extremities.

From this it will be apparent what skills the game demands. First, there is the size of your vocabulary, and the ability to visualize the construction of words from tiles on your own rack. Later in the game it is important to recognize ways of expanding words already on the board, and particularly in finding ways of linking letters separated from one another by one or more blank squares – that is, the sort of skill involved in playing *Ghost* (see page 14). Anagramming is an important ability, because there may be several potential words in your own rack and you will want to select one which most favourably covers a premium square. Manoeuvring your way towards premium squares, while simultaneously trying to deny them to your opponent, adds a positional element to the range of skills involved. It is this degree of player interaction that places Scrabble firmly in the league of deep strategic games.

All of which is a far cry from the simple and unpublished game of Lexico invented by an out-of-work Connecticut architect in the Depression year of 1931. A study of the games market led Alfred Butts to pick on words as the basis of a new development.

Lexico itself was not unlike its near-namesake Lexicon, in that the equipment consisted simply of tiles with letters, but no board. Following a procedure akin to Rummy, a fad card game of the time, the winner was the first player to successfully complete a seven-letter word and lay it face up on the table. To add a little variety, Butts later accorded point-values to the letters, and when one player went out the others could subsequently score for making words of four or more letters. He offered it in this form to several manufacturers, but without success.

Naturally, the architect Butts went back to the drawing board, and duly came up with the idea of adding a board to the equipment and placing tiles on it in crossword fashion. Crosswords (see page 127) were another relatively recent fad. Now renamed 'It', the game was offered again to the manufacturers, and again turned down. 'Too intellectual', they said, as games manufacturers are wont to do, following the business theorem that 'No one ever lost money by underestimating the intelligence of the public'. The new title can't have helped much either. 'It' had been a synonym for sex, as coined by romantic writer Elinor Glyn in the previous decade and applied to silent-film star Clara Bow. The game was evidently not as sexy as it sounded, which is perhaps ironic, in view of the later tendency to call upon 'playing Scrabble' as a phrase equivalent in euphemistic significance to *Private Eye*'s 'discussing Uganda'.

In 1939 Butts was introduced by a mutual friend to James Brunot, who had been looking for a suitable business to develop away from the city lights and rat-race. Brunot liked the look of the game, now called Criss-Crosswords, and started experimenting with it himself. War intervened to hold this up, and by 1942 Butts and his wife were making up sets and marketing them through one Chester Ives, a bookshop owner in Danbury, Connecticut, who undertook the manufacture of the boards. This came to nothing, and for a while it seemed as if Butts's brainchild would remain the Peter Pan of the games world.

Re-enter James Brunot, returning in 1947 from Washington, where he had been the wartime executive director of the President's War Relief and Control Board. Brunot had made one or two changes to the game, including the rule about starting across the middle instead of up in the top left corner, and, perhaps more inspirationally, changing the name of the game to Scrabble. No particular significance attached to the word: it just happened to be one of several nice-sounding possibilities that research showed had not already been registered as a trade name. (But would the game have been so successful had it been published, as it nearly was, under the title Logo-Loco?) Under a new arrangement between the two, Brunot would manufacture and market the newly named game through his business facility, the Production and Marketing Company.

In the three years from 1949 to 1951 the annual sales of Scrabble remained at the disappointingly low level of less than 10,000 per annum. In 1952, however, a certain Jack Strauss played it while on holiday. Having greatly enjoyed it, he was surprised on returning to work to learn that Scrabble was not to be found among the stock of New York City's famous department store, Macy's. It was fortunate for everyone concerned that Strauss just happened to be the Chairman of the Board of Macy's. Once there, everybody who was anybody started buying it. The game caught on and became a national craze. Within two years, Brunot's company had sold between four and five *million* sets!

Shortly after, Brunot sold to Selchow and Righter (who had long ago rejected Criss-Cross Words) the rights to the manufacture of the standard set, retaining for himself those for non-standard and speciality editions. He kept these until 1971, eventually selling out his entire interest to Selchow and Righter. Scrabble was introduced to Australia in 1953, being published there by T. R. Urban, and in 1954 to the UK through J. W. Spear and Son, who continue to market and promote the game.

Already established as a classic home favourite, it was in 1971 that Scrabble achieved the status of national tournament play through the enthusiasm of games fanatic Gyles Brandreth. Brandreth, who was then writing a book on British prisons, had been struck by the popularity of the game amongst the prisoners. Intrigued by its tournament possibilities, he placed an advertisement in *The Times* newspaper to see what sort of support such an idea might drum up. The response was overwhelming, and, with the ready cooperation of Spears Games, the British National Scrabble Championships have become an annual event attracting thousands of competitors.

Rainbow Scrabble. Spears produced a junior version of Scrabble in the 1970s. It involved a limited range of letter tiles bearing lower-case initials and lacking point-values. Very young players used one side of the board for completing a ready-printed pictorial crossword by placing letter tiles upon the matching letters of the crossword. Older children used the other side for a game following the same rules as adult Scrabble, but of course without premium squares because the letter tiles had no point-values. The pictorial crossword game fulfilled its function well, but something was clearly lacking from the game played on a board full of blank squares with (literally) pointless letter tiles. In 1987 Spears commissioned me to devise a more interesting version of the game intermediate between this and adult Scrabble, but still dispensing with tile points.

For this commission I developed a game called Rainbow Scrabble, which has since become the standard version intermediate between the junior and the adult forms. Clearly, what was needed was a more excitingly designed board and some other method of ascribing scores to words made on it. My solution was to colour the squares in seven different colours with values ranging from one to seven points for each colour. The value of any word made is that of the value of the colour in front of its first letter plus that of the colour following its last letter, thus dispensing with the need to lift tiles in order to record their values. To introduce players to the diagonally expanding premium squares of the main game, I followed a similar pattern of placing the lowest valued squares at the centre of the board, where play has to begin, and gradually increasing them towards the edges and corners where the highest values occur. Though I say so myself, Rainbow Scrabble is sufficiently interesting to be played by adults. Give it a try some time and see what you think.

BOGGLE
'The three-minute word game'
Invented by Alan Turoff, published by Hasbro UK Ltd
For 1–8 players (or more) aged eight to adult

Boggle is a well-presented embodiment of the simple game of making as many words as possible from a given word or phrase. First published in the USA in the early 1970s, it was introduced to the UK market by Parker Palitoy in 1976 and rapidly established itself as a favourite of British word-gamers too. It has the great advantage of being playable by any number, and the range has recently been complemented by the addition of a Junior and an Advanced version.

The standard game consists of 16 dice with a letter of the alphabet imprinted on each of their collective 96 sides, and a tray with 16 compartments into which the dice can tumble at random in such a way as to reveal only their topmost letters. A three-minute sand-timer and a transparent dice-shaker complete the equipment.

At each turn the dice are shaken up, allowed to fall, and jiggled about until they settle into their 16 spaces, producing a square of letters that might look something like this:

... except, of course, that they will rarely *all* read the right way up as depicted here.

The timer is turned and the players then have three minutes in which to write down as many words as they can make by mentally tracing a pathway through this maze of letters. Each word must be at least three letters long, and must be made by tracing a pathway from letter to letter, one at a time, horizontally, vertically or diagonally in a connected line. The same letter in the same space may not be used twice in the same word, nor the same word recorded twice though made in different ways. For example, in the illustration shown here you can make REED by starting on either of the two Rs, but only one of them counts. You may count as separate words a shorter contained in a longer, such as FEE and FEED, or even HEN and HENS in this example.

With time up, players stop writing and compare their lists. Any word appearing on more than one list scores nothing, so the real advantage accrues by finding words that nobody else has seen. Since, however, you dare not miss out the obvious ones for fear that someone else will score through being the only person to write them down, you still need to record everything you can see.

The best procedure for scoring is this. One player reads all the words on his or her list. If anyone calls 'Yes', indicating that they have that word too, then everyone who has that word crosses it off their list. This will eventually leave the first caller with a list of words of which some have been deleted. That player can then work out the score of the remaining words while the others continue with their own lists. If more than two are playing, the second player will then read out all the undeleted words remaining on his or her list, and the same procedure is followed. The only reason for requiring the last player to read out his or her list is to ensure that it contains acceptable words.

The scoring system, as presented in the rules, at first sight looks bizarre. You score 1 for each word of three or four letters, 2 for five, 3 for six, 5 for seven, and 11 for a word of eight letters or more. This may sound more reasonable if expressed as a score of 1 per word, with bonuses of 1, 2, 4 and 10 for words of 5, 6, 7 and 8 letters respectively. But in any case the higher scores are somewhat academic, as the dice rarely fall in such a way as to produce words of more than six letters.

Incidentally, there is no Q alone, but one side of one die is marked Qu. Presumably this counts as two letters, though the rules do not specifically mention it.

The turn-out displayed above is unusually fecund. I made 102 words (there may be more) for a highly theoretical score of 153 as follows (I did not limit myself to three minutes):

1 each for 31 three-letter words: *act, ash, con, cot, coy, dee, den, ens, eon, fee, foe, has, hen, her, hey, hoc, hot, nor, not, ore, red, roc, roe, rot, sac, sen, she, the, tor, try, yon.*

1 each for 37 four-letter words: *cash, chef, coed, core, deer, dees, dens, eery, feed, fees, fern, heed, hens, hoed, hoer, hoes, horn, need, neon, noes, reed, reef, rend, rocs, scot, seed, seen, seer, send, shed, shot, thee, then, tore, torn, tree, troy, yore.*

2 each for 24 five-letter words: *acorn, actor, ashen, cheer, chert, chore, cored, coyer, foyer, heedy, heron, north, notch, other, refer, score, sheen, sheer, shore, shorn, short, sneer, thorn, trees.*

3 each for nine six-letter words: *cashed, cheery, eothen, fender, render, scored, sender, shored, sneery.*

5 each for two seven-letter words: *notched, notches.*

(British players might reject *eon* as an American spelling, and *eothen* as absent from the SOED, though it appears in Chambers.)

In competitive play I expect to find an average of about 25 words, of which about half will be non-scoring duplicates, leaving the rest to yield a total of between 15 and 20 points. If you haven't already played this game, you won't be surprised to learn that the possibilities vary enormously. While this particular throw yielded more than a hundred words, a slightly earlier one had produced no more than five, there being only one vowel on display.

The play of Boggle is more of a procedure than a strategy. Given a fair sprinkling of vowels, one way of approaching it is to consider each letter in turn and use it as the initial of as many words as possible before passing to the next. Another is to pick on a promising cluster, such as EE or HOT in the above example, and milk it for all it is worth before passing on to another one. Usually, each group of words will produce one that leads on to another promising cluster. Given a severe shortage of vowels, you can often mentally black out areas of the grid that will certainly yield nothing, and concentrate only on those letters surrounding the vowels.

LEXICON
'The playing-cards word game'
Invented by David Whitelaw, formerly published by Waddingtons Games Ltd
Games for any number of players aged eight to adult

This classic word game with cards was patented in 1925, and so suited the tenor of the times as to have been played in Lexicon drives, like Whist drives, at tables of four. David Whitelaw is said to have invented it 'one morning', and to have made more money from it than from his fifty novels – including *The Lexicon Murders* (1945). I couldn't find it in the shops when I came to write this article, but am pleased to report that Waddingtons relaunched it before the first set of proofs came back from the printer. My own set is dated 1977, and I'm sure there must be many other ancient specimens knocking around in games-lovers' homes up and down the country.

The original Lexicon game is based on Rummy, a card craze of the early decades of the 20th century. A peculiarity of earlier forms of Rummy is that they were played and scored negatively – that is, you don't score a positive number for the cards you use but a negative number for the cards left in hand when one player has 'gone out'. For this reason, the letter values of Lexicon cards, unlike those of Scrabble tiles, are high for easy letters and low for hard ones. The distribution and values are as follows:

10	10	10	8	8	8	8	8	8	8	8	8	8	8	8	8	6	6	6	4	4	4	2	2	2	2
A	E	I	H	L	O	R	S	T	U	W	C	K	M	N	P	D	J	V	G	Q	Y	B	F	X	Z
4	4	4	3	3	3	3	3	3	3	3	1	1	1	1	1	1	1	1	1	1	1	1	1	1	1

A wild card or Joker, known as the Master-card, may be used to represent any letter and brings the pack total up to 52. The distribution and values are open to theoretical criticism, but in practice you tend not to notice the oddities.

A good feature of the Lexicon pack is that it is not merely a single game but a convenient set of equipment for playing a whole variety of word games.

The main game is played like basic Rummy. Each of two to four players receives ten cards. The rest are piled face down in one compartment of the playing tray to form a stockpile, and the top one turned face up into the other compartment to start a wastepile. The aim is to be the first to play out all your cards by laying them face up on the table in sequences forming words, or by adding them to other words already on the table. At each turn you may do one of the following:

1. Throw an unwanted card face up to the wastepile and draw, as a replacement, either the top card of the stock or the previous topmost waste card.

2. Make a word of two or more letters by taking the appropriate cards from your hand and laying them face up on the table before you.

3. Add one or more letters to another word, made by you or anyone else, to form a new word, but without disturbing the order of the existing letters. For example, to ROBE you could add P, L, M to make PROBLEM.

4. Steal one or more letters from an existing word and add them to your hand, provided that in the same turn you replace each of them with another letter that still produces a word without changing the order of the others. For example, you could take S, A, Y from DISPLAY and replace with, respectively, M, E, D to make DIMPLED.

Play ceases when one player goes out. The others record a negative score equivalent to the total value of the cards remaining in their hands. Further deals ensue. When players reach 100 minus points they drop out of play. The player who survives when everyone else has dropped out is the overall winner.

Also described in the accompanying leaflet are Lexicon versions of Clock Patience and a crossword game called Criss-Cross. The latter amounts in fact to the pencil-and-paper game *Wordsworth* (see page 86), the only difference being that letters are not called freely but from those turned from the shuffled pack.

More ingenious are some 25 additional games published by Waddingtons in a separate booklet, of which I have the second edition (1935, price one shilling). These include Lexicon versions of donkey, Newmarket, poker, cribbage, whist, and even bridge.

Lexicon appeals to me in my varied capacities as a fanatical card-player, word-gamer and games inventor. Even without the 1935 booklet it's not a hard matter to devise ways of playing with the cards that more or less duplicate the procedures of standard card games. So if you have a set hidden away somewhere, you may find it worthwhile re-exploring; and if you haven't, you can always get a new one now that it has made its comeback.

UPWORDS
'The 3D game of high-rise word-building'
Invented by Elliot Rudell, published by Hasbro UK Ltd
For 2–4 players aged nine to adult

The latest version of this crossword game for two to four players involves a board of 10 × 10 squares and 100 square letter-tiles. (The original had 8 × 8 squares and 64 tiles.) Each player takes seven tiles from the bag and a rack to put them on. Each player in turn places one or more tiles on the board in such a way as to make or extend one or more words reading either downwards or from left to right, then draws fresh tiles from the bag to make up seven again (or as many as may remain). All words must interlink. That is, any two or more adjacent letters on the board must form or belong to part of a valid word.

Sounds familiar?

Well, yes; and the superficial resemblance to Scrabble may make you wonder how anyone could have enough faith in such an idea to finish developing the game, let alone try to rival it on the open market. And yet – it works. Upwords is a different game, and I know players who prefer it to its well-established rival.

The original feature of Upwords, as implied by its title, is that you can build words not only from left to right and from top to bottom, but also in the third dimension from ground level *upwards*. In brief, you can change words by piling letter tiles on top of one another. For example, you can change NOVEL to HOVEL, or NAVEL, or NOMAD. Or you can build and extend it to make, for example, ENAMEL or INNOVATE – or even, with AIINNOT in you rack, INNOVATION, thereby gaining a bonus (albeit a miserly one) for using all seven tiles.

Another appealing feature of Upwords is that the letters do not have separate values, so the tiles are not cluttered up with distracting numbers. Instead, every word you make scores one point for each tile it contains. So, for example, a five-letter word with two tiles in each position scores ten, but if every letter tops a pile of five then it scores 25 points.

The other scoring elements are these:

1. A word consisting of single tiles only, none of them having yet been built on, scores double.

2. Each of five specially differentiated 'difficult' letters – J, V, Qu, X and Z – adds a bonus of two points to the nominal word score when first placed in position. The bonus does not apply on subsequent turns involving the same letter.

3. Using all seven of your tiles in one turn nets you a bonus of ten.

4. Unused letters at end of play count minus five each.

The other basic rules are:

1. The maximum permitted building height is five tiles.

2. You may not place a tile immediately on top of one bearing the same letter (A on A, B on B, and so on). But you may subsequently repeat a letter or a word that appeared at the next but one level down, or lower. For example, if the first player makes NOVEL and the second changes it to HAVEN, the original V and the E must remain showing at ground level. But the first can then change it back again to NOVEL; and so on.

3. On your turn to play, you may pass if you cannot or will not make a word. If you pass, you may (but need not) exchange one of your tiles for one in the bag if any remain. Presumably, though this is not stated, you should first turn one of your letters down, then draw a new one, then discard the one you turned down. You may think it mean to allow only one letter to be changed, but it is quite enough, as there are so many ways of getting a good score from even a single letter. In fact, I've never seen anyone exercise this option.

4. You may not use a turn merely to stick an S on the end of a word to make it plural (or, presumably, to make if a verb form, such as GIVE/GIVES). If you do add an S, you must play at least one other word-differentiating letter in the same turn. This rule has mysteriously disappeared from the new (10 × 10) version, but is still worth applying.

5. You may not completely obliterate a whole word by building on it – at least one letter must remain uncovered. This has also disappeared from the new version, but is equally worth reinstating.

Let's see how the scoring system works out in practice:

Suppose the first player kicks off with the five-letter word OLDEN, scoring ten points (five letters, doubled because all are at ground level). Let's also suppose that you also make a five-letter word on your first turn. Here are some different scoring possibilities.

1. You could use four letters to make a word crossing at the D, such as LADLE. For this you would score 10 for a five-letter word at ground level.

2. You could make a five-letter down-word such as CARRY with an R covering the N of OLDEN to make it OLDER. Now you score one for each letter of CARRY and one for each letter of the new word OLDER, totalling 10. Note that the R counts in each direction, but nothing is doubled as neither word lies completely at ground level.

3. You could make a five-letter down-word such as BAGEL with the G placed immediately in front of the existing O to turn it into GOLDEN. This gives you two words counting double because they are both at ground level, making 10 for BAGEL and 12 for GOLDEN, a total of 22.

4. Given the right letters, you could place the word PIANO horizontally beneath OLDEN, thereby scoring for your five-letter word and five two-letter down-words (UP, LI, DA, EN, NO, all of which are acceptable). Since all are at ground level, you score 10 for PIANO and 4 for each word of two letters, making a grand total of 30. The most you could make on this turn would be 44, which you would get for (say) PIANOLA, including the bonus of 10 for using all seven of your tiles.

This demonstrates that it is more profitable early in the game to make words at ground level that extend other words at the same level, so scoring for more than one word, and scoring them double for being at ground level. In fact, it is usually unprofitable to be the first to start building upwards. For example, for making the five-letter word BAGEL across the top of OLDEN (thereby observing the original rule requiring at least one letter to remain unchanged), you would score only 9 points. This would be doubly disadvantageous in the two-player game because of the effect of alternating play. For placing the first, third and fifth letters of a column on a particular square, you opponent will have scored 2 + 3 + 5 for it (the first one being doubled at ground level), totalling 10, as opposed to your paltry 2 + 4 = 6 for placing only the second and fourth.

So the general pattern of play becomes clear. Typically, players in the early stages will tend to cover the central area with multiply-interlocking words at ground level, thereby scoring for at least two words at a time, and scoring them double. The middle game begins when players cannot profitably extend the existing complex any further and are forced to start building at a low level. Once the relatively unprofitable two-level has been started, it becomes a scramble to see how many more points a word can be milked for by changing it with letters placed at successively higher levels up to five. Best of all is the situation in which two interlocking words are further improved by building on the square of intersection, thereby changing both at once and so scoring double.

The endgame starts when no more tiles remain in the bag. Now the object is to get rid of letters, often one at a time, in order to go out first, or not to have too many left over when someone else goes out. Now also is the time to get rid of your bonus letters (J, V, Qu, X, Z) if you haven't already done so. Fortunately, they don't count more than the standard five against you if ultimately left unplayed.

My experience of the game suggests that you should aim to use an average of two to three tiles per turn (more in the early stages, fewer later) for an average score of about 15 to 20, or about 7 per tile. On the whole, it's better to place a single letter for more than 10 points than three or more for less than 20. Making a lower than average score is a good strategy when you have a rack full of generally undesirable letters and feel the need to dump them in order to substantially change your rack scenery.

The new version of the game, enlarged to $10 \times 10 = 100$ squares, is something of an improvement on the smaller original. The 8×8 game tended to clog up rapidly, often leaving a large quarter of the board blank and unreachable. The larger game enables a good spread of ground-level words to be put into position, thus opening up many more opportunities for upward building (see diagram). However, one or two of the original rules have been revised, especially as regards the scoring, and I'm not convinced that all are for the better.

For example, the bonus of two points for first using a difficult letter is a needless frippery, especially as it is too niggardly to be worth counting in view of the expected average score of seven per letter. (In the original game it applied only to the Qu tile, which had a certain logic about it.) My suggestion is that you either abolish it altogether, or else make it worth having. A worthwhile score would be five in the early and middle game, ten if placed when no more tiles remain in the bag, and in either case doubled if it forms part of two words, one in each direction.

The bonus of 10 for using all seven tiles is even more niggardly, especially as it has been reduced from the original 20, which itself was hardly worth having. The fact is that it is more difficult to use all seven in Upwords than in Scrabble. In Scrabble, you can work towards it by getting rid of uncombinable letters and keeping your eye on an area of the board offering most opportunity for the slam. In Upwords, you tend to play fewer tiles at a time, so it is less easy to make a substantial change to your rack. In Scrabble, a word once placed remains unchanged, except by extension, whereas in Upwords any given area of the board may suddenly sprout a whole array of different words, making it impossible to plan ahead with any degree of confidence. To add to the difficulty, Upwords covers a smaller area, so that even when you do have a possible slam, you may not be able to use it because the letter you need to connect with is too near the edge and you therefore run out of space. Perhaps the bonus is kept low because, given a good initial rack, it is sometimes possible to make a slam on the first or second turn. If so, the answer is to vary the bonus according to the stage of the game at which it is made. I would suggest doubling the score made on any turn in which a player uses all seven letters. Alternatively, scrap it altogether as being not in keeping with the spirit of the game. After all, Upwords is all about changing words by building upwards. Making *long* words is beside the point.

Elliot Rudell, of Torrance, California, invented Upwords in 1982, using modified pieces of equipment from a game then published under the name Chinese Chess. The publisher Milton Bradley immediately expressed interest, but reported a tendency of players to keep building upwards to such an extent that the game became physically unstable and failed to develop properly in the basic two dimensions. Rudell countered this by the simple device of limiting stacks to five tiles and awarding double points to words entirely at ground level. In this form it took off with such success that, in true Californian tradition, the inventor now has UPWORDS as his personalized car number-plate. The game was less successful on the UK market and was withdrawn after a few years. However, 1995 saw its relaunch in the 10×10 form developed in house by Hasbro UK, which ought to give it a new lease of life.

Rudell reports an interesting history lineage note as follows:

'Alfred Butts invented Scrabble. Alan Turoff invented Boggle. I invented Upwords. Alfred Butts's nephew babysat Alan Turoff. My first job in the toy industry had me working in the office next to Caroline Poole, who subsequently married Alan Turoff.'

It's a small world, even in the USA.

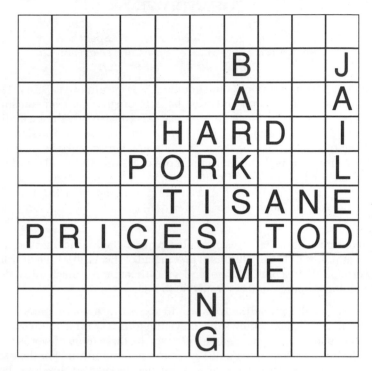

Upwords: This shows a typical foundation of words at double-scoring ground level before any building has been done. The last move was the addition of M to LI, making LIME and ATE for a score of 14. The next player started building by playing six letters to the vertical word HOTEL, scoring 11 for COMBATED, 5 for BARD, 5 for PARK, and 5 for DIME, totalling 26. (Heavily outlined squares indicate changed letters standing two high.)

COUNTDOWN

'All the fun of the popular and challenging TV game show'
An Armand Jammot game published by J. W. Spear & Sons plc
(Countdown is a Trade Mark of Yorkshire Television Ltd)
For 2–6 players aged ten to adult

Countdown, a quiz game with words and numbers, was introduced to British television screens by Yorkshire Television and was the first programme ever transmitted on Channel 4 when it opened in November 1982. It has consistently drawn audiences of between four and five million and enjoys a popularity that still shows no sign of abating. In it, contestants play against the clock and one another to make as long a word as possible from a row of nine letters selected more or less at random. To add variety to the format, there is a feature called Conundrum, in which contestants seek to perform the same feat on a previously determined anagram of a nine-letter word. There is also a number game working along similar lines which, as such, does not form part of our brief.

The equipment consists of 160 cards, a nicely textured playing mat marked with card-sized spaces appropriate to the patterns of play, a pad of sheets on which players record their answers and their scores, a 30-second sand-timer, and a mechanical device for generating all three-figure numbers from 000 to 999.

Countdown has all the properties you would expect of a board game based on a television game. A full game follows the television format of three rounds of the basic word game and one of the number game, followed by three more of words and one of numbers as before, and concludes with one round of Conundrum. For the basic word game, the 65-card pack of consonant cards is shuffled and placed face down beside the similarly shuffled 71-card pack of vowels. The oldest player calls either 'Consonant' or 'Vowel' until nine letters have been selected, and on each occasion the player on his or her left takes the top card of whichever pile is specified and places it face up in the nine-letter word space on the mat, working from left to right in order. Everyone then has 30 seconds in which to write down the longest word they can find using as many as possible of the letters displayed. You can't use any letter more often than it appears in the row.

With time up, each in turn reads out their word. Whoever makes the longest word records a score of one per letter, unless they use all nine, in which case the score is doubled to 18. If two or more players tie for the longest, they both score the appropriate amount. Players who fail to match the length of the longest word score zero for that round.

The same procedure is followed five more times (with the number game interpolated, if you like), resulting in six scores for the basic word game. The rules don't specify whether the job of selecting vowels and consonants remains with the oldest player, but it is obviously better to let this privilege rotate. Indeed, unless you want to reproduce the television version with complete fidelity, it is best to play as many rounds as there are players, so that everyone gets a fair crack of the whip.

The concluding game of Conundrum is played as follows. The number generator is set spinning until stopped by one of the players, a process that may be repeated as often as necessary to produce a number from 001 to 275. The number then showing is read off against a list of 275 nine-letter anagrams printed on the rule-sheet. The anagrams are nicely chosen to look like quasi-words – for example, No. 242 reads SEEDYDAWN. The selected anagram is reproduced by placing the appropriate letter cards on the mat, and everyone has 30 seconds again in which to find the word it makes. The first to discover the nine-letter word (in this case WEDNESDAY) scores ten points and the others nothing.

If a claimed answer is wrong, the round is annulled and another played without the participation of the defaulting claimant.

A problem we encountered may well be common to many TV-derived competitive games, namely, that whereas the TV games are played between contestants from different backgrounds who are unacquainted with one another, their home game equivalents are likely to be played by contestants who are well matched in skills and operate on the same mental and social wavelength. This would account for the fact that, when we play, the players almost invariably come up with words of the same length, if not actually the same words, thereby resulting in too many tied scores to make the game sufficiently competitive.

To counter this, you may want to skip the printed rules and scoring and introduce a more competitive mode of play. I suggest the following:

First, everyone scores the length of the word they make in every round (except Conundrum), with no bonus for using all nine. The player or players who make the longest words score that word length doubled – unless *all* the players' words are equal in length, in which case the doubling does not apply. Finally, if there is more than one word of the greatest length, a further doubling is applied to the word that comes earliest in alphabetical order.

For example, suppose the letters turned are EPOFTYMEL and four players come up with the words FLEET, TEMPLE, EMPLOY, PELMET. Because they are not all the same length, the five-letter word scores 5 but the six-letter words are doubled to 12 each. Of these, EMPLOY comes first in the dictionary, and is therefore redoubled to 24. Had the first player also found EMPLOY, all words would score a basic 6, and those who found EMPLOY would double this to 12.

Playing this way, the winner is the first to reach 100 points.

WORD FOR WORD
'The Game of the English Language'
A Paul Lamond game © 1993 by Creative Games Ltd
For 2–6 players aged 11 to adult

A relative newcomer, Word for Word is the word game member of the family of so-called 'trivia' games inaugurated in the 1980s by the extraordinarily successful Trivial Pursuit. The defining characteristic of trivia games is that the equipment consists largely of hundreds of cards containing questions and answers, to which correct responses enable players to make their competitive progress around the board.

Word for Word is thus essentially a race game. The board has a race track of 30 spaces arranged in a path round the perimeter of a hexagon, with one space marked as both Start and Finish. Each player takes a distinctively coloured counter and places it on Start, and the winner is the first to get back round to the same space again. Four packs of 100 cards each are shuffled and placed on appropriately labelled and coloured spaces inside the perimeter. These packs are headed Synonym, Definition, Rhyming, and Pot Luck.

Each player in turn rolls a die whose six sides are marked with coloured spots. The colour turned up specifies what sort of question must be answered for any advancement to be made – green for synonyms, orange for definitions, yellow for rhymes, red for Pot Luck. Blue gives the player a free choice of any of these, and purple results in the self-explanatory injunction to 'Miss a Go'.

The player's right-hand neighbour (play itself proceeds to the left) draws the top card of the appropriate pile and poses the question, with the following consequences.

● **Synonym**. Each player in turn, starting with the one who threw the die and excluding the card-holder, is asked to provide a synonym for the word stated on the card. Each synonym must be different, and only those printed on the card are acceptable. Success entitles that player to move forward one space. Presumably each player has one turn only, though the rules do not state this. A typical card sets the word PROJECT and offers 12 acceptable synonyms beginning *plan, proposal, venture, task, calculate*, and so on.

● **Rhyming.** The same procedure as above, except that players are asked to provide a rhyme for the word given, but only those on the card are acceptable. For example, the word OAK is followed by a list of 12 rhyming words – which do not, however, include all possibilities (*choke* but not *croak, yolk* but not *folk*, and so on).

● **Definition.** For the player who rolled the die this one has the advantage that no one else gets a chance to answer, and only he or she will be able to advance. A definition is given, and the player is required to give the conforming word. For example, given *careful, precise,* and *lacking in errors,* the player will advance one space for correctly responding with the only answer given on the card, which is ACCURATE.

● **Pot Luck** has the same advantage for the player who rolled the die. The questions here are more varied and interesting. They include synonyms, definitions, acronyms (e.g. *Give the full meaning of the acronym LASER*), rhyming slang (*Rabbit and pork = ?*), antonyms (*Give the opposite of DISAPPOINT*), collectives (*What is a group of bears known as?*), and other categories of the sort listed in the Playing with Words section (see page 111).

To add further variety to the game, the six corner squares are distinctively marked, and a player whose counter is on one of these has a different task to perform. For example, on the corner marked 'All Four' the player is asked the question on the top card of each of the four piles and so has an opportunity to move forward up to four spaces.

Word for Word is well designed and offers a pleasing range of variations on a theme. You may, however, want to relax some of the rules to make them less authoritarian and more dependent upon my rule of support by at least one opponent, especially as some of the answers given are not unflawed. For example, one card asks for the word that yields the definition *Giving voluntarily to those in need.* The answer given, supposed to be the only one acceptable, is CHARITY. Since, however, CHARITY is a noun and the definition a verb, many a player will similarly respond with a verb, such as DONATING. The fact that the definitions cited are reprinted (by permission) from the *Concise Oxford Dictionary* is no good reason for denying the validity of any other reasonable answer. Another grievance is the apparently arbitrary omission of some words from the list of acceptable rhymes. My rhyming dictionary gives more than 40 rhymes for OAK, whereas Word for Word offers only 12. There are also relatively minor lapses that do not in themselves detract from the playability of the game. For example, PVC is not an acronym but an initialism, as it fails to yield a pronounceable word.

Ultimately, like all games of 'trivia' lineage, Word for Word will play itself out as you get to know all the answers on the cards. On the way, however, you should get some fun and maybe learn something new.

4. PLAYING WITH WORDS

The big game hunter's alphabestiary of word-play

ABCese

A challenging task for minimalist word-gamers is that of writing more or less intelligible text consisting solely of the names of letters and numbers. For example, EFFIGY can be written as F E G, ENEMY as N M E, SEA ANEMONE as C N M N E, and Jupiter's bovine girlfriend Io as ... well, I O. (Unless Ogden Nash was right, and he really did call her 'Ten'.) IOU is an example of ABCese that has made it into the dictionary.

The traditional literature of ABCese features characters named LC, KT and LNR, but undoubtedly the best known, for reasons of alphabetical order, is Abie. Without him the following remarkable example of ABCese could not exist:

AB C D FEG

His finest role is probably that of the café proprietor in this somewhat less than Shakespearean dramatic interlude:

AB, F U N E X?
S, V F X.
F U NE M?
S, V F M 2.
OK, L F M N X.

To compose in ABCese, you can start by writing out the alphabet and the basic numerals, then apply your aptitude for phonetics and puns to the task of constructing a basic lexicon. Remember that Z can be pronounced *zed* or *zee*, depending on which side of the Atlantic you inhabit. So, after the speech of a male character, it is EZ (American) to write EZ (British). When you tire of the limited vocabulary of single letters, you can progress to disyllables by writing out all 676 combinations of two letters and seeing what you can make of them. And so on ...

This (slightly modified) prizewinning sample of ABCese, by Rosemary Walker, is from a competition set in an issue of the now defunct *Logophile* magazine. The scene takes place in the surgery of Doctor Essex, who is consulted about abnormal weight gain by a circus fat lady called Katie:

'O DR, KT,' Z SX, A G.P. 'I C Y U R CD: U R WR IDL MNCT. I F N FEKCS QR 4 OBCT. UL B AL N RT. O.K? IL B CN U!'

See also *Rebus* (page 166).

ACRONYM
(Greek, 'extremity-name')

An acronym is a word formed from the initial letters or syllables of a string of words. A pure acronym consists of initials only. For example:

BASIC   **B**eginners **A**ll-purpose **S**ymbolic **I**nstruction **C**ode

One consisting of initials and whole or part syllables may be called a compound acronym. For example:

CAMRA   **CAM**paign for **R**eal **A**le

One consisting entirely of syllables, in whole or part, is, strictly, a *portmanteau* word. For example:

OXFAM   **OX**ford Committee for **FAM**ine Relief

Not every set of initials is an acronym. It is merely an *initialism* if it either cannot be pronounced as a word in itself, such as:

BBC   British Broadcasting Corporation
GBH   Grievous Bodily Harm
NBG   No Bloody Good
PTO   Please Turn Over
RSVP   Répondez S'il Vous Plaît

or if it can be so pronounced but, for one reason or another, isn't:

AKA   Also Known As
ONO   Or Near(est) Offer
POW   Prisoner Of War
VIP   Very Important Person

Uncertain cases include RAF (Royal Air Force) and UFO (Unidentified Flying Object), which occur as one or the other according to personal preference.

Acronyms vary in the degree to which they do or do not coincide with real words. There are several gradations:

Non-words

AWOL   Absent WithOut Leave
BOLTOP   Better On Lips Than On Paper (*see* SWALK)
NIMBY   Not in My Back Yard
RO-RO   Roll-On, Roll-Off (ferry)
SWALK   Sealed With A Loving Kiss

Vaguely suggestive quasi-words

BOGSAAT   Bunch Of Guys Sitting Around A Table (decision-making procedure)
BOMFOG   Brotherhood Of Man, Fatherhood Of God (political sales pitch)
EETPU   Electrical, Electronic, Telecommunications and Plumbing Union
MOBIDIC   MOBIle DIgital Computer
POTUS   President Of The United States
SUNFED   Special United Nations Fund For Economic Development

Words real but irrelevant

CAT   College of Advanced Technology
CAVALCADE   Calibrating, Amplitude-Variation And Level-Correcting Analog-
               Digital Equipment
DIN   *Deutsche Industrie Normen*
NOSE   National Odd Shoe Exchange
OEDIPUS   Oxford English Dictionary Integrating, Proofing
               and Updating System
POETS   Piss Off Early, Tomorrow's Saturday
VAT   Value-Added Tax (Purchase Tax under an assumed name)
WASP   White Anglo-Saxon Protestant

| ZIP | Zone Improvement Plan (US addressing system) |

(DIN is spoken as a word in the context of electronic cable plugs. NOSE is a rare example of an organization whose name is funnier than its acronym. OEDIPUS, though irrelevant, is, of course, deliberate.)

Real words relevant but contrived

ASH	Action on Smoking and Health
CHRIST	Christians Heeding Righteousness Instead of Satanic Tyranny
STOPP	Society of Teachers Opposed to Physical Punishment
WAMPUM	Wage And Manpower Process Utilizing Machine
WATSUP	Wessex Association for The Study of Unexplained Phenomena (UFO spotters)

(WAMPUM is 'relevant' because it was coined by the US Bureau of Indian Affairs.)

The most successful acronyms are those which do not coincide with existing words but have been so well absorbed into the language that their acronymic origin is forgotten and they are written as real words. Barely two dozen can be enumerated, and many of these, such as LOX for liquid oxygen, are unlikely to be encountered outside specialized contexts. The best known are:

Gestapo	*Geheime Staatspolizei* (Secret State Police)
jeep	from GP, General Purpose vehicle
laser	Light Amplification by Stimulated Emission of Radiation
quango	QUasi-Autonomous Non-Governmental Organization
radar	RAdio Detecting And Ranging
scuba	Self-Contained Underwater Breathing Apparatus
sonar	SOund NAvigation Ranging
wysiwyg	What You See Is What You Get (term commonly used in computing)

In the Thatcher era one might have added *yuppie*, from Young Upwardly-mobile Person. It is recorded in the *Oxford English Dictionary*, but how long it will remain current remains to be seen. Also noteworthy is *ecu*, an obsolete foreign word reinstated as an acronym of European Currency Unit. RADAR spelt with capitals is an acronym of Royal Association for Disability and Rehabilitation.

Other successful acronyms are names of organizations, success being measured by the fact that generally only the initial is capitalized as a name-marker:

Acas	Advisory, Conciliation and Arbitration Service
Benelux	Belgium, Netherlands, Luxembourg
Fiat	*Fabbrica Italiana Automobile Torino*
Mori	Market and Opinion Research Institute
Nalgo	National And Local Government Officers (Association)
Nasa	National Aeronautics and Space Administration
Nato	North Atlantic Treaty Organization
Opec	Organization of Petroleum Exporting Countries
Unesco	United Nations Educational, Scientific and Cultural Organization

(Benelux, strictly speaking, is a portmanteau *word, see page 163.)*

The earliest known acronym is VAMP, used in 19th-century American fire-fighting circles for the Voluntary Association of Master Pumpers. An early British one was ANZAC, a First World War term for Australia and New Zealand Army Corps. Sporadic before the mid-20th century, acronyms proliferated in and through the outbreak of the Second World War. Paul Dickson, in *Words,* reports: 'The term *acronym* ... was first introduced to scholars in a 1943 issue of *American Notes and Queries,* which traced it to Bell Telephone Laboratories, which had created the word as a title for a pamphlet to be used to keep workers abreast of the latest initialized titles for weapons systems and agencies.' If most of the early ones were naturally American and military-oriented, they have since become worldwide and chiefly technical. Dictionaries of acronyms and portmanteau words now run into hundreds of thousands, and grow thicker by the year.

Many other words may be described as quasi-acronyms, or downright fakes, notably:

CABAL
: Traditionally thought to be derived from the intials of a band of conspirators against Charles II (Clifford, Ashley, Buckingham, Arlington, Lauderdale) it is actually from the Hebrew *cabbala*, a mystic secret.

MAFIA
: Sometimes claimed as an acronym, but no one seems to know what it stands for.

NEWS
: Traditionally said to derive from the points of the compass. Patent nonsense!

POM(E)
: Those transported to Australian penal settlements in the 19th century are said to have been described as Prisoners Of Mother England. The acronym was pronounced Pommie and shortened to Pom.

POSH
: Said to derive from initials painted on the sides of luggage of well-heeled passengers to and from India in the days of the Raj – those who could afford to keep on the side of the ship protected from the tropical sun, and so able to travel Port Out, Starboard Home.

SOS
: Undeniably stands for *Save Our Souls* (or *Save Our Ship*), but only by accident. The letters were selected without regard to meaning but for rapidity of transmission and recognition in Morse code.

WREN
: Female sailor, Second World War vintage. An interesting back-formation from WRNS (Women's Royal Naval Service), given an extra E to make it pronounceable, taken to denote the members themselves, and finally used in the singular for any one of them. It might be classified as a 'vaguely suggestive real word'.

> **Game**
> *Each player in turn announces the name of a person or corporate body, and everyone competes to see who can invent the best acronymous title for it. For example, shortly after Dillons, the bookstore, was bought out of its financial difficulties, someone promptly acronomized its name to Dumb Illiterates Look Lost In New Shops. See also*
> Acronimble *(page 28) and* Acronymous Bosh *(page 67).*

ACROSTIC
(Greek, 'across the tips of a line' [of verse])

A verse in which the initial letters of consecutive lines spell out a word, usually the name of the dedicatee. Acrostics reached their height of popularity and complexity in Queen Victoria's day, and were the staple delight of word puzzlers until the advent of crosswords. Lewis Carroll, inevitably, was a pastmaster:

> *'Are you deaf, Father William!' the young man said,*
> *Did you hear what I told you just now?*
> *Excuse me for shouting! Don't waggle your head*
> *Like a blundering, sleepy old cow!*
> *A little maid dwelling in Wallington town*

Is my friend, so I beg to remark:
Do you think she'd be pleased if a book were sent down
Entitled The Hunt of the Snark?'

'Pack it up in brown paper!' the old man cried,
And seal it with olive-and-dove.
'I command you to do it!' he added with pride,
'Nor forget, my good fellow, to send her beside
Easter Greetings, and give her my love'.

One of the most ingenious acrostics I have encountered occurs in Robert Robinson's *Landscape With Dead Dons,* in which the murderer writes one based on his own name, not foreseeing that it will eventually give him away.

It is not necessarily the first letter of the line which produces the hidden name. It may be the last letter, in which case it is technically a *telestich*, or the central or any numerically specified intermediate letter, in which case it is a *mesostich*. One in which the first and last letters spell the names is a double acrostic. In a triple acrostic, an intermediate column of letters forms a third. A diagonal acrostic, horribly difficult to construct, spells two names in an X-formation, using the first and last letters of the first line, the second and second to last of the second, and so on, up to the last and first of the last.

Further elaboration produced the double acrostic puzzle. In its standardized format, the first of a series of verses gives a clue to the whole, and each subsequent couplet provides the clue to a hidden word. Correctly identified and listed, the resultant words themselves form a double acrostic by means of their first and last letters. Lewis Carroll, again, conceals the names TRINA and FREDA in this ineffably twee effusion:

Two little girls near London dwell
More naughty than I like to tell.

Upon the lawn the hoops are seen
The balls are rolling on the green.

The Thames is running deep and wide
And boats are rowing on the tide.

In winter-time, all in a row,
The happy skaters come and go.

'Papa!' they cry, 'Do let us stay!'
He does not speak, but says they may.

'There is a land', he says, 'my dear,
Which is too hot to skate, I fear'.

The first couplet identifies the subject(s) of the acrostic. The solution to the second is TurF, giving the T and F of their two names. The rest you can work out for yourself.

See also: *Acronym* (page 111), *Crossword* (page 127), *Mnemonic* (page 153), *Word square* (page 176).

Games
Composing and solving acrostics is of necessity a solitary pastime, offering little by way of social entertainment. Vaguely relevant games include Acronimble *(see page 28),* Alphabet *(see pages 12 and 67) and* Telegrams *(see page 67).*

ADDITIVE

A word that can be, or has been, transformed into another by adding a letter. See *Charitable and hospitable words* (page 123).

ADVERB

For fun with adverbs, see *Tom Swifties* (page 47), and *Yours sincerely* (page 30) in the *Talking Games* section.

ALLITERATION
(Latin, 'throwing letters together')

A passage of text, usually verse, containing many repetitions of the same consonant, especially at the beginnings of words and stressed syllables. With metre and rhyme, it is a major constituent of the sound effects of poetry.

Medieval ballads revelled in it. *Robin Hood and the Monk* opens:

> *In somer, when the shawes be sheyne,*
> *and leaves be large and long,*
> *Hit is full mery in feyre foreste*
> *to here the foulys song.*

(*Shawes* are groves, *sheyne* relates to 'shiny', and *foulys* are fowls, i.e. birds.)

Romantic poets sometimes overdid it – as, perhaps, Coleridge, in *The Rime of the Ancient Mariner* (1798):

> *The fair breeze blew, the white foam flew,*
> *the furrow followed free:*
> *We were the first that ever burst*
> *into that silent sea.*

Welsh poetry continues the medieval tradition of employing it in patterns of two or three repeated sounds, producing a musical effect known as *cynghanedd*, or 'singing together'. Even if you can't pronounce it, you can see it employed in this Welsh proverb:

> *Dyn y ran da yn ei raid,*
> *Duw a ran da i'r enaid*

(Man feeds his body, God feeds his soul.)

Tongue-twisters are a jocular form of alliterative verse that became popular in the the 19th century. *Peter Piper picked a peck of pickled peppers* appeared in its most classic form in 1834. One of my favourites, which I think I may have elaborated somewhat, is:

> *How much wood would a woodchuck chuck*
> *If a woodchuck could chuck wood?*
> *The wood that a woodchuck would chuck*
> *Is the wood that a woodchuck could chuck*
> *If a woodchuck that could chuck wood would chuck wood.*

Some of the most effective tongue-twisters are the shortest. Try repeating *Red lorry, yellow lorry* several times in rapid succession and you will hear what I mean. Willard Espy based this one on a newspaper headline about a three-month truce:

> *If a three-month truce is a truce in truth*
> *Is the truth of a truce in truth a three-month truce?*

Games

Alliteration doesn't lend itself easily to competitive gaming, but you might set a subject and see who can produce the longest example of an epic in which successive lines alliteratively exploit successive letters of the alphabet. The classic example begins:

An Austrian army awfully arrayed
Boldly, by battery, besieged Belgrade;
Cossack commanders cannonading come –
Dealing destruction's devastating doom;
Every endeavour, engineers essay,
For fame, for fortune, fighting furious fray ...

Or see who can write the most sustained piece of alliteration based on the initial of its subject. Given 'Moose', for example, my offering was:

Melancholy Moose

With murgid movement, mirthless moos and moody mope
the Norse Moose moves;
Through mangled meadows, murky moors and muddy moat
the Norse Moose moves:
But many miles must be immured
And many mounds must be manured
Before the Norse Moose meets
its moosely moving mate.
All moodily it moves along its many miles
and stops awhiles
to ruminate.
And murmuring with mirthless murms
It moves its mouth and mutters
melancholy moos.

(No, I can't find MURGID, *either. It must be a cross between* MURKY *and* TURGID.)

ANAGRAM
(Greek, 'letters anew')

Two words or phrases composed of the same set of letters are anagrams of each other. Thus THUS is an anagram of both HUTS and SHUT, as also is each of the other. (An anagram consisting of a single word, as distinct from a phrase, is properly known as a *transposition*.) As they serve no serious or literary purpose, anagrams fall entirely within the realm of verbal recreation, being most frequently encountered as crossword clues. Sophisticated anagramming programs are nowadays readily available as software packages, and this has taken much of the fun out of discovering them for yourself. Consequently, the mere fact that one or more words are anagrams of one another is no longer of any interest in itself. There are, however, two main ways in which some new life can be breathed into this old pastime. One is the setting of specified anagram tasks, the other that of devising appropriately scurrilous anagrams for names of politicians, businessmen, criminals, and other celebrities.

An elementary but interesting anagram task, just about playable as a competitive game, is to find the longest possible series of mutual anagrams. Well-known names are acceptable.

For example:

3 letters	ASP, PAS, SAP, SPA = 4
4 letters	EVIL, IVEL, LEVI, LIVE, VEIL, VILE = 6
5 letters	ELGAR, GLARE, LAGER, LARGE, REGAL = 5
6 letters	DRAWER, REWARD, WARDER, WARRED = 4
7 letters	DETAINS, INSTEAD, SAINTED, SATINED, STAINED = 5

Another is to find anagrams of words and phrases that are mutually supportive:

A SHOPLIFTER	HAS TO PILFER
CHRISTIANITY	IT'S IN CHARITY
THE MORSE CODE	HERE COME DOTS
THE NUDIST COLONY	NO UNTIDY CLOTHES
WESTERN UNION	NO WIRE UNSENT

or self-contradictory (these are known as *antigrams*):

DIPLOMACY	MAD POLICY
ENORMITY	IT'S MORE TINY
FUNERAL	REAL FUN
MISFORTUNE	IT'S MORE FUN
UNITED	UNTIED

or otherwise amusing or at least remarkable:

CINERAMA	AMERICAN
DEMOCRATIC	RATED COMIC
NATIONAL LOTTERY	TOTALLY INANE ROT
WEIRD NIGHTMARES	WITHERING DREAMS

Making appropriate anagrams of people's names is an ancient practice. Examples from history include:

ADOLF HITLER	HATED FOR ILL
CLINT EASTWOOD	OLD WEST ACTION
FLORENCE NIGHTINGALE	FLIT ON, CHEERING ANGEL!
MARIA CALLAS	I CALL MRS 'AAA!'
MARIE STUART	I'M A TRUE STAR
PIET MONDRIAN	I PAINT MODERN
THEODORE ROOSEVELT	LOVED HORSE — TREE, TOO
WILLIAM EWART GLADSTONE	WILD AGITATOR MEANS WELL
WILLIAM SHAKESPEARE	I ASK ME, HAS WILL A PEER?
WILLIAM SHAKESPEARE	WE ALL MAKE HIS PRAISE
WILLIAM SHAKESPEARE	A WEAKISH SPELLER, AM I?

Anagramming names has since been elevated to the status of a media-sponsored national craze. Following a famous occasion on which PRESIDENT BORIS YELTSIN mysteriously failed to get off the plane to meet the Irish Prime Minister at Dublin airport, one anagram software packager ran the following advertisement:

ENDLESS INSOBRIETY TRIP
ONE ISN'T TERRIBLY PISSED
TIPSINESS DONE TERRIBLY

An equally challenging task is to devise an anagrammed alias or pen-name for oneself.

Voltaire, for instance, was born an Arouet. Equating U with V and I with J, as one did in the 18th century, his pen-name derives from AROUET L. J., where L J stands for *le jeune,* 'the younger'. CHARLES LUTWIDGE DODGSON, ignoring his surname, rejected EDGAR CUTHWELLIS before switching his first two names and anglo-latinizing them to LEWIS CARROLL.

Here, it must be admitted, some people have all the luck. Few can be as fortunate as RICHARD STILGOE, who once published a book of stories peopled by such anagrammatic aliases as:

> DR GLORIA ETHICS
> ERIC ROADLIGHTS
> GERALD I. OSTRICH
> GILES T. HAIRCORD
> GISCARD O'HITLER
> SIR ERIC GOLDHAT

P.S. What is the only word in the English language that is an anagram of itself? (See page 178.) See also *Huntergram* (page 141).

Games

A party game or puzzle consists in giving clues to answers of two meaningfully connected words, each of which is an anagram of the other. For example:

Knotted dog	LOOPED POODLE
Dozy bees buzzed	DRONES SNORED
Dull in bed	BEDROOM BOREDOM
Diddle don again	RECHEAT TEACHER
The Right Rev	PRELATIC PARTICLE
Aging saws	SENESCENT SENTENCES
Assessing flowers	MEASURING GERANIUMS
Darkest jumper	SWARTHIEST SWEATSHIRT

See also Acronymous Bosh *(page 67),* Name in vain *(page 64).*

ANGUISH LANGUISH

A peculiar form of punning, and the title of a book by Howard Chase, late of Miami University. The professor's extraordinary forte lay in reducing folk tales to 'anguish languish' by replacing every word with another similar in sound but unrelated in meaning. The introduction to one such tale begins with an explanation and example:

> *Heresy ladle furry starry toiling udder warts, warts welcher altar girdle deferent firmer once inner regional virgin.*

('Here is a little fairy story told in other words, words which are altogether different from the ones in the original version.')

Thus the saga of *Little Red Riding Hood*, in the guise of *Ladle Rat Rotten Hut,* begins:

> *Wants pawn term dare worsted ladle gull hoe lift wetter murder inner ladle cordage honor itch offer lodge dock florist.*

and ends:

> *Oil offer sodden throne offer carvers an sprinkling otter bet, disc curl and bloat Thursday woof ceased pore ladle rat rotten hut an garbled erupt.*

See p. 178 for a 'translation' of this.

Translooting is my term for a variation on *Anguish languish*. It involves translating from one language into another by choosing words most similar in sound to the original. The past-master of this linguistic perversion was Luis d'Antan van Rooten, whose collection of *Mots d'Heures: Gousses, Rames* appeared in 1967. This purports to be a late 18th-century manuscript of indefinitely older rhymes in somewhat garbled French. Try rolling that title around your tongue for a few moments until it seems to make sense, and then apply the same process to the first rhyme in the collection, which begins:

> *Un petit d'un petit*
> *S'étonne aux Halles,*
> *Un petit d'un petit*
> *Ah! Degrés te fallent ...*

The author helpfully interprets this by referring to the unfortunate product of a child marriage – one who is amazed at that famous Parisian market, *les Halles,* and is not intelligent enough to have gained any university degrees. With a little more tongue-rolling, you might recognize it as referring to the unfortunate history of an egg. If so, and if your French is up to it, you have the makings of a great word competition. To spur you on, here's one that is said to expound the virtues of the monks and curates of southern France, or Languedoc ('Oc' for short):

> *Et qui rit des curés d'Oc?*
> *De Meuse raines, houp! de cloques.*
> *De quelles loques ce turque coin.*
> *Et ne d'ânes ni rennes,*
> *Ecuries des curés d'Oc.*

Alternatively, you could entitle it *Mouse Time.*

Game

Agree on a well-known story and see who can produce the most anguished version of it in the space of ten minutes. If that's too ambitious, see who can come up with the longest list of anguished folk-tale titles in the space of one minute. Here are a few more:

> *Guilty Looks Enter Tree Beers*
> *Hands All on Grate Oil*
> *Jacantha Bins Talk.*

When you run out of folk tales, try Shakespearean plays:

> *Owls swill the tent swill*
> *Roe (miaow!) unduly ate*
> *Ann to neon clear batterer*

ANTIGRAM

A self-contradictory anagram. See *Anagram* (page 117).

APHORISM

(Via French and Latin from Greek, aphorismos, 'definition')

Primarily a brief statement of a scientific principle. Secondarily, an *epigram* (see page 130).

AUSTRALIAN

See *Strine* (page 173).

AUTANTONYM
(Greek, 'self-opposed name')

A word with two meanings that are not only different but actually contradictory. It's a pity there are so few examples, otherwise one could hope to compile a Contradictionary of them.

action	working: not working ('industrial action')
bent	crooked: levelled (of weapon)
bless	sanctify: curse (ironic)
cleave	adhere: separate
downs	depressions: uplands
dust	remove dust: spray with dust
effectively	to good effect (precisely): in effect (more or less)
infer	draw inference: make implication
let	allow: hinder
nyctalopia	having poor vision in dim light: seeing best in dim light
overlook	inspect: ignore
public	public (buildings): private (schools)
rout	rummage out: assemble
sweat	produce moisture: dry thoroughly
tickle	touch lightly: beat
trim	add to (embellish): take from (pare)
trip	move nimbly: stumble

(I share the common objection to equating *infer* with *imply*, but must acknowledge that it has been practised by eminent writers and is recognized by *The Oxford English Dictionary*.)

To this list can be added the homophones *raise* – lift up, *raze* – bring down.

An oddly related case is that of *inflammable*, which properly means 'easily ignited', but can justifiably be interpreted as meaning 'incapable of being ignited'. The latter has therefore been replaced by *non-flammable*, and *flammable* is now used to mean *inflammable*!

AUTOMATIC DOUBLET

A variety of cliché (see page 125), in which the appearance of one word automatically elicits that of its parasitic intensifier, especially in the mouths of politicians. For example, *inadequate* is inadequate without *woefully*, a *majority* without *overwhelming*, a *minority* without *tiny*, *clear* without *crystal*. A majority, if you do not form part of it, is not *overwhelming* but *technical*. A minority, if you *do* form part of it, is not *tiny* but *significant*.

See also *Underemployed word* (page 175).

BARBARISM (SOLECISM)

'A form of speech offensive to scholarly taste', according to Chambers. This poses the question (but doesn't beg it – see below): are you being pedantic in objecting to such current barbarisms as illustrated in the following?

1. Noisy neighbours continue to *flaunt* the law (for *flout).*
2. This is a relatively new *phenomena (*for *phenomenon).*
3. Conditions *mitigated* against setting new records (for *militated*).
4. Abel was one of Baker's most notorious *cohorts* (for *henchmen* – possibly by confusion with the phrase *in cahoots?).*

Some barbarisms arise not from choosing the wrong word but from unconsciously taking a wrong turning in enunciating the right word. I have recently heard such meanderings as *unindated, intregal* and *legarthic.* More fascinating is the imaginary word *miniscule.* The intended word is *minute.* Meaning *tiny,* it is pronounced along the same lines as *Canute.* With today's increasing illiteracy, many people seem unable to see the word without reading it as *minnit,* i.e. 60 seconds. This baffles them by failing to make sense in the context, so they reach for the nearest possible word with a similar meaning. What emerges is a cross between *mini,* made popular in the 1960s through *mini-skirt* and the *Mini* car design, and a genuine word *minuscule.* The fact that *minuscule* properly denotes a lower-case letter in the field of printing suggests that this particular barbarism was originally perpetrated by journalists. Newspapers are ineluctably the fastest medium of barbaric dissemination, and, as Willard Espy notes in *The Game of Words,* 'There is a form of Gresham's Law about barbarisms: they tend to drive out good usage, and in time become good usage themselves.'

Other barbarisms consist of using a word with a wrong grasp of its meaning. To *eke out* (a living) does not mean to secure one with difficulty but to supplement one from other sources; *of that ilk* does not mean of that family or name, but is a technical term asserting the identity of a family name with a property name. And to *beg the question* does not just mean to pose, set or raise the question, but merely to appear to answer it, without actually doing so, by assuming a fact not in evidence.

Another common species of barbarism is the tautologism. Take, for example, the ubiquitous *Free Gift!,* an advertisement that tends to haunt garage forecourts. By definition, a gift is free. But an advertiser's free gift is one you pay for without knowing it. Hence *Free Gift* may be the only specimen in captivity of two positives making a negative.

If you count misspellings as barbarisms, they outnumber all the rest put together. The most irritating in current use is BARBEQUE for BARBECUE, obviously derived from the mock rebus BAR-B-Q. The *Guardian*'s editorial column has offered us CANONISED with a doubled N, THRESHOLD with a doubled H, and CHOOSY with a redundant E. I rest my case.

See also *Malapropism* (page 149).

BEHEADING

Removing the first letter of a word. See *Charitable and hospital words* (see page 123).

BUZZWORD

A quasi-technical word employed for its effect rather than its meaning; a word chosen to impress rather than express. The sort of word which, when you hear it, makes you think 'Boy, does this guy operate at the cutting edge of the interface of today's state-of-the-art lifestyle.'

Some buzzwords, like *interface,* are genuinely technical terms that have merely been kidnapped to impart an air of precision to a tissue of waffle. New disciplines such as sociology, education and business studies are particularly rich sources of buzzwords. Indeed, Andrew Jackson maintained, in an article in *Logophile* (March 1978), that buzzwords emanate principally from business schools and the journals and people associated with them.

The flavour of buzzword-speak is well imparted by the following *BuzzWord Generator* published many years ago in *Computer Weekly*. To operate, think of any three-digit number at random and select the corresponding buzzword from each column to produce an impressive-sounding phrase. Use at least one such phrase in every sentence you utter.

1	balanced	digital	capability	1
2	compatible	incremental	concept	2
3	functional	logistical	contingency	3
4	integrated	management	flexibility	4
5	optimal	monitored	hardware	5
6	parallel	organizational	mobility	6
7	responsive	policy	option	7
8	synchronized	reciprocal	programming	8
9	systemized	third-generation	projection	9
0	total	transitional	time-phase	0

Not to be confused with *Weasel word* (page 176).

CHARADE
(Italian schiarare, *'to unravel', 'clear up', 'solve')*

A game or entertainment in which a polysyllabic word is to be deduced from a series of playlets, each providing a clue to one syllable, and the last a clue to the whole word. Metaphorically a charade refers to long-term behaviour which is a pretence, and so intended to deceive.

Games
See Performing Rites (page 29).

CHARITABLE AND HOSPITABLE WORDS

A charitable word is one that can give up a letter and remain a word, albeit a different one. A hospitable word is one that can accept an additional letter and remain a word, albeit a different one. For example, CHARITABLE is charitable, because it remains CHARTABLE after losing an I, and PEAR even more charitable, because whichever letter is removed it remains a word (EAR, PER, PAR, PEA). Conversely, the last four words are all hospitable, as is CHARTABLE.

Removing the first letter of a word is called a beheadment, losing the last a curtailment. Some exceptionally charitable words can be repeatedly beheaded or curtailed down to one letter. For example, SHEATHED yields successively SHEATHE, SHEATH. HEATH, HEAT, EAT, AT, A. Similarly, BUTTERINESS can be reduced to B, provided you allow the Italian painter BUTTERI (1540–1606) and the surrealistically meaningful BUTTER-IN.

A task often set by word-gamers is that of finding the longest possible non-curtailable word – that is, those which never yield a genuine word as successive curtailments are made. The 15-letter example PLAGIOSTOMATOUS can be beaten by one listed under the heading *Longest word* (see page 147).

Games
See Charity *and* Beheadments *(page 52).*

CHRONOGRAM
(Greek, 'time writing')

A word or phrase based on the letters of a date expressed in Roman numerals. Its meaning must relate to the year in some way, and every numeral letter it contains must be used in the date. The classic example appears on a medal of Gustavus Adolphus of Sweden minted in 1627:

> ChrIstVs DuX ergo trIVMphVs

meaning 'As Christ leads, so triumph follows'. Rearranged, the letters CIVDXIVMV yield MDCXVVVII, or 1627.

With so few letters available – C, D, I(J), L, M, U(V), X – some liberties have to be taken, such as the three consecutive 'V's in this example. Modern examples are rare. Paul Hallweg celebrated the first manned moon landing in 1969 with Men Can Make Lunar eXcursions in eXtravagance, substituting the rule about unused letters (two I's and a C are ignored) with a rule whereby the date letters appear in their true order as the initial letters of the sentence. (Well, almost …)

CLERIHEW

The invention of Edmund Clerihew Bentley (1875–1956), a four-line verse in free metre, rhyming AABB, of which the first is the name of a character and the remainder comments upon them. One of Bentley's runs:

> *Sir Christopher Wren*
> *Said 'I am going to dine with some men.*
> *If anyone calls*
> *Say I'm designing St Paul's.'*

His son Nicholas was responsible for:

> *Cecil B. de Mille,*
> *Rather against his will,*
> *Was persuaded to leave Moses*
> *Out of the Wars of the Roses.*

I can't remember who wrote this favourite of mine:

> *John Stuart Mill*
> *By a mighty effort of will*
> *Put aside his natural bonhomie*
> *And wrote* 'Principles of Political Economy'.

The following clerihew remains uncredited:

> *Jonathan Swift*
> *Never went up in a lift;*
> *Nor did the author of 'Robinson Crusoe'*
> *Do so.*

Here are two of mine, the second a parody of the clerihew form:

> *Catherine of Aragon*
> *Abhorred the taste of tarragon.*
> *She said it made her feel*
> *Like Eleanor of Castile.*

Attila the Hun
Said 'Let's have a bit of fun –
Let's build the biggest army ever assembled on
this side of the Ganges, sweep through Asia Minor,
nip across the Dardanelles, over to Macedonia,
up to the gates of the palace of Alexander the Great,
And ring his doorbell and run.'

Game
Players are presented with a name taken at random from the Dictionary of National Biography, *or the* Famous People *section of* Pears Cyclopedia. *The winner is the player who produces the best clerihew from it.*

CLICHÉ
(*French,* clicher, *'to stereotype'*)

The original cliché was a printer's metal block bearing a design relevant to a chapter-head or subject matter, and used to avoid the trouble of casting a one-off design. Hence, metaphorically it is a stock word or phrase automatically employed whenever one is unable or unwilling to come up with something more specific for the occasion. Current political clichés include:

We are (or aren't) in the business of ...,
I cannot speculate on ...,
Let me make it absolutely/perfectly/crystal clear ..., (etc).

Crystal clear a sub-class of cliché designated the 'automatic doublet'. No one nowadays dies of an ordinary heart attack, only of a *massive* one; nothing is inadequate but *woefully* so; no record is complete without its *track*; nothing is ever *inclement* but weather, and so, predictably, on.

Clichés are often used deliberately for jocular or satirical effect. For example, an invitation to a drink will often be heralded by *What's your poison?* Stephen Potter, in *Oneupmanship*, sees such clichés as the verbal equivalent of shaking hands, and accordingly refers to their use as 'shaking jokes'. The satirical magazine *Private Eye* revels in them. A bribe or sweetener will be quantified as *A sum not unadjacent to...* A prominent figure who says one thing and does another will be introduced as two separate people and castigated with *Are they by any chance related? ... I think we should be told*. In less accomplished hands such clichés amount to catchphrases.

Eric Partridge, late guru of the language police, produced several editions of his *Dictionary of Clichés*, listing thousands of the little devils which shouldn't be allowed to appear in a well-ordered society. Nicholas Bagnall, however, in *A Defence of Clichés* (London 1985), attacks the modern craving for originality at the expense of shared values and proposes a more restrained view. Whether or not a cliché is reprehensible, he argues, depends not upon its mere employment, but upon its context, its user's motivation, and whether or not it is apt. One must distinguish between the second-rate and the mere second-hand, and to forbid the use of any apt word combination that has ever been used before 'would be to wipe out whole tracts of the English language'. Bagnall himself does not hesitate to admit that some should be put out to grass; others, such as *If I may venture to suggest*, he graphically likens to rhetorical 'nose-pickings'.

As the old joke has it, clichés should be avoided like the plague.

COLEMANBALLS

See *Irish bull* (page 142), *Metaphor* (page 150).

COLLECTIVE

A specialized or technical term for a group of similar objects, such as a *herd* of cows, a *flock* of sheep, a *bevy* of beauties (or bishops, believe it or not) a *pack* of wolves (or cards), a *pride* of lions, a *clutch* of eggs, a *field* of (race-)horses, and so on.

Less common, but well known for the frequency in which they appear in such lists, are an *exaltation* of larks (often misquoted as *exultation*), an *ostentation* of peacocks, a *parliament* of owls, a *charm* of goldfinches, and a *pod* of seals.

Rex Collings, in *A Crash of Rhinoceroses* (London, 1992), lists many more. Most, however, are nowadays neither common nor well known for being noteworthy, leaving one to wonder whether more than a handful were ever anything more than one-off literary conceits. Among these may be mentioned a *thought* of barons, a *draught* of butlers, a *blush* of boys, a *collapse* of cricketers, an *incredibility* of cuckolds, a *fold* of Highlanders, a *devoutness* of monks and a *trogle* of snakes.

> **Game**
> *From composing a literary conceit to playing a game is but a short step, and much fun may be had in extending the list by a process of invention. One of the best I have heard is that for a collective of wheel-stoppers – namely, a* squeal *of brakes. Combining the collective with the pun, a group of Russian dictators would presumably be a* flock of Stalins. *This is spoilt only by the fact that the collective term for starlings is in fact a* murmuration.

CONCRETE POETRY

Poetry, or at least verse, which is typographically arranged on the page to produce a relevant visual effect. A classic example is *The Mouse's Tail* from *Alice's Adventures in Wonderland:*

```
        Fury said to
          a mouse, That
            he met in the
              house,'Let
               us both go
                to law: I
                 will prose-
                  cute you. -
                 Come, I'll
                take no de-
               nial; We
              must have
             a trial:
            for really
           This morn-
          ing I've
         nothing
         to do'.
          Said the
            mouse to
              the our,
               'Such a
                 trial, dear
                   Sir. With
                    no jury
                     or judge,
                      would
                       be wast-
                       ing our
                       breath'.
                     'I'll be
                    judge,
                  I'll be
                 jury.'
                Said
              cun-
              ning
              old
              Fury.
                 'I'll
                   try
                     the
                       whole
                         cause,
                          and
                           con-
                            demn
                        you to
                      death'.
```

CONSONANTS

See *Lost consonants* (page 148).

CONUNDRUM

This has various meanings, all turning on the idea of something unknown or unintelligible – such as (appropriately enough) the origin of the word itself. In word-play, it is a riddle with a punning answer. It is most typically introduced by the ritualistic formula *'What's the difference between ..?'*, as in the classic example: 'What's the difference between a riddle and a herd of elephants sitting on a cake?' – 'One's a conundrum and one's a bun und'r 'em'.

The trouble with conundrums, as with limericks, is that the clean ones are boring and the best ones obscene.

CROSS-BETWEENS

The crossing joke, or cross-between, has been credited to broadcaster David Frost (by Willard Espy in *The Game of Words).* For example:

Cross a zebra with an apeman and you get ..?
Tarzan stripes forever.
Cross a female entertainer with a cooked meal and you get ..?
Ma dinna
Cross Charles Laughton with a five-door saloon and you get ..?
The hatchback of Notre Dame

This form of word-play – which I am tempted to call a *lowbrid* (as opposed to hybrid) – can also be seen as a species of conundrum, being closely related to the (now extinct) elephant joke typified by:

What do you get if you cross a mouse with an elephant?
Enormous holes in the skirting-board.

CROSSWORD

An elaborate form of word square (see page 176), defined by Sir Anthony Dewlap as follows:

> *A crossword puzzle is a form of puzzle, milord, in which a number of numbered squares in a chequered arrangement of – er – squares, milord, have to be filled in with letters, milord, these letters forming words, milord, which words are read both horizontally and vertically, milord, milord – that is, both across and down, if your Lordship follows me ... As a rule, milord, the descriptions or clues provided are brief and the correct solutions are the names of mythical animals and Biblical characters, prepositions, foreign towns, classical writers, obscure musical instruments, vegetables, little-known adjectives, and so forth ...*

(From A. P. Herbert's *Misleading Cases,* in the case of the Bishop of Bowl, Earl Rubble, Evadne Lady Smail, John Lickspittle, General Glue, and others, versus Albert Haddock.)

The crossword is too popular to require further description, suffice to add that it derives naturally from the acrostic and the word square, its invention being credited to journalist Arthur Wynne. The first one appeared under the title *Word cross* in *The New*

York World in 1913. By the 1920s it had becomes a national and subsequently international craze. Of many variations in structure and content, two may be singled out as fundamental. That most favoured by American compilers and solvers consists almost entirely of checked letters (a checked letter is one common to a word in both directions) and few blanks, and is equipped with clues amounting to straightforward definitions. More favoured in Britain is the type containing relatively few checked letters – none of them consecutive – with a high proportion of blanks, and equipped with 'cryptic' clues involving elaborate forms of word-play in themselves. Here, for example, are three possible ways of giving a clue for the word ELABORATE:

- *To go into detail, the Spanish sailor. Alternatively, a brief note.*
- *Work up a bundle in reverse, then speak in public.*
- *Divinity able to recombine, to make more complex.*

A cryptic clue typically contains two parts, one for the meaning of the required word and one for its form. Above, the meaning of *elaborate* is variously expressed as *go into detail, work up,* and *make more complex.* As to form, the first may be explained as *el* – Spanish for 'the', AB – standard abbreviation for Able-Bodied Seaman, *or* – alternatively, *a* – 'a', *te* – a musical note in the tonic sol-fa system. The second analyses the required word as *orate* preceded by *bale* spelt backwards. In the third, the word *recombine* is one of many ways of indicating that the clue is an anagram, its component parts being ABLE, TO, and RE, standing for Religious Education, a subject known in some schools as 'Divinity'.

Thus the crossword is not just a word game in itself, but an excuse for indulging in all sorts of word play.

> **Games**
> Many a Cross Word ... *(page 80) is entirely devoted to crossword games.*

CRYPTOGRAM
(Greek, 'hidden writing')

A message transposed into a form that can be read only by those entrusted with the solution to the puzzle. Such a message may be in code or cipher. A code is a list of signs or symbols, each of which stands for a specific and invariable letter, word, number or concept. A cipher is a formula or process by which individual letters are transposed into other letters or signs, not necessarily the same ones each time.

Not all codes are designed for secrecy. Many are designed for purely practical purposes, such as the Morse code for wireless telegraphy, semaphore for manual communication out of earshot, sign language for communication within earshot but for the deaf, shorthand for speed in a professional context.

DOUBLE ENTENDRE

A way of having it both ways in public, the *double entendre* is an innocent line or phrase unintentionally offering a sexual or scatological interpretation to those of the requisite mental attunement. Willard Espy cites this classic example perpetrated by children's author Rose Fyleman:

> *My fairy muff is made of pussy willow ...*

Others include:

> She gave me tokens three:
> A look, a word of her winsome mouth,
> And a wild raspberry.
>   Francis Thompson, *Daisy*.

> Then, owls and bats,
> Cowls and twats,
> Monks and nuns, in a cloister's moods
> Adjourn to the oak-stump pantry.
>   Robert Browning, *Pippa Passes*.

It seems the word he was really looking for was *coifs*. The way it actually comes out throws an interesting alternative light on the word *pantry*.

The usual British way of noting that a phrase intended one way has been taken another is to respond with some such formulae as *'As the archbishop said to the actress'*, or *'As the art mistress said to the gardener'*, whichever is more appropriate in the context.

Double entendres are the stock-in-trade of good comedians and the obsession of bad ones. Marie Lloyd, the music-hall artiste, is said to have been ordered by the management of one theatre to clean up one of her songs that contained the refrain:

> She sits among the cabbages and peas.

Obligingly, she changed it to:

> She sits among the lettuces and leeks.

For effect, double-entendre jokes depend upon providing a polite explanation where an impolite one is apparently forced – a sort of *double*-cross-*entendre*. For example: 'What is it that a man does standing up, a woman does sitting down, and a dog does on three legs?'

For the answer, see page 178.

DOUBLET

Lewis Carroll's term for *Metagram*, (see page 150).

ENIGMA
(Greek, based on ainos, 'fable')

Loosely, a puzzle or mystery, as in Elgar's *Enigma Variations*. More specifically, a word-deduction puzzle in verse. As Tony Augarde points out in *The Oxford Guide to Word Games*, the only discernible difference between a riddle and an enigma is that the latter has more literary merit. Thus William Cowper:

> I am just two and two, I am warm, I am cold,
> And the parent of numbers that cannot be told.
> I am lawful, unlawful, a duty, a fault
> I am often sold dear, good for nothing when bought.
> An extraordinary boon, and a matter of course,
> And yielded with pleasure when taken by force.
> Alike the delight of the poor and the rich,
> Though the vulgar is apt to present me his breech.

Suitably attuned contemporaries of William Cowper would have appreciated the *double entendre* before coming up with the correct answer, 'a kiss'.

EPIGRAM
(Greek, epi, 'on top of', 'in addition to')

Strictly and classically, an epigram is a brief satirical verse with a sting in its tail. Loosely and contemporaneously, it is much the same as an *aphorism* – a smart-ass wisecrack about the human condition.

Classical examples abound in the work of the Roman poet Martial, who turned them into an art form:

> *Belliger invictis quod Mars tibi servit in armis,*
> *non satis est, Caesar, servit et ipsa Venus.*

> (Unconquered warrior – yes, because Mars supports you in arms.
> But that's not enough for you, Caesar – whom Venus herself supports too.)

As to pointed wisecracks, it's as hard to know where to start as when to stop:

> The race is not always to the swift, nor the battle to the strong. But that's the way to bet. *Damon Runyon.*

> Democracy substitutes election by the incompetent many for appointment by the corrupt few. *George Bernard Shaw.*

> In America, life is one long expectoration. *Oscar Wilde.*

> Conversation is the enemy of good wine and food. *Alfred Hitchcock.*

> France is the only country where the money falls apart and you can't tear the toilet paper. *Billy Wilder.*

> The two most beautiful words in the English language are 'cheque enclosed'. *Dorothy Parker.*

EPITAPH
(Greek, 'upon a stone')

Lines inscribed on a tombstone in praise of the deceased, or revealing something remarkable about them. The genuine ones tend to be unsurprisingly dull, and the amusing ones unsurprisingly apocryphal.

Typical of the apocryphal ones are those that evince apparently unintentional humour, such as:

HERE LIES

CAPTAIN
ERNEST BLOOMFIELD
~
ACCIDENTALLY SHOT BY
HIS ORDERLY
~
MARCH 2nd 1789

'Well done, thou good
and faithful servant'

More amusing are those suggested by various wits for their own graves. Dorothy Parker is credited with three:

And George Kaufman with:

Probably apocryphal is:

Better still are one-liners proposed by wits for others. Robert Benchley on a movie queen:

Here's an anonymous contribution:

proposed for the Tomb of the Unknown Hypochondriac.

Another old favourite is:

Various characters in history have had some sharp verses proposed for their epitaphs, not always before they were dead.

For Charles II, by John Wilmot, 2nd Earl of Rochester:

> *Here lies a great and mighty king*
> *Whose promise none relies on*
> *He never said a foolish thing*
> *Nor ever did a wise one*

For Viscount Castlereagh, by Lord Byron:

> *Posterity will ne'er survey*
> *A nobler grave than this:*
> *Here lie the bones of Castlereagh –*
> *Stop, traveller, and piss.*

More than one example is to be found in the literature of epitaphs (if not in the life) of the following observation:

> *Here lie the bones of Elizabeth Charlotte*
> *That was born a virgin and died a harlot*
> *She was aye a virgin till seventeen –*
> *An extraordinary thing for Aberdeen.*

Game
Well, obviously, everybody here present is charged to write a pithy epitaph for everybody else present. In case this sort of thing doesn't go down too well, you could substitute celebrities. Or, if you are all celebrities anyway, define your offering not as an epitaph but as a suitable title for an autobiography. One author has already done so, calling his autobiography Here Lies Eric Ambler.

EPONYM, EPONYGRAM
(Greek, 'given as a name')

A personal name from which is derived a place name, book title or word of general application. Thus Hamlet is the eponymous hero of *Hamlet, Prince of Denmark,* Alice the eponymous heroine of *Alice's Adventures in Wonderland,* and the Saxon deity Woden of the place-name *Wednesbury* and day-name *Wednesday.* In the case of a title, the name itself need not appear as such – which perhaps explains why I can never remember who is the eponymous friend of *Our Mutual Friend.* Generalized eponymous words are numerous and often surprising. *Sandwich,* for example, was invented by the Earl of Sandwich, *boycott* is what first happened to Captain Boycott of County Mayo, and *gun* is thought to be short for *Gunnhilda.* Other words, such as *namby-pamby* and *malapropism* (see page 149), derive from characters in fiction.

Eponyms have not figured largely in traditional word games, but have recently achieved prominence in one or two promising directions. Dan Glaister introduced a series in *The Guardian* under the heading 'eponygrams', defined as words 'designed to bring new uses to tired names'. For example:

Gump An oxymoronic moron ... may be a highly intelligent idiot, or a successful failure, and like a *newt* [also an eponygram] represents the triumph of anti-intellectualism.

Winnie A persistent and painful reminder of the past ... an embarrassment to the successful leaders of a political movement or revolution, harping on about ideals when the serious business of governance is at hand.

('Gump' comes from the film *Forrest Gump* whose simpleton hero achieves improbable fame, 'Winnie' from the estranged wife of South African president Nelson Mandela and 'newt' from Newt Gingrich, a conservative Republican who became Speaker of the US Congress in 1994.)

Eponygrams were probably inspired by a splendidly funny booklet called *The Meaning of Liff* (London, 1983), in which Douglas Adams and John Lloyd pointed out that 'the world is littered with thousands of spare words which spend their time doing nothing but loafing about on signposts pointing at things'. To give them something useful to do, the authors matched them to various phenomena for which no suitable word had hitherto been available, thus, as you might say, killing two words with one tome. For example:

Aberystwyth A nostalgic yearning which is in itself more pleasant than the thing being yearned for.

Liff A book, the contents of which are totally belied by its cover ...

Sidcup One of those hats made from tying knots in the corners of a handkerchief.

See also *Name* (page 154), *Toponym* (page 174).

Games

Each player in turn nominates a well-known place or prominent public figure until a list of ten or twelve has been compiled, and everyone then writes proposed new definitions for them as if they had become generalized words.

EUPHEMISM
(Greek, 'nice speech-ism')

A sweetening word or phrase that sugars the pill of an unpalatable concept, such as *pass away* for *die*, or *break wind* for *fart*. What constitutes 'unpalatable' varies with the times, but taboo areas of pretty universal extent include anything to do with sex, dirt, bodily functions, illness and death. Ridiculous extremes of euphemism are well referred to by Willard Espy, in *The Game of Words,* as 'Nice Nellyisms', which speaks volumes. Nice Nellyisms apply especially to the realm of underwear, as I was reminded recently in re-reading one of Erle Stanley Gardner's Perry Mason novels, where one of the characters states that in the murdered man's cabin were found 'certain intimate garments of feminine wearing apparel' (*The Case of the Perjured Parrot,* 1939). And I remember my mother telling me, when the man next door went into hospital for a prostate operation, that it was on account of 'a gentlemen's complaint'.

Another form of euphemism is the hypercorrection, as when the percussion instrument originally known as the Jew's harp is referred to as a 'jaws harp', or toasted cheese on bread is politely referred to as Welsh Rarebit instead of the originally ironic 'Welsh rabbit'.

If these examples of hypercorrection are intended to avoid any possible offence to an ethnic or social grouping, that of 'political correctness' goes even further in attempting to purge the language of anything that might possibly give offence to anyone of any minority grouping. It is the patent impossibility of such an aim that renders the whole concept so ludicrous (see *Political correctness,* page 161).

Some forms of euphemism amount to coded communication, as, for example, when talks between conflicting parties are described as a *frank* exchange of views, or involving a *robust* defence of positions, both adjectives being euphemistic code-words for a meeting that fell only just short of fisticuffs. A lot of underworld and criminal slang involves coded euphemism, from *light-fingered* to *concrete overcoat.* Others amount to evasions of unpalatable truths, as when the party in power, having suffered an ignominious by-election defeat or opinion poll survey, regrets that it has *'failed to get its message across'.*

Jocular euphemisms are those in which the pretence of code is adopted in order to engage the interest of the listener or reader. The satirical magazine *Private Eye* has developed a language all its own for this purpose, by which, for example, a notable figure – especially one in a position to sue for libel – is described as *tired and emotional* (drunk) or prone to *Ugandan discussions* (illicit sexual encounters). A wide overlap between jocular euphemisms and unabashed clichés is illustrated by phrases devised to suggest intellectual incapacity. One of the most obscure is *a bit behind the door,* which is short for ...*(S)he must have been behind the door when brains were being given out.* I think I encountered *Not firing on all four cylinders* in P. G. Wodehouse, and can certainly credit Cervantes with *The apartments in this gentleman's skull are unfurnished.* Many more are built along the lines of:

> *a few cards short of a full pack.*
>
> *a few sandwiches short of a picnic.*
>
> *five pence short of a shilling.*

> **Game**
> *Continue the above list.*

FAMOUS LAST WORDS

Famous last words, like epitaphs, and probably for the same reason, tend to be banal if genuine and apocryphal if witty. The following are noteworthy and reasonably well authenticated:

Louis XIV: *I thought dying would have been harder.*
Lady Mary Wortley Montagu: *It has all been very interesting.*
Lord Palmerston: *Die, my dear doctor? That's the last thing I shall do.*
George V: *Bugger Bognor.*
William Palmer, poisoner, on being told to step on to the trap: *Are you sure it's safe?*

> **Game**
> *Agree upon the names of five living celebrities and see who can devise the two most apt dying utterances for each of them, the first assuming natural death from old age, the second assuming judicial execution.*

FRANGLAIS

The French apply *franglais* to the excessive larding of their native language with English borrowings, such as *le week-end, le five-o'cloque* (afternoon tea), and so on. British writers employ the term for the language that emerges when English-speakers, to whom fluency in a second language is as desirable as garlic on the breath, try to appease the natives by using vaguely gallicized English words and translate English idiomatic expressions with word-for-word literality. As Miles Kington says, in the preface to *Let's Parler Franglais!* (1979):

> *Si vous êtes un fluent English speaker, et si vous avez un 'O' level français, Franglais est un morceau de gateau.*

Willard Espy quotes a poem in franglais that includes the verse:

> *Ce même vieux coon n'est pas quite mort,*
> *Il n'est pas seulement napping.*
> *Je pense, myself, unless j'ai tort,*
> *Cette chose est yet to happen.*

> **Game**
> *Si votre players avez un 'O' level français, voyez qui can produire le best translation of a donné nursery rhyme into franglais dans un minute or deux.*

GOBBLEDEGOOK
(An imitative word connected with gobble, *also spelt* gobbledygook)

Text which is dense to the point of unintelligibility. It doesn't necessarily denote technical language hard to understand by those unacquainted with the meaning of the appropriate technical terms. Whether or not that is gobbledegook depends on the quality of the writing in which they occur, which can only be judged by an appropriately literate technician.

Gobbledegook derives from linguistic incompetence combined with the pretentiousness of the Sunday writer. Here's a sample from page one of a potentially interesting book on the history of the Basques which I had to give up on a few pages later:

> *More recent phases of their history are, of course, also held to be of crucial significance, but what is tantamount to a politicization of normally abstruse and recherché anthropological arguments about the Stone Age is a distinctive feature of the ideological underpinning of modern Basque nationalism, in which the longevity of the people and the continuity of their occupation of their western Pyrenean homelands are arguments of central importance.*

This piece of literary constipation is mainly caused by pouring all the meaning into abstract nouns, leaving none to be carried by verbs. The only main verbs in this 69-word sentence are the colourless *are, is, is, are,* and the only concrete noun is *people,* whereas abstract nouns number 13 (*phases, history, significance, politicization, arguments, feature, underpinning, nationalism, longevity, continuity, occupation, arguments, importance*).

A lot of business-speak is goobledegook. This extract first appeared in *Logophile:*

> *It was planned that the preparation for the dispatch of the consignment of goods would have been carried out in time for it to be received by the consignee at the termination of a period of several days.*

The richest source of specimens of gobbledegook is the regular *Pseuds Corner* feature in *Private Eye.* The following passage, from a review of an art exhibition in Liverpool, is more pretentious than incompetent.

> *The placement of 'work' in this space seems almost a perverse act in itself. Yet in a sense these works do not occupy the space any more than a series of echoes defines the space which registers them. These works could be said to under-mine any prioritizing of intrinsic facticity in the viewer's assessment of the art object. Not that 'illusion' is a dominant characteristic – simply that the interpretive overspill generated in the interplay of looking at and 'reading' the object/image fills the space more certainly than the various objects and images which comprise the works.*

Gobbledegook also arises from two opposed extremes of psychological motivation. In one, the writer seeks to distance himself objectively from what is being expressed as a form of self-defence against any objection that might be raised to it. This underlies those dialects of gobbledegook known to everyone as officialese and legalese. In the other, the writer seeks to interpose himself subjectively between the topic and the reader in order to show the reader what a clever chap he is. If the former is dying out now, our thanks will be largely due to *The Campaign for Good English.* See also *Buzzword* (page 122).

GOLDWYNISM

An unintentionally humorous non sequitur or mixed metaphor rightly or wrongly attributed to the film producer Sam Goldwyn (1882–1974) of Metro-Goldwyn-Mayer. The following (from Boller and George, *They Never Said It!,* Oxford 1989) are typical Goldwynisms, except in so far as there is no evidence that he ever uttered a single one:

- *A verbal contract isn't worth the paper it's written on.*
- *Anyone who would go to a psychiatrist ought to have his head examined.*
- *Gentlemen, include me out.*
- *I'm very sorry that you felt it* [The Secret Life of Walter Mitty] *was too blood and thirsty.*
- *We can get all the Indians we need at the reservoir.*

Presumably Goldwyn must have said something noteworthily ridiculous at some time for others to have got into the habit of attributing such statements to him. According to Goldwyn, what he said was not *Gentlemen, include me out*, but *Gentlemen, I'm withdrawing from the association*. This is a pity, because anyone with an atom of wit would have laid claim to it without hesitation. Once he had acquired that reputation, other samples were either produced by garbling what he did say, or by crediting him with other people's utterances. The *verbal contract* remark is apparently an instance of garbling, the original being a compliment to the integrity of Joseph M. Schenk: *His verbal contract is worth more than the paper it's written on*. Many transfers must have been made from film director Michael Curtiz, the originator of *Bring on the Empty Horses*. (David Niven, who used this as the title for part of his autobiography, said of Hungarian-born Curtiz that he directed many of his films in a period of his life when he had forgotten all his Hungarian and had not yet learned to speak English. A genuine Curtizism, according to Niven, is *This'll make your blood curl*.)

If most Goldwynisms are apocryphal, it is simply because 'Goldwynism' has become the accepted modern term for what used to be called an Irish Bull, or a non sequitur.

See also *Misquotation and misattribution* (page 151).

GRAMMAR, RULES OF, UNGRAMMATICAL

1. Don't use no double negatives.
2. Make each pronoun agree with their antecedent.
3. When dangling, watch your participles.
4. Don't use commas, which aren't necessary.
5. Verbs has to agree with their subjects.
6. About those sentence fragments.
7. Try not to ever split infinitives.
8. Use apostrophe's correctly.
9. Correct spelling is esential.
10. Always read what you have written to see you any words out.

(Harold Evans, *Newsman's English*, cited in *Logophile III,3*.)

> **Game**
> *Invent some more 'ungrammatical rules' – bearing in mind,
> for starters, that no mention has yet been made of
> prepositions.*

HEADLINES

Few newspaper headlines today are straightforwardly informative: most are either deliberately jocular or irritatingly hyperbolic. Hyperbole manifests itself in the replacement of accurate words by their more graphic equivalents. Services are not REDUCED or CUT, but invariably AXED or SLASHED, the police never merely RAID but inevitably SWOOP or POUNCE, and so on. Hyperbole reaches the heights of ludicrousness in local newspapers. One of ours recently carried the mystifying headline REPORT SPARKS GLOOM.

Some follow peculiar grammatical structures of their own, making themselves wonderfully misleading. Of the then Labour leader, a Tory newspaper carried the headline KINNOCK IN 'NUTS' JIBE (or something equivalent – I quote from memory). Your first thought would naturally be that he had offended someone by calling them 'nuts'. Close reading of the small print revealed that he was in fact the target and not the perpetrator of the jibe, thus making a dubious political jibe out of a non-story.

The deliberately jocular ones tend to be feeble and repetitive when they depend on puns – as, for example, when the *Guardian* referred to anger over an epidemic as HOT UNDER THE CHOLERA. The most effective are those in which some kind of *double entendre* is implied by the way sentences are split between lines, or reduced to carefully selected telegraphese. Apart from the one about Winnie Mandela, which I collected myself, the following come from Fritz Spiegl's *Keep Taking the Tabloids* (London 1983).

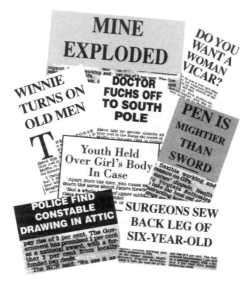

See also *Journalese* (page 143).

Game
Each player proposes an historical subject for a headline, which may be anything from the extinction of the trilobites to the flight out of Egypt to the umpteenth moon landing. Everyone then labours to produce a misreadable headline for every subject mentioned. The winner is the last player to die laughing.

HIGGLEDY-PIGGLEDY

A comic verse form based, like the Clerihew (see page 124) on a real or fictional character, but more elaborate. It was invented around 1950 by the American poet Anthony Hecht and is properly known as a Double Dactyl. Here's an example by Joan Munkacsi:

Higgledy-Piggledy
Oedipus Tyrannos
Murdered his father, had
Mama for sex.

This mad debauch, not so
Incomprehensibly
Left poor Jocasta and
Oedipus wrecks.

The essentials of the form are:

● Two four-line stanzas in the same metre as illustrated above, with the last line of each rhyming with the other.
● The first line to be 'Higgledy-Piggledy', the second the name of the subject.
● The sixth line to be an adverb of six syllables.

Apart from the strict metre, you're allowed a certain degree of leeway. *Higgledy-Piggledy* can be replaced by a perhaps more appropriate ejaculation, and the sixth line needn't be an adverb, though it must be one word. Here's another by James Lipton:

> *Misericordia!*
> *College of Cardinals*
> *Nervously rising to*
> *Whisper its will.*
>
> *'Rather than being so*
> *Unecumenical,*
> *Can't we just quietly*
> *Swallow the pill?'*

And one of mine:

> *Higgledy-piggledy*
> *President Kennedy*
> *Visited Marilyn*
> *After the show –*
>
> *Claiming the doctrine of*
> *Untouchability*
> *Didn't apply to that*
> *Kind of Monroe.*

> **Game**
> *Choose a character and see who can produce the best – or indeed any – Higgledy-Piggledy based on it between now and next time you meet.*

HOBSON-JOBSON

A word or phrase resulting from the corruption of a foreign original. The phrase *Hobson-Jobson* is itself an exemplary corruption of the cry *Yā Hasan! Yā Husain!* made, in memory of Mohammed's murdered grandsons, at the Islamic feast of Muharram. Surprising examples include *compound*, which derives from the Malay *kampong,* and *forlorn hope*, from the Dutch *verloren hoop*, meaning a lost expedition. Some derive not from a foreign language but from a misunderstood older form of the language. The classic example is *helpmate*, which comes from the (17th-century) Authorized Version of the Bible in the line *an help meet for him,* i.e. 'someone suited to help him' (Genesis, 2:18.) Others include:

belfry	from German via French for 'watch-tower' (not from *bell*)
humble pie	from pie made from 'umble' (liver and lights of deer)
shame-faced	from 'shame-fast' (held fast by shame)
stark-naked	from 'start-naked' (start – tail)

under way   from 'under weigh' (of an anchor)

> **Game**
> *Specify some words or phrases, suppose them to be Hobson-Jobsons, and see who can invent the most humorously suitable origins for them. For example:* touch and go *from the Spanish* tuchángo, *an energetic dance in which each participant alternately taps the other and trips away before being caught. See also* 'Orrible origins *(page 45) and* Fictionary dictionary *(page 90).*

HOMONYM
(*Greek, 'same name'*)

Homonyms are words with different meanings that are pronounced or spelt the same, or both. For example:

> READ (present tense) – REED
> READ (past tense) – RED
> LOVE (affection) – LOVE (zero score)
> MINUTE (60 seconds) – MINUTE (tiny)

They are the indispensable basis of *Puns* (see page 164).

HOWLER
(*Something that makes you howl with laughter*)

A verbal confusion or misunderstanding, resulting in a *non sequitur* or *double entendre,* and traditionally perpetrated by schoolboys of 'Billy Bunter' vintage. Many, of course, are apocryphal, but two of the mistranslations quoted below were genuinely perpetrated by a friend of mine at the age of 14. The rest are largely from the collections of Cecil Hunt, as re-presented by Russell Ash in *Howlers (Horsham, 1985).*

Mistranslations
Bouteilles de rhum – Rheumatism boots.
Il agitait son mouchoir – He twirled his moustache.
Il fit volte-face – He made a horrid face.
Il marchait sur les minces planches – He walked through the mint plantation.
Nemo mortalis sapit omnibus horis – No man is safe in a public vehicle with women.
Non hominum vide, non ego facta bonum – I see no man; I am not made of cows.
Quidquid in utraque parte – Two quid each way.
Le peuple, ému, répondit – The purple emu laid another egg.

Missing links
An abstract noun is something you can't see when you are looking at it.
'Gross darkness' mentioned in the Bible means it was 144 times as dark as ordinary darkness.
Leap year is instead of it being the next day on the same day next year it's the day after.
Poetry is when every line starts with a capital letter.
Queen Elizabeth liked Walter Raleigh so much she made him one of her nights.
The Israelites made a golden calf because they didn't have enough gold to make a cow.
The meaning of x^2 is curious. If x is an ox, x^2 is not two oxen because that would be 2x. In fact you can't describe the little '2'.
The names of the five members were Pym and four others.

The Oedipus Complex means liking your mother as if she were a normal woman.
The Seven Years War went on and off in a funny sort of way until the seven years were up.
There are four symptoms of a cold. Two I forget; the other two are too well-known to mention.

Ask a silly question
In what order do the gospels appear? – One after the other.
Name six animals found in the Arctic. – Three bears and three seals.
What happened in (a) 1483, (b) 1487? – (a) Luther was born. (b) Luther was four.
What is a simile? – A simile is a picturesque way of saying what you really mean, like calling your mother an old trout.
What is an isthmus? – An isthmus is a bit of land that juts inland.
What is half of five? – It depends on whether you mean the two or the three.
What is the capital of England? – 'E'.
What was the purpose of Cook's second voyage? – To see if America really was there.
Where is the elephant found? – The elephant, being a large animal, is rarely lost.

See also *Mistranslation* (page 152).

Game
See Daft definitions *(page 45).*

HUNTERGRAM

A puzzle verse in which words and phrases that are anagrams of one another have been blanked out. Named after Hunter Skinner, an enthusiast for them. Here's an example:

No ——— type of wine ———
 So little grasp of my affections
As Greek ———, which explains
 My ———' opposed directions.

The four blanks are all anagrams of one another. For the answer see page 178.

INCONGRUITIES

Asked by a non-pianist which element of the piano made it quieter, I automatically replied 'The right-hand foot pedal' – and was immediately taken aback by the incongruity of the term. In quest of further examples, I did think of taking a walk round the square, but then remembered that others had been there before me. It is usually those who do not come from a long line of English-speakers, like Victor Borge and B. Kliban (author and illustrator of *Never Eat Anything Bigger Than your Head*), who have the greatest facility for and take the greatest delight in pointing out the incongruities of the language. The humorist Denis Norden, in an article entitled *Words Flail Me* in *Logophile* magazine, explores the same field, and wonders how any foreigner can hope to learn a language containing such unmatched quasi-doublets as *maternity suit/paternity suit, old master/old mistress,* and *good-looking/looking good.* There's a world of difference between *If you're going to the cleaners will you pick up my skirt?* and *If you're going to the cleaners will you lift up my skirt?* And if an inhabitant of Poland is a Pole, why isn't an inhabitant of Holland a Hole?

How many more examples can you find?

See also *Oxymoron* (page 158).

INFLATED RHETORIC

The term applied by Willard Espy to a type of wordplay popularized by the pianist-comedian Victor Borge. It involves writing or rewriting a story or passage of text in such a way that any part of a word that looks or sounds like a number is increased by one. For example:

> Like his fivebears befive him, gangster Al Captwo was but nineteen-ager when he fired his second s-eleven gun. Hitherthree, his favourite sport was elevennis, though he found the basevens of the game somewhat asiten. In typically fifthright manner, he dix-septed the initiative and rapidly became a second-r-nine performer.

> **Game**
> Each player in turn proposes a category, such as places, flowers, animals, games. Everyone starts compiling a list of 'inflated' examples of that category. Places, for example, might yield Elevenessee, Oxfived, Threeting, and so on. The first to reach five examples stops the game. Players then score one point for each specimen they have collected, plus a bonus point for each one that no-one else thought of.

INSULT

See Sarcasm (page 171).

INVENTED WORD

See *Neologism* (page 155).

IRISH BULL

A statement which is humorously illogical or inherently self-contradictory; a non sequitur. The origin of the term is unknown. The first element undoubtedly relates to the traditional English view of the Irish as inhabiting a unique plane of logic, and the second may relate to a *cock and bull story* and to *bull* in its American sense of vaguely threatening codswallop. It can range in length from a shaggy dog story to the sort of earnestly nonsensical statement associated with Sam Goldwyn. The Marx Brothers' films abound in Irish bull one-liners, from Groucho's 'I'd horsewhip you, if I had a horse', to Chico's 'He's suffering from insomnia and he's gone to bed to sleep it off.' The classic Irish example is the response to a request for directions: 'If I wanted to get to there I wouldn't be starting from here.'

As the term is somewhat literary and out of date, and probably politically incorrect, it has tended to be replaced by other attributive designations, such as *Goldwynism* (see page 136). Splendid specimens are also regularly recorded under the heading *Colemanballs* in *Private Eye*:

● *This could be a repeat of what will happen at the European games next week. (David Coleman.)*
● *The advantage of the rain is, that if you have a quick bike, there's no advantage. (Barry Sheene.)*
● *I can't imagine what sort of problem Senna has. I imagine it must be some sort of grip problem. (Murray Walker.)*

- *If people had proper locks put on their doors, crime could be prevented before it happens. (Douglas Hurd.)*
- *I'm not a believer in luck – but I do believe you need it. (Alan Ball.)*
- *Then she met a bloke called Fritz. Literally. That was his name. (Simon Bates.)*
- *Nearly all the Brazilian fans are wearing yellow shirts. It's a fabulous kaleidoscope of colour. (John Motson.)*
- *There's no such thing as a lack of confidence. You either have it or you don't. (Rob Andrew.)*
- *Brazil, the favourites – if they are the favourites ... which they are. (Brian Clough, with faint echoes of Winnie the Pooh.)*

JOURNALESE

The peculiar style adopted for newspaper reports and stories, especially tabloids. The theory behind it is to keep the language snappy and graphic. The practice results in a sort of code from which no one dare deviate for fear of being misunderstood, and which in itself becomes a string of clichés. Its characteristic features are analysed by Fritz Spiegl in *Keep Taking the Tabloids* (London, 1983). They include specialized vocabulary, such as *beleaguered, bronzed and fit, confirmed bachelor, crucify, flying high, kiss-and-tell, lash out, pundit, red-faced, rumpus, saucy* and *track record*. It is regularly spoofed in *Private Eye's* sports page satire. For example:

> *The soccer world was rocked to its foundations last night when Neasden's ashen-faced manager Ron Knee complained that no one had offered him any money all season. Said the tight-lipped mastermind of the eleven-man defence system ...*

A distinctive use of adverbs as sentence-openers is presumably designed to ensure that the reader is led to make a desired response to the news it heralds, instead of being allowed to read the report and perhaps draw conclusions that might run counter to the editorial slant. Spiegl satirizes it pithily by applying it to the journalist's rewrite of Genesis as follows:

> *Initially, God created the heavens and the earth. Basically, the earth was without form, and void. Noticeably, darkness was upon the face of the deep. Reportedly, the spirit of God moved upon the face of the waters. Loftily, God said Let there be light. Predictably, there was light. Brilliantly, God called the light Day ...*

See also *Headlines* (page 137) and *Cliché* (page 125).

Game
Agree on any well-known story and rewrite it in journalese. Then compare the results. Unlike most word games of this sort, the aim is to avoid writing anything original. Instead, wherever two or more players have used the same cliché, each one of them scores as many points for it as the number of players who used it.

LADDER

See *Metagram* (page 150).

LAPSUS LINGUAE

A slip of the tongue. See *Spoonerism* (page 173).

LAST WORDS

See *Famous last words* (page 135).

LIFF-WORD

A place-name to which a more useful meaning has been attached, from Adams and Lloyd, *The Meaning of Liff*. See *Eponym* (page 133).

LIMERICK

> *There was a young writer called Lear*
> *Who made limericks his career*
>   *Till now they're so popular*
>   *No one can stop. (You'll a-*
> *gree* they're as many as we're.)

Evidently named after the Irish county or town, possibly through a misunderstood connection with recitation festivals known to have been traditionally held there, the limerick is described (by W. S. Baring-Gould, in *The Lure of the Limerick*) as the only true form of English folk ballad still extant. In other words, the best ones are anonymous, bawdy and strangely compelling.

> *The limerick's a verse form complex*
> *Whose topics run chiefly to sex –*
> *It's famed for its virgins*
> *And vicars with urgin's*
> *And vulgar erotic effects.*

I quote from memory. If the wording is not precisely as it appears in your own repertoire, remember that the essence of folk art lies in spontaneous re-creation by the performer.

Limericks are popularly thought to have been invented by Edward Lear, but he truthfully claimed no more than to have exploited a verse form already current at his birth, and which was not to receive the name limerick until after his death. Lear's 212 limericks are typified by the following example:

> *There was an old man with a beard*
> *Who said 'It is just as I feared –*
> *Two owls and a wren,*
> *Four larks and a hen*
> *Have all made their nest in my beard'.*

The verse form itself can be traced back much further. Its stress pattern (1-2-3, 1-2-3, 1-2, 1-2, 1-2-3) is an obvious variant of the traditional ballad quatrain exemplified by *The Rime of the Ancient Mariner* – i.e. 1-2-3-4, 1-2-3, 1-2-3-4, 1-2-3, with 1-2-3-4 sometimes varied to 1-2, 1-2 by means of an internal rhyme. Similar in form are children's rhymes such as *Tell-tale tit, Your tongue shall be slit,* and *One, two, three, Mother caught a flea.* Also similar is the form employed by Edward Fitzgerald for his umpteen similar paraphrases of the *Rubáiyát of Omar Khayyám*, of which the first and best appeared in 1859:

> *'Tis all a chequer-board of nights and days*
> *Where Destiny with men for pieces plays:*
> *Hither and thither moves, and mates, and slays,*
> *And one by one back in the closet lays.*

Stanzas in quasi-limerick form can be found in Shakespeare, in the poetry of Elizabeth I, and as far back as *Sumer is a-cumen in* (c.1300):

Ewè bleateth after lamb
Low'th after calvè cou:
    Bullock starteth,
    Buckè farteth,
Merry sing cuckoo!

At least four features distinguish the true limerick from such possible ancestors. One is its anapaestic rhythm (*de-DIDdly-DIDdly-DEE*) as opposed to the more traditional iambic rhythm (*de-DUM-de-DUM-de-DUM*). Elizabeth Tudor's quasi-limerick shows how poorly the iamb fits the stress pattern:

The daughter of debate
Who discord aye doth sow
    Hath reaped no gain
    Where former reign
Hath taught still peace to grow.

Another is its perfect self-containment – it has its own beginning, middle and end, and its end is not that of a free-chain poetic molecule. The beginning normally introduces a subject and a place in the first line, and a potentially embarrassing peculiarity of the subject in the second. The rhyming couplet forming the middle brings about the very circumstance most inimical to the potential embarrassment, and the last line rams home the inevitable but unobvious consequence. Sagas have been composed in a succession of limerick stanzas, but this is like basing a symphony on a folk-tune: as Constant Lambert once said, all you can do is keep repeating it, only a bit louder each time.

A third is its distinctive rhyme scheme (AABBA), and the fourth its wit, preferably ribald in flavour.

Given these strict constraints, it is in the ingeniousness of its rhyme that the limerick offers the greatest scope for creative exploration and surprise:

There was a young lady of Chichester
Who made all the saints in their niches stir;
    One morning at mattins
    The shape of her satins
Made the Bishop of Chichester's breeches stir.

Even so, I have a particular liking for limericks that deliberately don't rhyme, such as the one about the old man of Dunoon, who always ate soup with a fork. Here are two of mine:

There was a young fellow of Llan-
fairpwllgwyngyllgoger-
    ychwyrndrobwll-
    llantysiliogo-
gogoch. So he moved. (To Japan.)

There was a young fellow of Ryde
Who decided to walk for a change.
    When they said 'It don't rhyme'
    He replied 'I should coco –
Neither does Paradise Lost'.

Game
Each player in turn selects a place-name from a gazetteer and everyone writes a limerick with the place-name at the end of the first line.

LIPOGRAM
(Greek, 'lacking a letter')

Composing text with no occurrence of a given letter is an ancient literary exercise. The 5th-century Greek poet Tryphiodorus wrote an epic about Ulysses in 24 books, the first omitting alpha, the second beta, and so on throughout the Greek alphabet. The Roman writer Fulgentius performed a similar feat in 23 books for the Latin alphabet. The difficulty of composition varies in direct proportion to the relative frequency of the omitted letter. An outstanding *tour de force* of modern times is Ernest Vincent Wright's 50,000 word novel *Gadsby*, published in 1939, in which the most common letter in the English alphabet, E, never appears. More remarkably, Georges Perec's French lipogrammatic novel *Disparition* (1969), which also omits E, was published in 1994 in an E-qually lipogrammatic English translation by Gilbert Adair, and Paul Gray's review of it in *Time* magazine (27 February 1995) performs precisely the same feat.

Rewriting well-known passages of text in lipogrammatic form makes a good game or competition. Lacking E, Hamlet's soliloquy begins *Living or not living – that is what I ask,* while Edgar Allan Poe's *The Raven* begins:

> *'Twas upon a midnight tristful I sat poring, wan and wistful,*
> *Through many a quaint and curious list full of my consorts slain...*

and incorporates the recurring refrain:

> *Quoth that Black Bird 'Not again!'*

The American word-gamer A. Ross Eckler constructed several versions of *Mary had a little lamb*, omitting a different common letter each time. What's missing from this one (apart from J, X and Z)?

> *Mary had a little lamb*
> *With fleece a pale white hue,*
> *And everywhere that Mary went*
> *The lamb kept her in view;*
> *To academe he went with her,*
> *Illegal, and quite rare;*
> *It made the children laugh and play*
> *To view a lamb in there.*

Lipopangram. More ingenious is the compound of a lipogram with a pangram which employs every letter of the alphabet except the one to be omitted. The challenge is increased by compressing this feat into a rhyming quatrain. Willard Espy quotes an anonymous poem of three such verses omitting E:

> *Bold Nassan quits his caravan*
> *A hazy mountain grot to scan;*
> *Climb rocks to spy his way,*
> *Doth tax his sight, but far doth stray.*

> *Not work of man, nor sport of child,*
> *Finds Nassan in that mazy wild;*
> *Lax grow his joints, limbs toil in vain*
> *Poor wight! why didst thou quit that plain?*

> *Vainly for succour Nassan calls,*
> *Know, Zillah, that thy Nassan falls;*
> *But prowling wolf and fox may joy*
> *To quarry on thy Arab boy.*

For the reader, the trouble with lipograms is that in order to appreciate them you have to concentrate on what is not there, which makes it hard to appreciate the remainder.

A related puzzle, though not strictly a lipogram, is that of a piece of text in which a frequently occurring letter has merely been suppressed. Espy, again, offers this C-less passage on the Coptic Creed:

> *The opti reed has a haste harm. It hose, one assumes, not to be lever; it neither heats the ripple, nor hides the razed sinner for his rude rime; it is not old. Then leave to it; ere thy grave loses, thou mayst find here the hart to the rest thou ravest to limb.*

LOGOGRAM
(Greek, a 'word-letter')

A sign or symbol standing for a word, like the sign ♥ in the sticker

If intended as a puzzle, it is a *logograph*. Both terms have been used for various games involving series of words which have letters in common, such as those appearing in the games section under titles like *Beheadals, Curtailments,* and *In-words.* A once popular Victorian puzzle involved a series of verses containing clues to a series of words that can all be made from a keyword. Here's an elementary example that I've just made up. The verse reads:

> *My lady brewed a honeyed cup*
> *That brewed her mother's anger up.*

The keyword DAME *(my lady)* yields the subsequent words MADE *(brewed),* MEAD *(honeyed cup),* DAM *(mother),* MAD *(angry).*

> **Game**
> *If you set this as a competition you can hardly fail, between you, to come up with something much better.*

LONGEST WORD

What's the longest word in the English language? When I was in primary school the answer was 'Elastic, because it stretches'. That remains the only sensible answer today, for if you try to take the question seriously, you find that it only raises more questions than it answers. Firstly, *whose* English language? Is the English of Shakespeare the same as that of James Joyce, or the *Oxford English Dictionary,* or *Mary Poppins,* or of modern biochemistry? Secondly, is any proposed word really English? Thirdly, is it really useful? To demonstrate the problems raised in practice, here's a critical list of some contenders:

HONORIFICABILITUDINITATIBUS (27) Shakespeare's longest word means 'honourableness' and occurs in *Love's Labour's Lost,* but it is obviously more Latin than English.

ANTIDISESTABLISHMENTARIANISM (28) remains the only English word likely to entertain any hope of becoming topical again. You can lengthen it by prefixing *pro-, ultra-, pseudo-,* etc, though to no great effect.

FLOCCINAUCINIHILIPILIFICATION (29) 'The act of despising as worthless' – remains the longest in the *Oxford English Dictionary,* but, again, sounds more Latin than English.

SUPERCALIFRAGILISTICEXPIALIDOCIOUS (34), an adjective of approbation, was coined for the film *Mary Poppins*, and has since found its way into less discerning dictionaries.

HEPATICOCHOLANGIOCHOLECYSTENTEROSTOMY (37) is a surgically created connection between the gall bladder and a hepatic duct and between the intestine and the gall bladder.

PNEUMONOULTRAMICROSCOPICSILICOVOLCANOCONIOSIS (45) is a miners' disease causing shortness of breath – 'in more ways than one', as somebody once remarked.

OSSEOCARNISANGUINEOVISCERICARTILAGINONERVOMEDULLARY (51) appears in Thomas Love Peacock's novel *Headlong Hall* as a facetious but etymologically defensible way of describing the structure of the human body.

AEQUEOSALINOCALCALINOCERACEOALUMINOSOCUPREOVITRIOLIC (52) was concocted by Dr Edward Strother in the 18th century to describe the spa waters at Bath.

The most fertile source of long words is to be found in the field of complex chemical compounds, though it could be argued that they are not so much words as list of words stuck together like long-chain molecules. Although longer ones have been concocted, the longest that has actually been published in a genuine context is the 1185-letter name for a strain of the Tobacco Mosaic Virus. It consists of repetitions, in various combinations, of the components ACETYL, ALANYL, GLYCYL, GLUTAMINYL, LEUCYL, PARAGINYL, PROLYL, SERYL, THREONYL, TRYPTOPHYL, VALYL, and a few others. You'll find it in full in a book by Hellweg republished as *The Wordsworth Book of Intriguing Words*. Alternatively, you could just write them all on blank cards and pull them out of a witty retort, which is probably what those chemists did in the first place.

LOST CONSONANTS

A form of illustrated word play devised by Graham Rawle and published regularly in the *Guardian* newspaper. Each item is a photomontage appropriately illustrating a phrase from which one consonant has been deliberately omitted – a *monolipogram*, I suppose. One that I don't think has yet been used would be a picture of a marquee covered with snow, and captioned *Now is the winter of our disco tent*.

> **Game**
> *Everybody draws a picture and everybody else has to guess
> what consonantally challenged caption it illustrates.*

MACARONIC

A passage of text, usually verse, written in two different languages randomly juxtaposed – originally Latin and one's own vernacular. The term probably comes from *macaroni*, used as a metaphor for a meaningless jumble. In this example the four languages are virtually isolated from one another:

> *Un an plus tard ma femme me dit*
> *Wir bleiben doch zu Hause, wie?*
> *Si, Cara, faccio ci che vuoi,*
> *(Congratulations – it's a boy!)*

(From *Pauvre Henri*, a saga by A. E. Hopkins, *Logophile* Vol.II, No.5)

However, the effect is more satisfying, not to say funnier, when they are more thoroughly mingled, as in this anonymous Anglo-Latin macaronic quoted by Willard Espy:

> Parvus Jacobus Horner
> Sedebat in corner
> Edens a Christmas pie:
> Inferuit thumb,
> Extraherit plum
> Clamans 'Quid sharp puer am I!'

In the long-lost days of classical education, a much favoured recreation was the production of verses in so-called Pig Latin, which may be allowed to squeak for itself:

> Lightibus outibus in a parlorum
> Boyibus kissibus sweeti girlorum;
> Daddibus hearibus loudi smackorum,
> Comibus quickibus with a cluborum.
> Boyibus gettibus hardi spankorum,
> Landibus nextibus outside a doorum;
> Gettibus uppibus with a limporum,
> Swearibus kissibus girli nomorum.

Several examples of macaronic verse in Medieval Latin and Old French occur in the lyrics of *Carmina Burana,* made famous by Carl Orff's concert setting. The one beginning *Dies, Nox et Omnia* may be done into English and modern French as:

> Be it night or be it day
> In my timeless disarray
> Hearing maidens bavarder
>   Me fait complaindre:
> And the more I sigh away
>   Plus me sens craindre.

A macaronic variation is that in which a passage in one language is written as if it were a passage in another, producing an effect comparable to that of *Anguish languish* (see page 119). As Molesworth Junior noted in *Down with Skool!* (by Geoffrey Willans and Ronald Searle), all Latin masters have one joke, viz:

> Caesar adsum jam forte, Brutus aderat

which actually means 'Caesar, here perchance I am; Brutus came before', but may be read as 'Caesar 'ad some jam for tea, Brutus 'ad a rat'. But at this point macaronimania passes into the stage of 'translooting' — for which, see *Anguish languish* (page 119).

See also *Franglais* (page 135), *Howler* (page 140), *Mistranslation* (page 152).

MALAPROPISM

The use, through ignorance, of a word similar to but different in meaning from the one intended. The resultant word is consequently not *à propos* but *mal à propos,* thereby furnishing Sheridan with the name of his best-known character. Mrs Malaprop, in *The Rivals* (1775), produces the classic line 'If I reprehend anything in this world, it is the use of my oracular tongue, and a nice derangement of epitaphs'.

Malapropisms are a species of solecism or barbarism (see page 121). But whereas barbarisms tend to be widepread and irritating, malapropisms are characteristically individual and humorous, albeit unintentionally. One is more likely to laugh at than castigate the statement : *There's a dirge of light music on the radio.* And Richard Nixon is quoted as eulogizing Adlai Stevenson thus: *'In eloquence he had no peer, and very few equals.'*

METAGRAM (PARAGRAM)
(Greek, 'change word')

A series of words each differing from the next by one letter. Under the title *Doublets*, Lewis Carroll seems first to have proposed the puzzle, in a letter to *Vanity Fair*, of converting one word into its opposite by such means. The example he quoted was HEAD to TAIL in five steps as follows:

0.	H	E	A	D
1.	H	E	A	L
2.	T	E	A	L
3.	T	A	L	L
4.	T	A	I	L

Chains of five-letter words are feasible, and six-letter chains are occasionally attempted. Word chains are closely related to *Word squares* (see page 176).

METAPHOR
(Greek, 'bearing a change')

A metaphor is a word or concept standing for another word or concept, typically for an artistic or striking effect, or to soften an otherwise harsh idea, in which case it is a *euphemism* (see page 134). For example, when a camel is described as the ship of the desert, the desert is real and the ship is metaphorical. In the Arab world, on the other hand, a ship might be referred to as the camel of the sea, in which case the sea is real and the camel metaphorical. Similarly, passing a camel through the eye of a needle is more of a metaphorical than a practical proposition.

Word-gamers are more interested in 'mixed metaphors'. Metaphors become mixed when their perpetrators switch between two incongruous images, or confuse the elements of two or more individual specimens. Real-life examples are regularly exhibited in the *Colemanballs* column of *Private Eye*:

● *It all depends on whether there are any more hot potatoes waiting to come over the horizon. (Tory MP for Bedford South West, Radio 3)*
● *That shot knocked the stuffing out of his sails. (Frew McMillan, BBC 2)*
● *After 11 days, we're still sharp as a button. (David Vine, BBC 2)*
● *Beckenbauer really has gambled all his eggs. (Ron Atkinson, ITV)*
● *There's one more result to give you, just to put the jigsaw into focus. (Andy Peebles, Radio 1)*

Some often repeated phrases entangle their metaphorical roots so subtly that that you hardly notice them in everyday speech. A computer is advertised as being *based around* a particular chip; a topic of conversation is said to *centre around* this, that or the other. It is only when you look at these inanities literally that you recognize the inappropriateness of the metaphor. What you do with a base is set something *on* it, not around it; and what you do *around* something is not *centre* but *revolve.*

METATHESIS

See *Spoonerism* (page 173).

MINGLISH

A term devised by journalist Paul Jennings to denote the sort of mangled English produced by those who translate into the language without being able to speak it, and some variations of English that produce a similar effect on the British ear or eye. For the former, see *Mistranslation,* page 152. The latter is not necessarily due to mistranslation – quite often it derives from varieties of English that have become naturalized in other parts of the world and followed local developments. Apart from the misprint *quene* for *queue,* the following extract from an advertisement in an Indian newspaper may well sound unremarkable to its readers:

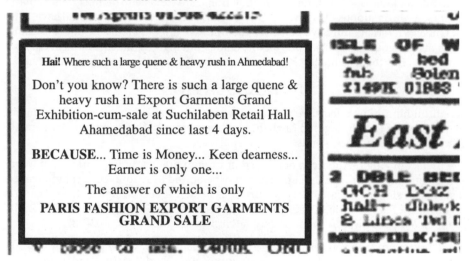

MISQUOTATION AND MISATTRIBUTION

Misquotations are often clichés derived from lines of literature or history whose original features have been eroded into vague generality, like regal images on coins worn smooth by circulation:

● John Bright (1811–1889) wrote *England is the mother of parliaments.* He is routinely misquoted as naming Parliament itself as the mother of parliaments, even by MPs, who ought to know better.

● Every other writer to a newspaper correspondence column avers that Topsy, in *Uncle Tom's Cabin,* 'just grew'. Her actual words were '*I 'spect I grow'd.*'

● Sherlock Holmes didn't quite say 'Elementary, my dear Watson', though he did say 'Elementary!' on being congratulated by Watson on a piece of deduction (in *The Return of Sherlock Holmes*).

● Neil Armstrong didn't quite say 'That's one small step for man, one giant leap for mankind.' That's how it sounded, owing partly to a radio blip and partly to an idiosyncrasy of articulation, but the actual spoken words included an indefinite article: 'one small step for a man'.

● Winston Churchill didn't quite offer 'Blood, tears and sweat', but in his inaugural speech as Prime Minister to the House of Commons in 1940 said 'I have nothing to offer but blood, toil, tears, and sweat.'

● Humphrey Bogart didn't say 'Play it again, Sam' in *Casablanca*. Somebody did say 'Play it, Sam; play *As Time Goes By*', but that was Ingrid Bergman, which makes it a misattribution as well.

● Hermann Goering didn't say 'Whenever I hear the word culture, I reach for my pistol.' He may have misquoted a line from Hans Johst's play *Schlageter* (1934), which translates as 'Whenever I hear the word culture, I get out my Browning.' If so, he missed the point of the punch line, as Browning is both a poet and a machine gun.

● David Jenkins, as Bishop of Durham, didn't describe the Resurrection as merely 'A conjuring trick with bones' – he specifically said it was *'more than'* just a conjuring trick with bones.

Some misquotations, or even imagined quotations, are excusable on the grounds that if the person who is supposed to have said them didn't, they nevertheless should have. Who but Queen Victoria could have delivered the line 'We are not amused'? Michael Caine, in his autobiography *What's it all About?*, denies having originated 'Not many people know that'. But then, as Mandy Rice-Davies really did say, 'He would, wouldn't he?'.

MISTRANSLATION

Delightful humorous effects are produced when non-English-speakers boldly undertake the task of translating into English, or when perfectly fluent writers deliberately parody them to humorous ends.

The dialect of Anglo-American employed in foreign menus, hotels and tourist literature around the world, to which perhaps may be added the more recent phenomenon of surrealist slogans on Japanese tee-shirts, has been dubbed 'Minglish' (see page 151) by journalist Paul Jennings. Here are some gems from a guidebook to *San Gimignano by the Beautiful Towers*, as reported by Julian Bower (in *Logophile*, III-3):

> *Trade expansion was alive and florid for almost two hundred years ... It was just during this year ... that San Gimignano's independency from grass ear ... A few families, the richest ones, try to impose their sovereignty through the joke of reincharges ... The war vicissitudes are a ruffled ball ... [the church] has three naves in carved travertine and is offering a rude mystic spectacle.*

A famous ancestor was a book of Portuguese–English dialogues by P. Carolino, first published in Paris in 1855, of which the English section was reprinted in 1883 under the title *English as She is Spoke.* It was clearly concocted by translating word for word from the French bits of an equivalent Portuguese–French guide. The preface reads:

> *A choice of familiar dialogues, clean of gallicisms and despoiled phrases, it was missing yet to studious portuguese and brazilian youth; and also to persons of other nations ... We expect then, who the little book (for the care what we wrote him, and for her typgraphical correction) that may be worth the acceptation of the studious persons, and especialy of the Youth, at which we dedicate him particularly.*

The dialogues include such titbits as:

> *You hear the birds gurgling? Which pleasure! Which charm!*

The trouble with bilingual phrasebooks is that the natives never seem to have learnt their lines. Jerome K. Jerome recounts, in *Three Men on the Bummel*, what happens when George tests their effectiveness by entering a bootmakers and pretending to be foreign. He raises his hat and says 'I have been recommended to your shop by my friend, Mr X.' In response, the man should have said 'Mr X is a most worthy gentleman; it will give me the greatest pleasure to serve any friend of his.' What he did say was 'Don't know him; never heard of him.' George abandons 'Mr X', and turning back to a previous page, takes a sentence at random ... 'One has told me that you have here boots for sale.' This starts the bootmaker on a tirade which begins 'What d'yu think I keep boots for – t' smell 'em?' and concludes 'Do you think I decorate the shop with 'em to make it look pretty? What d'you take me for – a prize idiot?' (See *Sarcasm*, page 171).

As J. remarks, 'What we wanted was some English equivalent for the well-known German expression *Behalten Sie Ihr Haar auf* ('Keep your hair on').

As for parody, here's Mark Twain demonstrating how much more sexist English would sound if, like German, it dignified nouns with capital initials and marked them as grammatically masculine, feminine and neuter:

> **The Tale of the Fishwife and its Sad Fate** *It is a bleak Day. Hear the Rain, how he pours, and the Hail, how he rattles; and see the Snow, how he drifts along, and oh the Mud, how deep he is! Ah, the poor Fishwife, it is stuck fast in the mire; it has dropped its Basket of Fishes; and its hands have been cut by the Scales as it seized some of the falling Creatures; and one Scale has even got into its Eye, and it cannot get her out. It opens its mouth to cry for help; but if any Sound comes out of him, alas, he is drowned by the Raging of the Storm.*

If this specimen represents English flavoured with German, travelling further along the line produces German flavoured with English. Willard Espy quotes (in *Another Almanac of Words at Play*) some alleged entries from USAF technical literature such as:

> Guided missile: *das sientifike Geschtenwerkes Firenkrakker*
> Rocket engine: *der Firesphitter mit Smokenundschnorten*
> Guidance system: *das Schteerenwerke.*
> Control system: *das Pullenundshovenwerke*
> Warhead: *das Laudenboomer*
> Nuclear warhead: *das Eargeschplitten Laudenboomer*
> Hydrogen device: *das Eargeshphlitten Laudenboomer mit ein Grose Holegraund und Alle Kaputt.*

See also *Anguish languish* (page 119), *Franglais* (page 135), *Howler* (page 140), *Macaronic* (page 148).

Game
The Portuguese–English phrasebook quoted above includes translations of well-known phrases or sayings, such as He is not so devil as he is black, The stone as roll not heap up not foam, After the paunch comes the dance. *Get everyone to devise ten mistranslations along similar lines.*

MNEMONIC

A device for recalling long or intricate lists of things by translating them into a more easily remembered series of associations. Thus the seven classical colours of the rainbow – red, orange, yellow, green, blue, indigo, violet – are made memorable by turning their initials into the sentence 'Richard Of York Gave Battle In Vain'. The order of the geological periods from prehistory till now may be remembered by the observation that 'Camels Often Sit Down Cautiously. Perhaps Their Joints Creak? Early Oiling Might Prevent Permanent Rheumatism'. Or so Gyles Brandreth claims in *Pears Book of Words*. Personally, I find it easier to remember Cambrian, Ordivician, Silurian, Devonian, Carboniferous, Permian, Triassic, Jurassic, Cretaceous, Eocene, Oligocene, Miocene, Pliocene, Pleistocene, Recent. The problem is not so much one of memory as that every time you look away the geologists change them. (Wasn't there a Palaeocene at some stage in the proceedings? Or has it been abolished?)

Psalm 119 is divided into 22 sections, each beginning with a letter of the Hebrew alphabet and all in alphabetical order. The poet may have been indulging in word play, but he has also provided a device by which the reciter can more easily remember the correct order of sections in this exceptionally long psalm.

Mnemonics may also be used to memorize numbers. Pi, best known as the ratio of the diameter to the circumference of a circle, is an endless irrational number approximately equivalent to to 3.1416. Every so often somebody sets a computer to increase the number of places to which it is calculated. In 1983 the record stood at 16,777,216. As few people can remember more than about eight digits at a time without outside help, a popular sport of recreational mathematicians is to devise a passage in which the lengths of consecutive words correspond to the figures to be remembered. Thus pi can be reconstituted 20 decimal places (3.14159265358979323846) by recalling: 'How I wish I could remember to strike while the irons heatedly desecrate clothes. Smoothing out an old elephant gets boring.'

MY FIRST IS IN ...

See *Riddle* (page 169).

NAME

One of the word-gamer's greatest delights lies in devising – or even spotting, because they do occur in real life – names that pun on the character or activity of their subjects. When I was at primary school the height of humour consisted in quoting such book titles and authors as *Lean and Hungry* by Norah Bone, *Caught the Train* by Justin Time, and *Exciting Adventures* by Helen Highwater. I also recollect a strip cartoon called *Just Jake* in the *Daily Mirror,* one of whose characters was a bus conductor called Aubrey Tight. And if you get that, or can even remember what bus conductors are, you must be as old as I am. (Another strip featured a family named *The Flutters,* who lived in a pun called Letsbee Avenue.)

The temptation to make puns of people's names, or names of people's puns, is one which every teacher is naturally drawn to but should at all costs be resisted, as there is nothing more upsetting to the young mind than to have its integrity impugned by a joke on its name. Fortunately, we are not all teachers, and most of us can play about with names to our hearts' content.

Knock-knock jokes are one form of name game. Another is that of occupational names. Staple characters in comics include dentists called I. Pullem and grocers named P. Green, to whom deliveries are made by Laurie Driver. Ida Down would have been a renowned maker of quilts, and Evan Jellicle a local preacher. My own researches in this field have thrown up an unfulfilled boy wonder called Peter Doubt and a happy-go-lucky Bombay builder known as Ram Shackle.

If it wasn't occupations, it was appropriate ranks and titles. No army was complete without its Major Breakthrough, Private Property, or General Lee Speaking, and no navy without Abel Seeman and, your humble servant, Cap'n Hand.

Rather more difficult, but worthwhile if you come up with anything good, is the task of devising questions to which the answer is a single name. For example:

> *What's a good name for a grate?* – Alexander.
> *What's a good name for an eel?* – Achilles.
> *What do you call a man in a hole?* – Doug.
> *How do you greet a flower called Cynthia?* – Hyacinth.

The longest-running outlet for pun-names is that of appropriate authors for carefully concocted book titles. *Feeling Hungry* by Norah Bone is followed by:

Dinner's Up	by Sally Vate
Ethnic Dishes	by Iris Stew
On a Diet	by Einar Fungry
Nearly Didn't Make It	by Justin Thyme
Didn't Make it at All	by Mr Buss
On the Whole	by Brian Large
Various Things	by Miss Ella Neous

I have recently unearthed a history of the slave trade, a joint project by N. Oboe, D. Nose, D. Trubble, R. Seen.

But the real challenge lies in discovering punning names that do *not* appear in the comprehensive list on page 21 of Leslie Dunkling's *Guinness Book of Names*, from which I can't resist citing:

Aaron C. Rescue – Barry D. Hatchett – Erna Living – Gloria Mundy – Iona Mink – Lettice Prey – Lynn C. Doyle – Orson Buggy – Warren Peace.

See also *Eponym* (page 133), *Toponym* (page 174).

> **Games**
> *You can turn any of these exercises into a game by simply getting each player in turn to quote a book title, occupation, rank or title, or whatever it may be, and awarding a point to the first player to remember or deduce the appropriate name – with an extra point to anyone who invents a better one than intended by the setter. If nobody comes up with a good name within a suitable period of time, the point is scored by the player who set the trap.*

NEOLOGISM
(Greek, 'newness' or 'novelty')

The invention of a new device, the discovery of a new phenomenon of nature and the awareness of a new social experience are examples of circumstances which require someone to coin a new word (*television, helicopter, dinosaur, jet lag*) or extend the range of meaning of an existing word (*atmosphere* was first borrowed from meteorology and applied to mood by Coleridge Taylor). Neologisms are often resisted. Phillips's *New World of Words* (1678) listed as 'objectionable' such novelties as *agonize, bibliography, ferocious* and *misogynist*. Most of the words we use unquestioningly today were once neologisms, and many enjoy known ascriptions. For example, Aristotle coined the word from which *energy* derives, and Cicero those from which we get *indifference, moral,* and *quality.* The opposite of Rabelais's *gargantuan* is Swift's *lilliputian.* Others have given us *pandemonium* (Milton), *serendipity* (Walpole), *international* (Bentham), *boredom* (Carlyle, reputedly), and *agnostic* (Huxley). Richard Turner of Preston, a temperance campaigner with a stutter, accidentally transformed *total* into *teetotal* in 1883. Remarkably, the word *pacifism* did not appear until the 1914–18 war, from which period, equally surprisingly, dates *camouflage.*

More interesting to word-gamers are those invented for one-off or humorous effects – so see, instead, *Nonce word* (below).

NONCE WORD

A word invented for the nonce, i.e. for a one-off occasion. The phonetic resemblance to *nonsense* is as appropriate as it is fortuitous, as such words are most often devised for humorous effect. The truly felicitous ones may be admitted as members of the regular lexicon, having first passed through the state of *neologism,* which is akin to purgatory. Invented words that have emerged from purgatory to the paradise of the dictionary include Lewis Carroll's *chortle* and the mathematician Kasner's *googol* (for the number written as 10^{100}, or 1 followed by 100 zeros). The *quark,* one of three elementary particles, was named after a word coined for purposes other than sub-atomic physics by James Joyce in *Finnegans Wake* (1939), which is written almost entirely in the Anglo-Irish dialect of Nonce. But the source of *widget* remains a mystery.

Children are a great source of nonce words. At the age of three, my daughter described a roof with a sloping edge that appeared serrated in outline as *sperky.* She also announced that when the cat settled down in her toy-box 'I had to *hodge her out*'. We've used *hodge* ever since.

Some adults have the happy knack of devising nonce words. The American humorist Gelett Burgess was one – he gave us, for example, *bromide* (for a bore), and *blurb,* and many other coinages that have not been so successful, yet have a charm of their own. They include:

> *allibosh* – a glaringly obvious falsehood
> *cowcat* – a person whose main function is to occupy space
> *diabob* – a tasteless piece of decoration or amateur work of art
> *jujasm* – a much-needed relief, long desired satisfaction
> *voip* – food that gives no gastronomic pleasure, is filling but tasteless
> *yamnoy* – a bulky or unmanageable object, one you don't know how to carry

James Thurber invented words to incarnate certain hitherto rare or non-existent letter combinations. For -sgr- he proposed:

> *blessgravy* – a minister or cleric, head of family, or anyone else who says grace
> *fussgrape* – one who toys with his food; a scornmuffin, a shuncabbage
> *kissgranny* – a man who favours older women

The reverse of coining words to denote hitherto unrecognized phenomena is that of ascribing meanings to plausible but hitherto non-existing word forms. It forms the subject of many a magazine competition. Some prizewinning entries from *Logophile* include:

> *trellable – describes a climbing plant (c.f. trellis)*
> *porry* – a startling mixture (from potpourri)
> *hambo* – correct response to a toast such as 'Cheers!' or 'Here's mud in your eye', roughly equivalent to 'And the same to you'
> *modition* – (statistics) a method of interpolating least-square fits in a bivariant

distribution by considering the mode of one variable while allowing the other to take arbitrary values in an elliptic range

Closely related, and generally funnier, are *Liff-words* – words derived by the attachment of more useful meanings to place-names, primarily by Douglas Adams and John Lloyd. See *Eponyms* (page 133).

> **Games**
> *See* Fictionary dictionary *(page 90)*, Fabulary vocabulary *(page 92)*. *Also: Each player in turn proposes a rare letter combination, such as* -SGR-, *and everyone invents five words, plus definitions, that embody it. Score how you like, if at all.*

OUNCE, DICE, TRICE

The title of a book by Alister Reid, published in 1958, which, for all its slimness, is worth its weight in Goldilocks for a series of quasi-numerals of the following type:

OUNCE	INSTANT	ACREAGE
DICE	DISTANT	BROKERAGE
TRICE	TRYST	CRIBBAGE
QUARTZ	CATALYST	CARTHAGE
QUINCE	QUEST	CAGE
SAGO	SYCAMORE	SINK
SERPENT	SOPHOMORE	SENTIMENT
OXYGEN	OCULIST	OINTMENT
NITROGEN	NOVELIST	NUTMEG
DENIM	DENTIST	DOOM

> **Game**
> *Read these out until everyone has got the idea and then allow five minutes to see who can come up with the most amusing variation. Our efforts incorporated other spontaneous variations, such as counting up to 12* (Uncle, Ducal, Treacle, Focal, Fizzle, Sizzle, Settle, Ogle, Nigel, Deckle, Electoral, Duodenal) *and forming a series from paired compounds* (Won-Ton, Free-Fall, Fire-Ship, Servant-Maid, Mine-Stone).

OVERSPECIALIZED WORD

A word whose meaning is so obscure or long-winded, or both, that you wonder why anyone bothered to coin it in the first place. Ross Eckler, the American word-gaming expert, introduced them in *Logophile* magazine, and elicited some further excellent examples from interested readers (of long-winded dictionaries). They include the following, all recorded in the *Oxford English Dictionary* unless otherwise attributed:

ambilevous – left-handed on both sides
anemocracy – government by wind
nosarian – one who argues there is no limit to the possible largeness of a nose (*Webster's Second*)
nudiustertian – pertaining to the day before yesterday
paneity – the state of being bread
qualtagh – the first person to enter a house on New Year's Day

serein – fine rain falling from a cloudless sky after sunset
shrewstruck – struck by a shrew (Yes; obviously – but why? And how?)
(Webster's Second)
supermuscan – beyond the power of a fly (as in what isn't?) *(Webster's Second)*
ucalegon – a neighbour whose house is on fire *(Random House Unabridged)*

Some contributors offered words from other languages:

hvannrock – cliff-ledge where angelica grows *(Norwegian)*
ling – a horse passing wind after eating corn *(Chinese)*
megarizein – to throw piglets into holes in the ground *(Greek)*
mihrap – a woman still beautiful though no longer young *(Turkish)*
nemimi – the ears of someone asleep *(Japanese)*
rhaphanidoun – to thrust a radish up the fundament *(Greek)*
sin – the mournful feeling occasioned by observing the fall of a leaf in autumn
(Chinese)
t'han – to pretend to look near whilst cherishing distant views *(Chinese)*

See also *Underemployed word* (page 175).

OXYMORON
(Greek, 'sharply foolish')

A figure of speech which unites opposites for a pointed effect; an apparent contradiction in terms. The classic example is from Tennyson:

His honour rooted in dishonour stood,
And faith unfaithful kept him falsely true.

Everyday language throws up many apparent yet unquestioned contradictions in terms. Unless they are created for deliberate effect, they can hardly be dignified with the literary term, but that is no reason for them to escape the notice of the true word-gamer. How about, for example, such terms as *Military Intelligence*, or *Progressive Conservative?*

> **Game**
> *See who can compile the longest list of oxymoronic, or at least self-contradictory, phrases you might hear in everyday speech. A few that spring to my mind are:* pretty ugly, jolly sad, barely clothed, thoroughly superficial, basically over the top, disgustingly healthy. *And I have just invented* utterly ineffable, *which I suppose is an oxymoronic pun, or poxymoron.*

PALINDROME
(Greek, 'running backwards again')

A word, phrase or sentence that can be meaningfully read in either direction. Several types may be distinguished. As I am not aware of any standardized terminology for them, I will propose my own.

1. An optical palindrome is one that reads intelligibly upside down or mirror-wise (bilaterally rotated), or both. An example that always works is NOON, and MOW is acceptable if printed in the correct typeface. Some only work in handwriting, as illustrated by this version of chump:

chump

2. A symmetrical palindrome is one that reads the same in either direction. The classic example is the supposed first introductory utterances made in the Garden of Eden:

> *He:* Madam, I'm Adam.
> *She:* Eve.

3. An asymmetrical palindrome reads differently in opposite directions. Not surprisingly, most palindromes are of this sort. My favourite is:

> *A man – a plan – a canal – Panama!*

(Largely because I love the following parody of it: *A man – a plan – a canal – Suez!*)

4. A verbal or syntactic palindrome is a sentence, passage of text, or even a whole book, in which it is not the letters of individual words but the words themselves that are reversed. These may also be symmetrical or asymmetrical. Here are two by J. A. Lindon:

> *So patient a doctor to doctor a patient so!*
> *Girl, bathing on Bikini, eyeing boy, finds boy eyeing bikini on bathing girl.*

Palindromes were not unknown to Classical Greeks and Romans, but the first published in English was by John Taylor, the Water Poet, who in 1614 offered five shillings to anyone who could improve on

> *Lewd did I live, & evil I did dwel.*

Not bad for a beginner, despite the suspect ampersand and the 17th-century liberty of spelling. No one is reported to have accepted the challenge until long after Taylor's death, when, in 1821, it was re-issued in *The Monthly Magazine and Literary Journal*, and yielded a flock of palindromes including the now classic

> *Able was I ere I saw Elba* (a reference to Napoleon).

Of the many more that have been devised since, some of the most noteworthy are:

> *Dennis and Edna sinned.*
> *Dog, a devil deified, deified lived a god.*
> *Draw pupil's lip upward*
> *Egad, a base tone denotes a bad age.*
> *Live dirt, up a side-track carted, is a putrid evil.*
> *Satan, oscillate my metallic sonatas.*
> *Straw? No, too stupid a fad. I put soot on warts.*
> *Sums are not set as a test on Erasmus.*

Others will be found, as these were, in the pages of the great masters such as Willard Espy (*The Game of Words*) and Tony Augarde (*The Oxford Guide to Word Games*). Devising palindromes offers little to an evening of social entertainment. It is a pastime best pursued in an ivory tower in the middle of a jungle on a desert island on a wet Tuesday afternoon.

PANGRAM
(Greek, 'all (the) letters')

One of the first things I learnt from *The Children's Encyclopaedia* was which verse of the Bible was the shortest (John 11:35), closely followed by which one contained every letter of the alphabet:

> And I, even I, Ataxerxes the King, do make a decree to all the treasurers which are beyond the river, that whatsoever Ezra the priest, the scribe of the law of the God of heaven, shall require of you, it be done speedily. (Ezra 7:21)

Oh, unless you count J as a letter of the alphabet. (What a pity Ataxerxes did not finish *It shall be done with jolly great speed.*)

A passage of text containing every letter of the alphabet is a pangram. A well-known pangram formerly used for testing second-hand typewriters is *The quick brown fox jumps over a lazy dog.* As pangrams go, this one is not particularly efficient. It contains 33 letters, which represents a redundancy of nine over the 26 letters of the alphabet, or an 'efficiency' of 74 per cent ($26/35 \times 100$), though it can be improved to 32 letters (76.5%) as shown below. On the other hand, it does make for a reasonable degree of sense when compared with others of similar length. For the sorry fact of the matter is that as the number of redundant letters decreases in the quest for the ultimate goal of a 100% efficient 26-letter pangram, a corresponding increase is noted in the degree of explanation required to explain what the sentence is purporting to convey. Thus:

> 35 Many-wived Jack laughs at probe of sex quiz.
> 34 Xylophone wizard begets quick jive form.
> 33 The quick brown fox jumps over a lazy dog.
> 32 Chunky Jap quizmaster gave flawed box.
> 32 Pack my bag with five dozen liquor jugs.
> 32 Quick, brown fox, jump over the lazy dogs!
> 31 Jackdaws love my big sphinx of quartz.
> 30 Judges vomit; few quiz pharynx block.
> 29 Quick wafting zephyrs vex bold Jim.
> 28 Waltz, nymph, for quick jigs vex Bud.
> 28 Blowzy frights vex, and jump quick.
> 27 Brick quiz whangs jumpy veldt fox.
> 26 Quartz glyph job vex'd cwm finks.

The last of these represents the headline that might be encountered in an archaeological magazine, when some treacherous people from a Welsh valley found themselves irked at the discovery of a (presumably forged) rock carving in quartz.

> **Game**
> *Each player in turn nominates a current news story, and the winner is the player who, within two minutes, devises an appropriate headline containing as many different letters as possible.*

PARAGRAM

See *Metagram* (page 150).

PARODY

(Greek, a 'burlesque poem' or 'song')

A passage of text written in exaggerated imitation of an author (or anonymous work), whether for the purpose of ridicule or for humorous effect in its own right. As in so many areas of humorous literature, you can't beat Lewis Carroll, whom it is always a delight to quote, especially now that he's out of copyright. My particular favourite is *Hiawatha's Photographing*, which begins:

> From his shoulder Hiawatha
> Took the camera of rosewood,
> Made of sliding, folding rosewood;
> Neatly put it all together.
> In its case it lay compactly,
> Folded into nearly nothing;
> But he opened out the hinges,
> Pushed and pulled the joints and hinges,
> Till it looked all squares and oblongs
> Like a complicated figure
> In the Second Book of Euclid.

And gets even funnier as it goes along.

> **Game**
> *One player selects a short poem, or a self-contained passage from a long poem, and reads it out, or (preferably) comes equipped with photocopies of it. The obvious requirement is for everyone to write a parody of it within a specified period of time, say 15 minutes. As a refinement, another player, before knowing what the selection is, specifies the obsession of the parodist. Players may accordingly be required to rewrite Wordsworth's* Daffodils *from the perspective of an opposition backbencher, or* The Stately Homes of England *from that of a burglar.*

PARONOMASIA

See *Pun* (page 164).

POLITICAL CORRECTNESS

An American use of language originating in the desire to avoid giving offence to individuals or minority groups – a practice laudable in itself but open to ridicule when carried to extremes. It is for example:

● **sexist** to refer to adult females as *ladies*, and some object to *women*, holding that it should be spelt *wimmyn* in order to avoid the suggestion that they are a non-standard variation of *men*.

● **ageist** to refer to *the old folks at home*. Now that even *senior citizens* has gone out of fashion it is better to employ a more positive-sounding phrase like *the chronologically gifted at personal residential units*. (I originally wrote *familial residential units*, but then discovered that such language was *familist.*)

● **ableist** to describe cripples as *handicapped* or *physically disadvantaged*: they are *differently abled*. The phrase *I see what you mean* is ableist, discriminating as it does against those who who enjoy alternative degrees of eyesight. Replace with *I understand you*, even if this does discriminate against those who find you totally unintelligible.

● **anthropocist** or **speciesist** to refer to animal companions as *pets*, and some harbour suspicions about the word *animal* itself – why not just *companions*, without drawing attention to their democratically exercised right of not belonging to the same genus as ourselves? (Not *human race,* of course – *human* is sexist, and *race* is racist, and never the twain shall meet.) Some recommend *protectors*, but this makes little impression on my four cats, to say nothing of the guinea pig.

The particular language we speak shapes the way in which we view the world and hence the particular thought and culture we develop. It is but a short step from this to the idea that you can change people's undesirable attitudes to others by getting them to change their language. The practical problem is, however, the same as that with euphemisms (see page 134) – namely, that after a while the euphemistic term itself becomes imbued with the negative concept lying behind it, and has to be replaced with something new. Political correct terms, like euphemisms, resemble clean dressings on wounds: they get soiled by seepage and have to be replaced yet again. And by the time one wound has gone, another one opens up somewhere else. Thus *cripple* is now virtually a swearword, *handicapped* is reprehensible, and *physically disadvantaged* slightly suspect. By the time this book is published *differently abled* may well be on the way out, to be replaced by goodness knows what. Another problem is the lack of any centralized authority on political correctness. Terms promoted by some people are denounced as heretical by others, with the result that any outsider trying to play the game is simply stepping through a minefield established by several opposing camps.

Another problem is that so much of it is motivated by ignorance. An example of this is the objection to *fellow* in the mistaken belief that it is an inherently masculine word. I recently came across the assertion that the terms *homo-* and *hetero-sexual* were coined as a form of verbal discrimination against gays. A more objective pair of words would have been hard to find at the time they were coined. The writer probably thought *homo-* derived from the Latin for a male person, which is wrong on both counts. *Homo-* actually derives from the Greek word meaning 'same'.

A peculiar spin-off from PC language in its euphemistic mode is the insistence on falsifying bad news to make it sound good. While this is understandable in the case of *partially sighted* for the more meaningful *partially blind,* it becomes risible in the case of the weather-forecast reporter who was sacked from the Californian radio station KMJ for refusing to re-word *a chance of rain* to *a probability of sunshine,* and *partly cloudy* to *largely sunny.* (See the *Guardian,* 29–4–95, p.16.)

On the plus side, PC language (an abbreviation which to my ears makes it sound even more like a product of the Thought Police) has given rise to some endearingly ingenious modes of expression. It is a game in itself to seek to distinguish between a genuine politically-correct term and a spoof. The following terms, though not the interpreta-tions, are all genuine. (Source references are quoted in Beard, Cerf, *The Official Politically Correct Dictionary and Handbook,* London–New York–Toronto 1992.)

additional preparation	remedial classes
efemcipated	freed from male domination (or, possibly, constipation)
involuntarily leisured	out of work
over-exploited nations	underdeveloped nations
sinistromanualism	oppression of left-handers by right-handers
sobriety-deprived	pissed as a newt
socially misaligned	psychotic
straw-person	scare-bird (*scarecrow* is crowist)
temporally challenged	habitually late
terminally inconvenienced	dead

P.S. The politically-correct form of *Eskimo Nell* is *Inuit Eleanor.*

PORTMANTEAU WORD

Lewis Carroll coined this term, from the French for a type of suitcase with two compartments, for an invented word formed from the combination of two or more words already existing. He thus explains the word *slithy,* in the poem *Jabberwocky,* as a cross between *slimy* and *lithe.* Not that he was the first to do so: William Blake, you may recall, addressed a poem to *Nobodaddy.* The portmanteau has subsequently become a regular device for creating useful words and names, almost as popular in this respect as *acronyms* (see page 111), with which it overlaps. Many are devised as trade names, notably *Brymay* for the brand of matches made by Bryant and May Ltd – now sadly defunct.

Portmanteaux that have entered the language so successfully as to require no further explanation include:

brunch	= breakfast + lunch
chunnel	= channel + tunnel
electrocute	= electric + execute
guestimate	= guess + estimate
motel	= motor + hotel
motorcade	= motor car + cavalcade
Oxbridge	= Oxford + Cambridge
smog	= smoke + fog
workaholic	= work + alcoholic

(Curiously, *chunnel* has dropped out of use since it became a reality. Nearly everyone now refers to it as *the Channel tunnel.*)

As to portmanteaux that have not caught on, who shall number them? Here are a few that strike me as having something to recommend them:

beautility	= beauty + utility
cosmosis	= process by which matter oozes through the spatial void
cremains	= cremated + remains (= ashes)
feebility	= feeble + debility
jubiloon	= one who writes poems celebrating anniversaries
illiterature	= tabloid newspapers
posthumorous	= published after you died laughing
prounce	= prance + flounce

swelegant   = swell + elegant
(tele)videot   = television (or video) + idiot

> **Game**
> *Invent some more.*

PREPOSITION, SENTENCE, END OF, AT

The idea that sentences shouldn't end with prepositions is part of the same pedantry as the objection, on principle, to the use of split infinitives and of *hopefully* as a clause-modifier. Unlike split infinitives, it provides word-gamers with the perennial challenge of concocting sentences ending with the longest possible string of prepositions. For many years the record was held by *What did you choose that book to be read to out of for?* This was later improved by making it an Australian book, expanding the ending to *to out of up from Down Under for?* Further expansions can be made, but, like pangrams, the sentences they yield suffer from requiring long-winded explanations. In any case, the whole idea is flawed by the fact that many of the words objected to are not in fact prepositions but adverbs *(e.g. out, up, down).*

PUN

(Ultimately from Latin punctum, *'point', possibly via Italian* puntiglio. *The technical term is* paronomasia, *from Greek 'similar naming'. Formerly known as a* clinch *or* quibble.*)*

The pun is often defined as 'a play on words', but as this applies to almost anything from Spoonerisms to *Eskimo Nell* it can hardly be described as definitive. More precisely, it is an ambiguous word or phrase which is approached in one sense and departed in another, thus leading the listener up the proverbial garden path. 'Two disparate strands of thought tied together by an acoustic knot' is how Arthur Koestler put it. A pun is perfect if it sounds identical in both senses, as in Thomas Hood's couplet:

> *He went and told the sexton, and*
> *The sexton tolled the bell.*

Or in a rhyme I thought of to teach children certain basic distinctions about their relatives:

> *Some can do card tricks*
> *and some can't:*
> *some are called 'uncle',*
> *and some – aren't.*

Or almost anywhere in the Marx Brothers' *oeuvre*, such as this from *Duck Soup* (1933):

> Margaret Dumont: *Notables from all over the world are gathered here in your honour. This is a gala day for you.*
> Groucho: *Well, a gal a day's enough for me. I don't think I could handle any more.*

Or in this putative headline from a 1950s newspaper:

STALIN BURIED IN COMMUNIST PLOT

A perfect pun is not necessarily a good one. Someone recently asked me if I had seen *Red Shoes*, the ballet film by Powell and Pressburger. 'Who on earth is Reg Hughes?' I responded, quite innocently, being hard of hearing and not expecting a question about films. Had the pun been intentional, it would have been acoustically perfect, but not 'good'. A good pun should make equal sense in both its meanings. Since neither of us knew a Reg Hughes, the pun would have been flawed through being made purely for its sound and without regard for its meaning. A pun that is both good and perfect is exemplified by this exchange from the Mad Hatter's tea party: '"But they were *in* the well," Alice said to the Dormouse ... "Of course they were," said the Dormouse: "well in."'

A transpositional pun is one in which new light is thrown on an old saying by transposing two (or more) of its elements. A classic example is that of the critical audience, who left no turn unstoned. A better one is this one-liner from *The Marx Brothers Go West:* 'Time wounds many heels.'

The ideal pun is one that is made off the cuff, is acoustically perfect, and casts an alternative but equally valid light on the subject. Some people hardly ever make puns; others are at it all the time. How they spring to some minds with such rapidity is a constant mystery, unless it is merely a case of practice making perfect. A friend of mine once consulted my wife about a culinary matter. He had had friends to dinner the previous night, had made a gooseberry fool for dessert, had made far too much, and wondered if it would still be edible. 'Of course it will,' I interrupted, without pausing for thought: 'There's no fool like an old fool.' The curious thing was that I had no idea I was going to say it until I'd said it. Obviously, pun is from heaven.

A bad pun, on the other hand, requires an artificial set-up and sheds no valid alternative light on anything. To describe Quasimodo's sandwiches as *The lunch-pack of Notre Dame,* or quote Dracula's favourite song as *Fangs for the Memory,* is to perpetrate a bad pun, for the simple reason that no one can have any sensible interest in the former's eating habits or the latter's musical tastes. They also happen to be acoustically imperfect, but that is not the root cause of their badness. Some of the most brilliant puns are patently less than perfect, including the first of the two contained in Anthony Burgess's dictum *Let sleeping dogmas lie.*

Theoretically, a pun evokes laughter. Conventionally, the correct response is not a laugh but a groan. Why should this be? The main reason is that the richness and flexibility of the English language engenders bad puns, predicated on sound only and making no particular sense in the context. Such puns deserve the contempt they attract. The real art of punning lies not in spotting acoustic resemblances but in knowing when to keep quiet.

But why groan at a good one? While a bad pun merely causes a temporary diversion in the train of thought, a good pun throws it on to a completely different track to which there is no apparent ending. It takes people by surprise, and some people, especially those of an authoritarian nature, hate being taken by surprise.

> The third is its slowness in taking a jest.
>   Should you happen to venture on one
> It will sigh like a thing that is deeply distressed:
>   And it always looks grave at a pun.
>   Lewis Carroll, The Hunting of the Snark

For snarks, a groan is as appropriate a response to a pun as to a poke in the ribs with a stiletto. To the making of puns there is no end: myth, history and literature abound in them. As for the beginning, the very name *Adam* has its roots in the Hebrew word for *earth.* Jesus punned in renaming Simon *Peter,* equating it with *petros,* 'rock', a pun that works equally well in Greek as in Aramaic (and with the French *Pierre*). St Augustine punned in describing youthful British slaves as *Non Angli, sed angeli* ('Not Angles, but angels'). Elizabeth I punned in describing Lord Burleigh as *burly* and as causing *less stir* in her reign than *Leicester*. Shakespeare was at it all the time. And so on. Joyce's *Finnegans Wake* is an endless cascade of surrealistic punning, as when everyone fell to eating noisily and *All chime din with eatmost boviality*.

A Joycean flavour might be detected in the sort of whole-sentence puns common in my own household. (Homespuns? Finneganisms?). For example: An excuse for being unable to do something burdensome is *the piggy swilling but the fleshy squeak*. On being presented with a cup of tea or coffee, the recipient may be assured that it is *sugared ant's turd*.

> **Games**
> *See the games section headed* Pun is from Heaven *(page 42).*

PUNCTUATION
(Latin, 'pointing')

Punctuation used to be a device for pointing out relationships between the various components of a passage of text – the lubricant of language, as someone neatly put it. Nowadays it has become a shower of vaguely dotty things sprinkled randomly over text like salt and pepper over a meal. Hence no one is likely to be unduly perturbed by sentences of this sort that amused me as a child:

> *Charles I walked and talked 20 minutes after his head was cut off.*
> *Caesar entered on his head his helmet on his feet his sandals.*

> **Game**
> *Prepare, in advance, copies of a passage of text from which you have eliminated all punctuation, including capital letters. Get everyone to rewrite the text with their idea of suitable punctuation. When all are ready, reveal the results, and stand well back while they argue about their various interpretations. (Note: This game is only marginally more fun than drilling your own teeth.)*

REBUS (DINGBAT)

Non verbis, sed rebus: 'Not in words, but by means of things.' The 'things' referred to are objects which can be pictured – hence, a rebus is a piece of text consisting of or incorporating picturable objects which can be pictured in place of written words.

Not all forms of picture-writing are rebuses. If you represent a bee by drawing a bee instead of spelling it out, you produce a pictogram but not a rebus. A rebus is what you would make if you drew a bee to represent the verb *be*. In short, a rebus is a pictogram used as a pun, or the graphical equivalent of a charade.

Early forms of writing usually thought of as pictographic, such as Egyptian hieroglyphics are actually rebuses, incorporating the punning element required to express abstract concepts. It was by similar means that the alphabet developed. For example, the Hebrew word *aleph* means ox, and the letter aleph, which represents the first sound of the word, derives from the simplified drawing of an ox-head. Similarly, *beth* means house; the simplified drawing of a house represents the sound B; and so on. Our modern capital A is ultimately an ox-head looking up.

Rebuses came into their own in the field of heraldry. A well-known instance is the crest of the Fordyce family, which depicts four dice. That of a possible ancestor of mine features a parrot, as being the nearest pun of the surname Parlett which can be pictured.

Rebuses have long been popular as puzzles and amusements, and still form a staple ingredient of children's puzzle books. In this capacity they soon came to involve two devices additional to the punning pictogram. One is the use of a letter or numeral name to represent sounds or syllables, such as 'C' for 'sea' or 'see' and '2' for 'to' or 'too'. The other involves marking the addition, subtraction or alteration of letters in the word derived from a pictogram in order to represent another. For example, 'loved' could be represented by drawing a glove in association with a crossed-out 'G' and an added 'D'.

Using all these devices, we can now start translating Shakespeare into a rebus:

Shakespeare in rebuses? Is nothing sacred? Well, no, actually: somebody once went so far as to translate the scriptures into rebus format, publishing the whole thing under the title *The Hieroglyphic Bible* in 1893.

Besides combining letters and numbers with pictures, rebuses go even further by dispensing with pictures altogether and concentrating solely on letters and numbers. The classic

YY U R YY U B I C U R YY 4 me

('too Y's you are', etc) goes back to the mid-18th century. Hardly more recent, but requiring a little more thought, is:

If the B mt put :
If the B. putting :

Which is to be interpreted: If the grate B empty, put coal on: if the grate B full stop putting coal on.

More variety can be introduced by expressing simple relations of space and time by the relative positioning of letters, syllables and words on the page. Voltaire is said to have received the following invitation from Louis the umpteenth:

$$\frac{P}{venez} \quad à \quad \frac{6}{100}$$

Correctly interpreting this to read 'Come and dine [with me] at Sans Souci' ('*Venez*' *sous 'P' à 'cent' sous 'six'*), Voltaire riposted with this elegant acceptance:

G a

or, '*J'ai grand appétit*' ('*G' grand, 'a' petit*).

Typographical rebuses. Rebuses do not depend entirely upon pictures, but may make use of pictorial or other graphic symbols. The simplest are numerals, which, in the hands of a master mathematician-*cum*-word-gamester like Lewis Carroll, produce such effects as:

Yet what are all such gaieties to me
　　Whose thoughts are full of indices and surds?

$$x^2 + 7x + 53$$
$$= \frac{11}{3}$$

From here it is but a short step to the use of printer's symbols, or dingbats, as American printers call them, employing a term equivalent to British 'thingummies'. (A string of dingbats, such as @&*%Ω*!, is traditionally used in comics to indicate foul language.) The following example is taken from Irish humorist Myles na Gopaleen and appeared in *Literary Criticism*:

> *My grasp of what he wrote and meant*
> *Was only five or six %*
> *The rest was only words and sound*
> *My reference is to Ezra £.*

Typographical rebuses are now common in books of word puzzles. Typical examples include:

1	BUREDGH
2	DNAIVTH
3	A C D E F G H ...
4	'DI' 'DI' 'DI'
5	! !
6	ONXLD

They tend to be more subtle but less complex than Victorian examples such as:

faults _____ B _____ faults
man quarrels wife

Answers on page 178.

RHYME (RIME)

(Greek rhythmos *'flowing', Late Latin* rithmus *'measure', perhaps conflated with Germanic* rim = *'number')*

Words rhyme if their last stressed syllables are phonetically identical, with the exception of the initial consonant or consonant cluster. Thus the following words rhyme with one another:

> BATE
> DATE
> SLEIGHT
> STATE
> STRAIGHT

EIGHT and the American pronunciation of ATE also rhyme, despite lacking an initial consonant (apart from a glottal stop, which appears only in phonetic script).

Words ending on a stressed syllable form masculine rhymes; feminine rhymes are followed by one or more identical unstressed syllables (honey/bunny; scribbling/ dribbling). A feminine rhyme with an extra unstressed syllable is a *triple* rhyme, and so on. English, having lost its declensional forms, tends to end in iambs or stressed syllables, resulting in a preponderance of masculine rhymes. Perhaps this is why feminine rhymes are more often associated with humorous verse – the more ingenious the rhyme, the funnier it is. One of my favourites is the line from Groucho's song *Lydia the Tattooed Lady*, in *The Marx Brothers at the Circus*:

> *Here is Spalding exploring the Amazon*
> *Here's Godiva – but with her pyjamas on.*

Words whose endings are spelt alike but sound different are described as eye rhymes. An interesting task is to see who can compose the longest list of words that are eye rhymes without any two of them being ear rhymes. Here's a set of six:

BOUGH
COUGH
DOUGH
LOUGH (Irish equivalent of LOCH)
THOROUGH (British pronunciation)
THROUGH

Consonant rhymes are like sandwiches, with identical consonantal bread enclosing different vocalic jams: fine/phone; trapped/tripped.

Half-rhymes, by the same analogy, resemble open sandwiches: step/grip; art/light.

Occasionally in English a rhyme characteristic of Welsh verse appears, in which the two words bear different stresses – for example:

> *Fischer always made a hit*
> *Starting with the queen's gámbit.*

I suppose you might call this an offset rhyme – or perhaps, since it is a cross between masculine and feminine, hermaphrodite.

A humorous effect is achieved, especially in the quest for a difficult rhyme, by the cheating method of splitting words across line endings – as in Lewis Carroll's:

> *Who would not give all else for two p-*
> *ennyworth only of beautiful soup?*

Some words are notoriously, or at least traditionally, incapable of carrying a rhyme. The classic example is ORANGE, but there are equally classic ways of cheating. How many ways can you find of incorporating the word ORANGE into a verse in such a way as to produce a technically correct rhyme? Some solutions are given on page 178.

> **Games**
> *Rhyming games include* Crambo *(page 27) and* Defective
> detective *(page 47).*

RIDDLE
(From the same root as read, *and German* Rede, *'discourse' etc.)*

A trick question, whether explicit or implied, whose correct answer must be reached by some form of mental dexterity or lateral thinking. As Aristotle observed, the true riddle depends upon metaphor and deception, as:

> people are more clearly conscious of having learned something from their sense of surprise at the way in which the sentence ends and their soul seems to say 'Quite true and I had missed the point'. This, too, is the pleasure afforded by clever riddles; they are instructive and metaphorical in their expression' (*Rhetoric*, trans. Crossley-Holland)

Closely related are the *enigma,* which is strictly defined as a riddle in verse, and the *conundrum*, which is a riddle based less on a metaphor than on some form of word play, such as a pun or *double entendre.*

Metaphorical riddles are perhaps the oldest form of word play. Often connected with myth and magic, they tested the mental prowess of heroes just as their physical ability was tested by wrestling with monsters and rescuing damsels. (Or was it wrestling with damsels and rescuing ... No, surely not.) Oedipus saved Thebes – at the cost of rendering his own life more complex – by solving the riddle of the Sphinx, namely, 'What creature is it that goes upon four legs at dawn, two at midday and three in the evening?' The answer, was 'Man', who crawls in babyhood, walks unsupported in maturity, and uses a stick in old age. Solving the riddle requires the recognition of times of day as metaphors for stages of life.

More elaborate riddles were favoured by the Anglo-Saxons. This one, at least a thousand years old, is from *The Exeter Book Riddles*, translated by Kevin Crossley-Holland (No. 44 in the *Penguin Classics* series):

> *A strange things hangs by a man's hip*
> *hidden by a garment. It has a hole*
> *in its head. It is stiff and strong*
> *and its firm bearing reaps a reward.*
> *When the retainer hitches his clothing*
> *high above his knee, he wants the head*
> *of that hanging thing to find the old hole*
> *that it, outstretched, has often filled before.*

This is a fine example of *double entendre* (see page 128), the socially acceptable answer being, in all probability, 'a key'.

Making connections is the essence of solving the riddle. Typically, you do not so much attack it with direct thought as walk around it, looking the other way, until you suddenly fall in. In the days before television, riddles were hurdles erected by uncles and aunts that had to be cleared before they would release the coins lurking in their pockets and palms. Children were thereby well motivated to learn about trick questions and so develop a sense of lateral thinking long before Edward de Bono gave it an identity.

Through the ages, riddles have revolved around a stock of common themes. The Sphinx's was found by Iona and Peter Opie to be still current among children in Kirkcaldy in the form:

> *Walks on four feet,*
> * on two feet, on three:*
> *the more feet it walks on*
> * the weaker it be.*

Many a riddle is based on representing a bell in a tower as a creature that makes a noise only when pulled by the tail. The bell-beast can be decorated with other descriptive elements, such as nodding its head, never touching the ground, requiring no food, and so on. Others purport to describe strange creatures with peculiar numbers of legs, which on closer examination prove to be biological compounds. Thus *A New Collection of Enigmas,* published in 1810, asks 'What creatures are those which appear closely connected, yet upon examination are found to be three distinct bodies, with eight legs, five on one side, and three on the other; three mouths, two straight forwards, and the third on one side; six eyes, four on one side, two on the other; six ears, four on one side, and two on the other?' The answer — a man and a woman on horseback — involves the 'catch' that the woman is riding side-saddle. When I was a teacher, the equivalent was:

> Q: *What's yellow and has 22 legs?*
> A: *A Chinese football team.*

That well-known cliché *a chicken and egg situation* derives from the now-in-danger-of-being-forgotten riddle 'Which came first, the chicken or the egg?', (first recorded in the earliest printed collection of English riddles, Wynkyn de Worde's *Demaundes Joyous* of 1511). Wynkyn's answer, 'The chicken, because God created it', might now be countered by the evolutionist's answer 'the egg, because an egg is an egg regardless of what laid it'. A related but borderline riddle is the ancient catch question 'Have you stopped beating your wife yet?' Assuming you don't, the logically correct answer is 'No', since, if you haven't started, you can't possibly have stopped. Also related are the riddles whose 'catch' consists in sidestepping the catch and answering the question literally rather than metaphorically – as in 'Why did the chicken cross the road?' Classic chicken-and-road riddles include:

> Q: *What makes more noise than a pig squealing under a gate?*
> A: *Two pigs squealing under a gate.*

> Q: *What does a cat looking out of a window look like?*
> A: *A cat looking into a window.*

Complementary to metaphorical riddles, though generally cruder and easier to invent, are literal or alphabetical riddles such as:

> Q: *Why does the letter D cause domestic squabbles?*
> A: *Because it makes ma mad.*

> Q: *What occurs once in a minute, twice in a moment, but not once in a thousand years?*
> A: *The letter M.*

Its extreme form is that of the riddle-me-ree, in which a word is to be discovered from its spelling by a process of deduction and induction:

> *My first is in apple but never in pear,*
> *My second in ogle but never in star ...*

and so on.

SARCASM
(Greek, sarx *'flesh'*, sarkazein *'gnash'*)

Sarcasm, whose Greek roots have been metaphorized into biting or wounding irony, has, like punning, been described as 'the lowest form of wit'. But of course it is not in itself a form of wit, more a form of verbal spite that may incorporate a shaft of wit as a sting in its tail, aimed more at a bystander than the victim. Basic sarcasm consists merely in saying the opposite of what you mean in a particular tone of voice, and may be so lacking in wit as to border on the meaningless: 'Well, you're a fine one, I must say', expresses no more than mild disapproval. 'Take the dog out? Oh yes, I've got nothing else to do all day but take the dog out for a walk', is more pointed but no wittier. 'I've got better things to do with my time than sit around all day taking the dog out for a walk' – is perhaps softened by a witty component, but is not thereby transformed into a species of wit. In short, it would be truer to say that the lowest function of wit is to embellish a sarcasm.

Sarcasm widely overlaps insult, especially the indirect insult, in which the sarcastic remark is addressed to a third party within the hearing of the victim. In this context wit is requisite. Amusing the third party engages his or her complicity in the cleverness of the remark, and thereby attracts their support: without it, the insulter runs the risk of merely sounding rancorous and so directing sympathy to the victim. Indeed, sarcasm minus wit equals invective. Groucho Marx was the arch exponent of sarcastic wit, whether on screen or in real life. From *Duck Soup* (1933):

Of Chico: Gentlemen, Chicolini here may look like an idiot, and speak like an idiot – but don't let that fool you. He really is an idiot.

Of Margaret Dumont: Remember, men, you're fighting for this woman's honour, which is probably more than she ever did.

Not an insult, but wittily sarcastic, is this line from *The Marx Brothers at the Circus* (1939). Pushed by Chico into a puddle in the pouring rain, and warned to get up in case he gets wet, Groucho replies 'Oh nonsense – if I were any drier I'd drown.' This format is paralleled in the comment 'If only she calmed down a bit, she'd be a nymphomaniac', which is so often quoted as to have lost its source.

The sarcastic insult is not so much indirect as remote when the victim is absent from the scene of utterance. Such is the case in literary and dramatic criticism, of which the pastmistress was undoubtedly Groucho's contemporary, Dorothy Parker, who sometimes wrote under the pen-name Constant Reader:

Of Katherine Hepburn: She ran the whole gamut of emotions from A to B.
Of The House at Pooh Corner: Tonstant Weader fwowed up.

Equally witty, if less vitriolic, is the *Guardian* newspaper's television critic Nancy Banks-Smith. For example: 'I've never seen a memorable production of Shakespeare on television – or, if I have, I've forgotten it.'

I once wrote a review that read 'No waste-paper basket is complete without this book'. Which amused me, even if it hardly competes with Dorothy Parker's 'This is not a book to be cast aside lightly. It should be thrown with great force.'

Politics is another great area for sarcasm. A wonderful collection compiled by Greg Knight MP under the title *Honourable Insults* reveals the sort of gems you would expect from those who live as much by their wits as their whips.

● *Disraeli, of an obscure MP:* He only had one idea, and that was wrong.
● *David Lloyd George, of Herbert Samuel:* When they circumcised him, they threw away the wrong bit.
● *Margot Asquith, queried by Jean Harlow as to the pronunciation of her first name:* The T is silent, as in Harlow.
● *Dorothy Parker, on hearing that President Coolidge had died:* How can they tell?
● *Churchill, of Attlee:* An empty taxi cab drew up at the House of Commons and Clement Attlee got out.
● *Harold Wilson, of Tony Benn:* He immatures with age.
● *Dennis Healey, of Margaret Thatcher:* The Prime Minister says that she has given the French President a piece of her mind. This is not a gift I would receive with alacrity.

Games
You might try ad-libbing a Monty Python *sketch, in which various society wits take it in turns to report to a humourless royal figure an insult made by one of the others, who is then obliged to embark upon a mollifying metaphorical explanation beginning 'Ah, what I really meant by that, Sire, is …'*

SPOONERISM (METATHESIS)

The technical term *metathesis*, from Greek roots meaning 'change places', denotes the transposition of nearby sounds in speech, as when '*a battle of wit*' emerges as '*a wittle of bats*'. If the result is amusing the preferred term is that derived from its best-known exponent – or perhaps we should say victim, as he was often unaware of his lapses and embarrassed at having them pointed out. It was first applied by fellow academics at New College, Oxford, of which the Rev William Archibald Spooner was a Fellow in the 1890s and Warden from 1903 to 1924. No doubt there were as many apocryphal Spoonerisms as, later, there were to be apocryphal Goldwynisms (see page 136). The only one Spooner admitted to was announcing a hymn as *Kinquering Kongs*, though he is also credited with '*In a dark, glassly*'. Surely apocryphal, because they are too good to be true, are:

> *A well-boiled icicle …*
> *A blushing crow.*
> *Our shoving leopard.*
> *Our queer old Dean.*
> *You have hissed my mystery lectures; you have tasted a whole worm. You will leave Oxford on the next town drain.'*

Tony Augarde, in *The Oxford Guide to Word Games,* notes that many of Spooner's genuine utterances were nevertheless not genuine Spoonerisms. On one occasion, for example, he compared a distance to that between '*Land's End and John of Gaunt*'. This is a plain case of aiming at a word and getting a near miss – a not uncommon failing, and one which caused a former colleague of mine to speak of someone suffering from *spina Biafra*. Nor were Spooner's lapses merely verbal, as witnessed by the following ear-witness account:

> *Spooner:* I want you to come to tea next Thursday to meet Mr Casson.
> *Casson:* But I am Mr Casson.
> *Spooner:* Come all the same.

Which puts me in mind of an exchange in *Animal Crackers*:

> *Groucho:* I once knew a fellow looked just like you. His name was Emmanuel Ravelli.
> *Chico:* I'm Emmanuel Ravelli.
> *Groucho:* You're Emmanuel Ravelli?
> *Chico:* I'm Emmanuel Ravelli.
> *Groucho:* Well, I still insist there is a resemblance.

Genuine Spoonerisms are thought of as involving initial consonants (*Lawyers sitting on their beery wenches*), but they may involve vowels, syllables, and even whole words. Two nice examples of word transposition are *too true to be good* and *time wounds many heels*. More than two syllables may be juggled around, as in the self-contradictory assertion '*I'm not as thunk as drinkle peep I am.*' While not Spoonerisms, further elaborations of this kind produce such contrasted utterances as:

- I'd rather have a bottle in front of me than a frontal lobotomy.
- Before a canny judge, prompting evidence can be tempting providence.
- You can't be optimistic with a misty optic.

STRINE

Australian pronunciation (to British ears) of the variety of English spoken in Australia, as revealed by Afferbeck Lauder in *Let Stalk Strine* (Sydney, 1965). (I have just realized that it could equally well have been called *Let Strine Talk.)* Examples include:

air fridge	not extreme
baked necks	a breakfast dish
egg jelly	in fact
egg nishner	a mechanical room-cooling device
flares	blossoms
furry tiles	stories beginning *One spawner time* ...

To which, presumably, one may add the author's pen-name:

Afferbeck Lauder   what the above examples are in.

TOM SWIFTY

A cognate adverb with jocular intent. For example:

> *'Must fly' said Tom, swiftly.*
> *'I've eaten a nasty herb' said Tom, ruefully.*
> *'I've lost my buttonhole' said Tom, lackadaisically.*

It originated in Edward Stratemeyer's American strip cartoon of the 1920s about the inventions of Tom Swift and the Motor Boys, or Tom Swift and his Electric Plane, each episode of which began with such a phrase. Although they are less common now newspapers do still run the occasional Tom Swifty competition.

What adverbs follow the following? Answers on page 178.

- *'I've just eaten your brother William' said the cannibal ...*
- *'Tweet, tweet' said the baby chick ...*
- *'I think I'll sharpen my quill on the cheese-grater' said the bard ...*
- *'I've just finished scraping my quill on the cheese-grater' said the bard ...*

Composing Tom Swifties can be played as an amusing rather than competitive game in its own right, and accordingly reappears in the Games section (page 47).

TONGUE-TWISTER

See *Alliteration* (page 116).

TOPONYM
(Greek, 'place name')

Place names exert a fascination all their own. A typical piece of fascination is exerted by the discovery that Torpenhow Hill, in Devon, is a fourfold tautology. *Tor* is an Old English word for hill, *pen* is the Brythonic Celtic word for hill, *how* comes from the Old Norse for hill, and – I seem to have forgotten what *hill* means. *Buslingthorpe* will be recognized by all good word-gamers as a place-name of 13 letters, all different. At least two others can be found in Britain (see page 178). Can you beat 13 letters? One player proposed *South Cambridge* for 14, but as no such area is officially so called it was not accepted as valid. *Knightsbridge* is of interest for containing six consonants in a row. Can you equal or beat that?

See also *Eponym* (page 133), *Name* (page 154).

Games
See Categories *(page 53). See also who can produce the
longest passage of text or dialogue in which place-names are
used as puns. A classic American example begins* 'What did
Delaware?' – 'Don't know: Alaska'.

U AND NON-U

Forms of speech serving as indicators of social class, as propounded in 1954 by Professor A. S. C. Ross in an academic paper entitled *Linguistic Class Indicators in Present-day English*, and subsequently by Nancy Mitford in an article on the English aristocracy in *Encounter*. 'U' stands for Upper Class, but could equally stand for 'Us', as in the phrase 'Not One of Us' reportedly current in the Hon. Miss Mitford's childhood.

In the following list of equivalences, one member of each pair is the 'U' form and one the 'non-U'. Each pair is presented in alphabetical order and your task is to correctly identify which is which. If you are 'U' you will get them all right. If you care whether you get them right or not, you are definitely non-U.

Bicycle	Cycle
Have you sufficient?	Have you got enough?
I was ill on the boat	I was sick on the boat
Jam	Preserves
Loo	Toilet
Looking-glass	Mirror
Note-paper	Writing paper
Pardon?	What?
Serviette	(Table) napkin
Your family	Your people

Answers on page 178.

UNDEREMPLOYED WORD

A perfectly ordinary and innocent-looking word with, however, the peculiarity that exists almost exclusively in conjunction with one other word, which it lives on like a parasite. In effect, half a cliché. You might like to match them up properly:

bottomless	weather
brook no	stupidity
crass	state
fulsome	rights
inalienable	praise
inclement	point
moot	pit
parlous	lies
tissue of	denial

You might also amuse yourself by looking up the basic meaning of *fulsome*.

See also *Automatic doublet* (page 121), *Overspecialized word* (page 157).

Game
Unearth some more.

UNIVOCALIC

A word containing only one vowel but in multiple occurrences, such as *banana, leveret, mini-skirt, octopod, cumulus*. These each contain three of the same vowel. Since Y counts as a vowel for this purpose, it may not be included in any word other than that based on multiple occurrences of itself. (The list just quoted omits Y because I only know of one example containing three and you may prefer to find it for yourself.)

A tough literary challenge is to write univocalic verse. You should be pleased with a successful rhyming couplet, and need not attempt to emulate this *tour de force* reported by Roger Millington in an issue of *Logophile:*

> *Dull, humdrum murmurs lull, but hubbub stuns.*
> *Lucullus snuffs up musk, mundungus shuns.*
> *Puss purrs, buds burst, butts butt, luck turns up trumps;*
> *But full cups, hurtful, spur up unjust thumps.*

> **Game**
> *Quoting only the example of* banana *to give the general idea, get everyone to write one word containing multiple occurrences of one vowel for each of the six vowels. The winner is the player whose list contains the greatest number of vowels. A tie is broken in favour of the list containing the smallest number of consonants.*

WEASEL WORD

A fashionable word or phrase automatically reached for by the fundamentally inarticulate, especially when being interviewed, and hence akin to a cliché (see page 125). Examples include *at this moment in time* for 'now', *at the end of the day* for 'eventually', *prior to* for 'before', *in excess* of for 'over', and *democratic* for nothing in particular except that it's a word with a good feel about it and will hopefully get the non-thinking listener on your side. In her review of the book *Weasel Words* by Philip Howard (London 1979), Kathryn Harrison admirably describes them as 'not chosen as tools to do a specific job, but … slapped into sentences as a kind of linguistic Polyfilla'. A *Logophile* correspondent subsequently explained the term as deriving from the American phrase *to weasel out*, meaning to evade an obligation.

Hopefully has been condemned as a weasel word in the way I have used it above, but I would defend it to the death. (Of the critic, that is.)

WORD SQUARE

An arrangement of *n* words of *n* letters each in a square of n^2 squares. The classic example, unearthed in Roman remains at Pompeii and Cirencester, is:

This is technically an acrostic, rather than a mere word square, because it reads as a sentence: *Arepo the sower guides the wheels with care.* It may have had a mystic significance to early Christians, as it consists entirely of letters derived from the Latin opening of the Lord's prayer (*Pater noster*).

Mere word squares contain words reading across and down but not forming a sentence. Squares of order two to five are so easily constructed that the real challenge lies in making them 'double' word squares, with the across words all different from the down words. Single and double squares of orders four and five are:

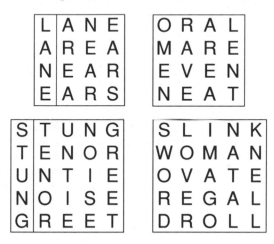

One of the best seven-letter word squares was compiled by Henry Ernest Dudeney:

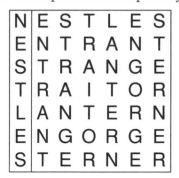

Squares have been constructed up to order 10, but of necessity involve the use of names, foreign words, rare spellings and other forms of cheating. As Willard Espy says, quoting Dr Johnson, they are 'like a dog that has learned to stand on its hind legs. It is not done well, yet you are surprised to find it done at all.'

Victorian word-puzzlers increased the interest of word squares by leaving them blank and providing clues to their contents. In this they proved to be the forerunners of the modern crossword (see page 127), which have replaced them in popularity with the exception of a few dedicated enthusiasts.

See also *Buzzword* (page 122).

Games
See section devoted to word-square and crossword games.

ANSWERS

Anagram (p. 119). The only word I know of that is an anagram of ITSELF is STIFLE.

Anguish languish (p. 119). Once upon a time there was this little girl who lived with her mother in a little cottage on the edge of a large dark forest … All of a sudden throwing off the covers and springing out of bed, this cruel and bloodthirsty wolf seized poor little Red Riding Hood and gobbled her up.

Double entendre (p. 129). What the dog does on three legs is to shake hands.

Huntergram (p. 141). Nastier retains retsina retinas.

Rebuses, typographical (p. 168). 1. Ed-in-burgh, 2. Back and fo(u)rth, 3. Be-gone!, 4. Three DI-mentions, 5. Eyes down, 6. In olden times.
  The Victorian rebus carries the meaning: Be above quarrels between man and wife. There are faults on both sides.

Rhymes for ORANGE (p. 169). The simplest but least elegant solution is to write about someone bearing the surname Gorringe. The only other way is to cheat by means of a split rhyme. Here's a politically correct one by Willard Espy:

> *The four eng-*
> * ineers*
> *Wore orange*
> * brassieres.*

This works less successfully in British than American English, so here's an alternative:

> *I used to feed my foreign ge-*
> *(e)rbil on an orange.*

Or you can split the word ORANGE itself:

> *When he cut his orange, a*
> *pip popped up pa's porringer.*

Tom Swifty (p. 174). Wilfully. Cheaply (or, perhaps, chirpily). Pensively. Expensively.

Toponym (p. 174). Other place-names which contain 13 different letters are *Buckfastleigh* and *Rumboltswhyke*.

U and non-U (p. 175). The 'U' forms are *Bicycle (or Bike), Have you got enough? I was sick on the boat, Jam, Loo, Looking-glass, Writing paper, What?, (Table) napkin, Your people.*

APPENDIX: USEFUL WORDS AND FIGURES

I like the story of the nurse who was given the nickname 'Appendix' because all the doctors wanted to take her out. The difference between writers and doctors is that writers prefer to put appendixes *in*. This appendix is devoted to a miscellany of information about words and letters which I find useful in devising, playing and policing word games.

NAMES AS NOUNS

The following 165 names, mainly personal forenames, are acceptable as common nouns without needing to be spelt with a capital letter. Some are names that have taken on a generic meaning, such as *abigail*–a lady's maid. Others are totally unrelated words in their own right, such as *ken*–know. Deliberately omitted are names too well known as common words to need listing, especially flowers used as girls' names (or vice versa), such as *heather, pansy, violet*, etc. You may be surprised to find that neither Oscar nor Emmy, an entertainment award, is acceptable without a capital.

abigail	craig	jasmine	madras	peregrine
abram	crispin	jeff	magdalen(e)	perry
alexanders *(pl)*	davenport	jemima	margarite	peter
alexandrine	derrick	jemmy	marguerite	poll
alma	dick	jenny	martin	polly
amazon	dick(e)y	jereboam	maud	regina
amelia	dickens	jerry	mavis	rex
ann *(Scots)*	ebenezer	jersey	maxwell	reynard
anna	emma	jess	may	roger
ava	eric	jimmy	mick	rory
barney	erica	jo	mick(e)y	rosemary
basil	fanny	joanna	micky	ruth
benedict	fay	jobe	mike	sally
benjamin	flora	joey	mina	saul *(Scots)*
bertha	flossy *(not -ie)*	jo(h)annes	molly	sheila
beryl	french	john *(US)*	molly	sophia
betty	gemma	joss	mona	stephane
biddy	gene	jud	mungo	stepney
billy	georgette	judas	myrtle	talbot
blanch *(no e)*	gloria *(Latin)*	judy	nancy	timon *(obs)*
bob	gregory	julienne	nanny	timothy
bobby	harry	juvenal	neddy	toby
carol *(no e)*	henry	kelvin	nelly	tom
cecils *(pl)*	homer	ken	ngaio	tommy
celeste	ingram *(obs.)*	kitty	norma	tony
celestine	iris	lambert	norman	valentine
charlie	isabel	laura	oliver	valerian
charley	isabella	lewis	otto	veronica
cicely	jack	lill *(Scots)*	paddy	vesta
clarence	james	lionel	pam	victor
clement	jane	louis	patty	wally
clementine	jean	madge	paul	wellington
collie	japan	mag	peggy	willy

TWO-LETTER WORDS

aa	at	*di*	er	he	ka	me	ob	op	re	to	wo
ab	aw	do	*es*	hi	*ki*	mi	od	or	*ri*	ug	xi
ae	ax	*dy*	ex	ho	ko	mo	oe	os	*se*	uh	xu
ag	ay	ea	*ey*	id	*ky*	mu	of	ou	sh	um	ya
ah	*ba*	ee	fa	if	la	my	oh	ow	si	un	ye
ai	be	*ef*	fy	in	li	na	oi	oy	so	up	yo
am	*bi*	eh	*gi*	io	lo	ne	*ol*	pa	st	ur	yu
an	bo	el	go	is	*lu*	no	om	pi	ta	us	*za*
ar	by	em	*gu*	it	*ly*	nu	on	po	te	ut	zo
as	da	en	ha	jo	ma	*ny*	oo	*qi*	ti	we	

The 119 two-letter words tabulated above appear in either or both of *The New Shorter Oxford English Dictionary* (1993) and *The Chambers Dictionary* (1993). Eleven appear only in X (Oxford) and nine only in C (Chambers), leaving the 99 printed above in bold type common to both – though not always with the same denotation. In the more detailed table below, comments in the third column relate to the language of any word not native to English, and to any other possible basis for a validity exclusion order under your own house rules.

word and meaning	source or style	in
aa volcanic lava	Hawaiian	X, C
ad advertisement	Colloquial	X, C
ae one (*pronoun*)	Scots	X, C
ag agriculture	US colloquial	X –
ah *interjection*		X, C
ai three-toed sloth	Tupi > Portuguese > French	X, C
am be		X, C
an *indefinite article*		X, C
ar *letter R*		X, C
as conjunction		X, C
at *preposition*		X, C
aw *interjection*	Mainly Scots & US	X, C
ax axe	US spelling	X, C
ay 1. ever 2. *interjection*		X, C
ba soul of the dead	Ancient Egyptian	– C
be exist		X, C
bi bisexual	Colloquial	– C
bo 1. *interjection* 2. friend	US colloquial (2)	X, C
by *preposition*		X, C
da 1. dad 2. Burmese knife		X, C
di *plural of deus – god*	Latin	– C
do act, perform		X, C
dy lake sediment	Swedish	X –
ea stream, channel	Obsolete except dialectal	X, C
ee 1. eye 2. *interjection*	1. Scots, 2. Lancashire	– C
ef *letter F*		– C
eh *interjection*		X, C
el 1. *letter L* 2. elevated train	2. US	X, C
em 1. *letter M* 2. printer's measure		X, C
en 1. *letter N* 2. printer's measure		X, C
er *interjection*		X, C

es *letter S*		–	C
ex former spouse	Colloquial	X,	C
ey 1. *interjection* 2. *egg*	Obsolete	X	–
fa *musical note*		X,	C
fy *interjection*	Obsolete spelling	X,	C
gi = gie: judo or karate costume	Japanese	–	C
go proceed		X,	C
gu crude violin, Shetland		–	C
ha *interjection*		X,	C
he *pronoun*		X,	C
hi *interjection*		X,	C
ho *interjection*		X,	C
id 1. fish 2. part of unconscious	Latin	X,	C
if *conjunction*		X,	C
in *preposition*		X,	C
io 1. moth 2. *int*	Greek	X,	C
id be		X,	C
it *pronoun*		X,	C
jo sweetheart	Scots	X,	C
ka soul	Ancient Egyptian	X,	C
ki oriental shrub (*also* ti)	Hawaiian	X	–
ko 1. dagger 2. position in game of Go	Chinese	X,	C
ky kye, kine, cows	Scots	–	C
la *interjection, musical syllable*		X,	C
li 1. unit of length 2. right behaviour	Chinese	X,	C
lo *interjection*		X,	C
lü musical syllable	Chinese	X	–
ly *variant of li*	Chinese	X	–
ma *mother*	Colloquial	X,	C
mi *musical syllable*		X,	C
mo moment	Colloquial	X,	C
mu 1. *Greek letter* 2. micrometre	Greek	X,	C
my *possessive adjective*		X,	C
na no, not	Scots	X,	C
ne not, never	Archaic	X,	C
no *negation*		X,	C
nu *Greek letter*	Greek	X,	C
ny nigh	Obsolete spelling	–	C
ob 1. half penny 2. objection	Obsolete	X,	C
od 1. *interjection* 2. a hypothetical force	Archaic. Arbitrary	X,	C
oe grandchild	Dialectal	X,	C
of *preposition*		X,	C
oh *interjection*		X,	C
oi *interjection*		X,	C
ol hydroxyl group	Rarely uncompounded	X	–
om 1. *interjection* 2. *mantra*		X,	C
on *preposition*		X,	C
oo *interjection*		X,	C
op 1. opus 2. operation	Latin. Colloquial	X,	C
or *conjunction*		X,	C
os bone	Latin	X,	C
ou 1. *interjection* 2, honey-creeper	Scots. Hawaiian	X,	C
ow *interjection*		X,	C

ox animal		X, C
oy *interjection (also variant of* oe*)*		X, C
pa father		X, C
pi 1. *Greek letter* 2. *geometric ratio*	Greek	X, C
po chamber pot	Colloquial	X, C
qi life force, material principle	Chinese	X, C
re concerning (from *in re*)	Latin. Colloquial	X, C
ri *unit of length*	Japanese	X –
se Chinese zither	Chinese	X –
sh *interjection*		X, C
si *musical syllable (=te)*	Obsolete	X, C
so *conjunction*		X, C
st *interjection*		X, C
ta thank you	Colloquial	X, C
te *musical syllable*		X, C
ti 1. *musical syllable* 2. Cabbage-tree	Polynesian (2)	X, C
to *prep*		X, C
ug 1. inspire dread 2. *interjection*	Dialectal	X, C
uh *interjection*		X, C
um *interjection*		X, C
un one, him	Dialectal	X, C
up *adverb*		X, C
ur *interjection*		X, C
us *pronoun*		X, C
ut *musical syllable*	Obsolete	X, C
we *pronoun*		X, C
wo *interjection (=whoa)*		X, C
xi *Greek letter*	Greek	X, C
xu 1/100th of a dong (currency)	Vietnamese	X, C
ya you	US colloquial	X –
ye you	Archaic	X, C
yo *interjection*		X, C
yu 1. Chinese vase 2. precious jade	Chinese	X, C
za pizza	US, colloquial	X –
zo Himalayan cattle hybrid	Tibetan	X, C

Two others are sanctioned by *Official Scrabble Words* (1991) and *Official Scrabble Lists* (1991), but without definition or explanation:

ch appears in Chambers as a contraction of *ich, a* dialectal form of the first person pronoun. As it is only recorded in compound verb forms such as *cham* for *I am,* it cannot be considered an independent word.

wa appears in the Oxford dictionary, but only with a capital letter as an ethnic name, and in Chambers, but only with an apostrophe as the Scots version of *wall.* These are good reasons for omitting them.

Many others appear in other sources and dictionaries. Peter Newby, in *Pears Advanced Word-Puzzler's Dictionary* (1987), records no fewer than 229 two-letter combinations which may or may not be regarded as words. He rightly discounts 'plurals' of letters of the alphabet, such as Bs, Cs, and so on, even though they are listed as such in the largest dictionaries. For most word-gaming purposes other than crossword-solving, these should in any case be discounted as being spelt with a capital initial. On the same grounds, Newby's own list can be reduced by a number (I haven't counted them) of names and proper nouns spelt only with a capital initial, starting with Ao, the personification of light in Maori myth and legend.

More could be added by accepting two-letter combinations from the following sources as valid words:

Interjections. Both *mm* and *zz* are widely recognized representations of expressions of agreement and slumber, respectively. Dubiety is also expressed by *h'm*, but this may be rejected as requiring an apostrophe. Surprisingly, neither X nor C acknowledges *ee!* as a well-known Lancashire interjection. Have none of their compilers ever watched a George Formby film?

Alphabets. Disregarding two-letter combinations already listed above, we could add *pe* from the Hebrew alphabet, and *ra* from the Arabic, plus *ya* and *za* in case Arabic letters are preferred to American colloquial abbreviations. Incidentally, the letters spelt *ef, el, es* in Chambers are spelt *eff, ell, ess* in Oxford.

Solmization systems. The Tonic Sol-fa system runs *doh-ray-me-fah-soh-lah-te*, with various alternative spellings including *mi, fa, la* and *ti*. You might as well allow all the resultant two-letter words, as all but *fa* have other meanings as well. Also included in the SOED is *ut*, an older equivalent of the tonic *doh*. The system also indicates sharpened and flattened notes required for modulation into other keys. If you consider these acceptable, you can extend the two-letter word-list by adding *de, fe, le, ra*. There are others, but they already appear for other reasons (*ma, me, re, se, ta*). You can extend the list by scraping the barrel of obsolete 16th- and 17th-century solmization systems. The Bebization system runs *la-be-ce-de-me-fe-ge*, the Bocedization (or Bobization) has *bo-ce-di-ga-lo-ma-ni*, and the extended precursor of Tonic Sol-fa has *ut-re-mi-fa-sol-la-bi*.

'Y' IS A VOWEL NOT A VOWEL?

Rules of word games and competitions are often spoilt by confusion over the status of the letter Y, which, because it is technically described as a semi-vowel, is generally regarded as a consonant. This is nonsense. Y is nearly always a vowel, being merely a written variant of the vowel I. It is only a semi-vowel, or quasi-consonant, at the start of a syllable when followed by a different vowel, as in *yes, yam*, and *yo-yo*. I calculate Y to be a fully-fledged vowel in about 97 per cent of all occurrences. It certainly is so in the following 53 words, which contain no other. I have arranged them by length in letters and number of Ys.

2L	3L		4L	5 & 6L	2 & 3Y
by	cry	shy	cyst	crypt	dryly
dy	dry	sky	fyrd	lymph	gyppy
fy	fly	sly	hymn	lynch	gypsy
ky	fry	spy	lynx	myrrh	pygmy
ly	gym	sty	myth	sylph	shyly
my	gyp	thy	wych	tryst	slyly
ny	hyp	try	wynd		thymy
	ply	tyg	xyst		wryly
	pry	why			xylyl
	pyx	wry			
		wyn		rhythm	syzygy

Of words you may not be acquainted with, *fyrd* is an old English army or militia, *hyp* an archaic word for depression (from *hypochondria*), *syzygy* a period of new or full moon, *tyg* a mug with two handles (C.17-18), *wyn* a letter of the Runic alphabet equivalent to W, *wynd* a narrow town backstreet or alley (Scots), *xyst* a covered portico, and *xylyl* a chemical radical. See also the list of two-letter words (above).

Three more are sanctioned by *Official Scrabble Words*. Of these, *lym* is a conjectural Shakespearian form of *lyme,* and *nys* a Spenserian verb form equivalent to *isn't*. The third, *bys*, I cannot find either listed or implied in either Chambers or Oxford. No one in their right mind would accept any of them.

JUMPING THE NON-U QUEUE

There are some games in which it's helpful to know what words can take a Q not followed by a U. Here are 25 or so. The ones you choose to allow is a matter of agreement. Although *qinghao* appears in Oxford and *qadi* in Chambers, neither does so as a headword. The 17 listed in *Official Scrabble Lists*, and therefore acceptable in the National Scrabble Championship, are based on those in Chambers. They include alternative spellings of *tsaddiq* and its plural (-*im*).

	meaning and alternative spelling	language	in	
burqa	*burka* loose garment for Muslim women	Arabic	X,	C
cinq	*cinque* five, as on a playing-card or die	French	X,	–
inqilab	revolution	Urdu	X,	C
muqaddam	*mokaddem* leader, headman (India)	Arabic	–	C
qadi	*cadi, kadi* Islamic judge	Arabic	X	–
qaimakam	*kaimakam* regional governor (Turkey)	Turkish < Arabic	X	–
qalamdan	*kalamdan* Persian writing-case	Persian	–	C
qanat	*kanat* underground channel	Arabic	X,	C
qasida	a monorhyme poem of eulogy	Arabic	X,	C
qat	*kat, khat* shrub yielding a narcotic	Arabic	X,	C
qere	*kere* alternative reading in Hebrew O.T.	Hebrew	X	–
qi	*chi, ch'i* physical life force	Chinese	X,	C
qibla	*kiblah* proper orientation for Islamic prayer	Arabic	X,	C
qigong	meditational exercises	Chinese	–	C
qindar	*variant of qintar*	Albanian	X	–
qinghao	medicinal plant (Artemisia)	Chinese	X	–
qinghaosu	chemical derived from *qinghao*	Chinese	X	–
qintar	1/100th of a *lek* (currency)	Albanian	X,	C
qirsh	1/20th of a *rial* (currency)	Arabic	X	–
qiviut	under-wool of musk ox	Inuit (Eskimo)	X	–
qursh	*variant of qirsh*	Arabic	X	–
qwerty	keyboard layout	English	X,	C
suq	*souk* market-place, bazaar	Arabic	X,	C
talaq	*talak* a form of divorce (Islamic)	Arabic	X,	C
tsaddiq(m)	*tzaddiq(m)* righteous man	Hebrew	X,	C

All but four are transliterations of foreign words normally written in a non-Roman alphabet, and most of these can be transliterated in more than one way. My inclination would be to ban transliterations and accept only words normally written in the Roman alphabet: *cinq, qindar, qintar, qiviut, qwerty*. The latter is acceptable as a quasi-acronym that has become naturalized in the same way as *radar* and *scuba*.

LETTER FREQUENCIES

Word-gamers are naturally interested in letter frequency and distribution – that is, with how commonly the common letters occur and how rarely the rare ones in relation to them. Such information has always been useful to cryptographers, and many such lists have been compiled. In Table Two, the list headed 'in text' comes from Fletcher Pratt, *Secret and Urgent* (1942), and purports to present the number of occurrences of each letter per 1000 letters. It must, however, be treated with caution, as letter frequency varies according to the context. In *The Cambridge Encyclopedia of Language* (1987), David Crystal quotes figures for frequencies in specimens of American English relating to press reporting, religious writing, scientific writing, and general fiction, no two of which show precisely the same order. Their average order is shown in the second row of Table One (the first row is the order according to Fletcher Pratt). The order I learnt by heart as a child was that of row three, the order used by Samuel Morse and based by him on the relative quantities of type found in a printer's office.

Table One

1. ETAONRI SHDL FCMU GYPWB VKXJQZ
2. ETAOINS RHLD CUMF PGWYB VKXJQZ
3. ETAINOS HRDL UCMF WYGPB VKQJXZ
4. EAIRTONLSCUPDMHGBYFVWKXZQJ

Rather than quote the actual figures, it seems more useful, for the purposes of comparison between the three lines, to show how all produce the same letter groupings. The fourth row does not follow the same group characteristics because it represents the same letter frequency of words listed in the dictionary as opposed to passages of text. It is the same as the second column of Table Two.

To the word-gamer, however, these figures are largely irrelevant for the simple reason that they are all based on *running text*. In other words, the frequency of some letters is inflated by the fact that they are used in more frequently occurring words. The letters T, H and E, for example, are increased by the relative frequency of such common words as THE, THEY, THEM, THERE, THIS, THEN, THESE, and so on. In word games and puzzles, however, no such weighting applies. What the word-gamer is interested in is the relative frequency of letters in all the words *listed* in the dictionary, each of which occurs once only. Having never encountered any statistics along these lines, the first job I did with my first computer was to produce such an estimate. This I did by analysing a list of 2000 words found by taking the first word in bold type (not necessarily the headword) on each page of *Chambers Twentieth Century Dictionary,* and adding another 500 or so by an equally random method. The result appears as the fourth row in Table One and in the second column, headed 'in list', in Table Two. From this you will see, as you would expect, that the relative frequencies are flattened – that is, the figures for common letters are generally reduced and those for rarer letters generally increased. And although E remains the commonest letter, the T and H associated with the commonest words are now considerably reduced.

Table Two

in text		in list		in text		in list		in text		in list	
E	131	E	109	D	38	C	49	W	15	F	14
T	105	A	91	L	34	U	37	B	14	V	10
A	82	I	78	F	29	P	34	V	9	W	10
O	80	R	75	C	28	D	32	K	4	K	9
N	71	T	72	M	25	M	30	X	2	X	3
R	68	O	69	U	25	H	28	J	1	Z	2
I	63	N	62	G	20	G	23	Q	1	Q	2
S	61	L	61	Y	20	B	21	Z	1	J	2
H	53	S	58	P	20	Y	19				

Letter frequencies by position. The following table may be found helpful for word games played with letter-cards or tiles, and in several written word games. In Wordsworth, for example, given a Y, you will immediately see that it is much more useful in last position (fourth most frequent after S, E and T) than in first (in which position only Z and X are more useless).

| *Initials* | **SPCAM** | **TBRDF** | **HEIWG** | **LOUNV** | **KJQYZX** |
| *Finals* | **SETYN** | **LRDCA** | **HMGPO** | **KFWBX** | **IUZJQV** |

The table is based on my own research into frequencies of letters in listed words rather than in running text. Letter S counts high as a final only because of its grammatical uses as a marker of plural nouns and singular verb forms. By my estimate, some 60 to 70 per cent of words can take an S ending for one reason or another. If the rules of a game prohibit words ending in a grammatical S, its relative frequency as a final ranks below D and above C.

Letter combinability. Another property of a letter of interest to word-gamers is its relative usefulness in combination with other letters. For example, E is the most combinable letter, since it can be preceded or followed by almost any other in the alphabet. On the other hand, Q comes low on the list, as few letters can precede it, and it is almost invariably followed by U. By my calculations, the order of letters from highest to lowest degree of combinability is as follows:

EIAOR UTLSC PNDMG BHFYV WKQXZJ

The most commonly occurring pairs of consonants, from highest to lowest, and excluding words ending with a grammatical S, are as follows: ST, NT, TR, CH, LL, ND, TH, NG, BL, NC, SS, PR, SH, CT, CK, PH, SC, RT, PL, NS, MP, SP, GR, SM, TT, RD, CL, RR, RC, DR, RS, RN, FF, MB, RM, GH, LD, DL.

These all occur with above-average frequency.

The commonest diphthongs are: OU, EA, IO, IA, OO, EE, AI, IE, UE, AU, EO, OI, OW, UA.

The third of these is more common than might be expected because of the many words ending in -TION.

INDEX